LEAVING
CURRENCY
BEHIND

How We Transition from Human Labor for Survival
Toward a Fully Automated Economy

RICHARD GUITAR ZEN

Leaving Currency Behind

How We Transition from Human Labor for Survival Toward a Fully Automated Economy

Richard Guitar Zen

ISBN (Print Edition): 978-1-09831-589-4

ISBN (eBook Edition): 978-1-09831-589-4

Leaving Currency Behind © 2020. After Thought Publishing LLC.

Website: Richardguitarzen.com

Contact: Message@richardguitarzen.com

Table of Contents

Introduction

The currency system is a system of inequality that has never served the common people. As we move forward during the next 50 years, the currency system is on a collision course to fail, due to unrestricted laws allowing outsourcing, artificial intelligence and advancements in automated labor. We've reached a tipping point of sorts in our technology development, where our focus should be on eliminating all human labor through automation, with the ultimate goal of running our economy without income or expenses. At this point we can't change the game, we can only change the rules by which it's played to build a different type of economy—a new economy, a technology-based economy—that distributes technology rather than currency as its focal point to our entire population, and frees its citizens to pursue the highest and best use of their free time.

The only way you will free yourself from the endless drudgery of 40-hour work weeks is by lowering your overhead, and the only way that can be done is to apply superior technology to our ever-increasing overhead cost problems.

Did you know that the majority of the American population lives paycheck to paycheck and is not prepared financially for any type of an emergency, natural disaster, job loss or economic downturn? Did you know that we're on the verge of developing and distributing technology in our country that will eliminate the majority of jobs and the 40-hour work week as we know it, in just the next few decades? Did you know that the United States has no specific plans to stop the development of technology that will replace most of our jobs and cut us off from earning the income we all need now to survive?

What if there was a simple solution to all these problems? What if there was a specific economic plan to drastically reduce your overhead costs like housing, transportation and healthcare every month, with the long-term intent of reducing those costs even further over time? How many hours a week would you need to work, if your rent or healthcare costs were a fraction of what they are today? What if you were able to purchase your home with a credit card or cash rather than being tied down to 30-year loan financing? A currency-based economy will never answer these questions or resolve our greatest financial problems; in fact, the currency-based economy we participate in today ensures that your future housing, healthcare and transportation costs will always cost more over time than what they do today. Higher prices and higher profits are the incentivized goals for all companies and corporations, in a for-profit, currency-based economic system. In order to reduce our working hours and overhead, I have developed a new economic system that is simple to understand, benefits everyone and ensures that our overhead stays low and continues to progress even lower decade after decade. So as our technology advances we will welcome its progress rather than fear its inevitability. This dynamic solution also transfers the voting power of economic issues away from federally corrupt officials and back to each individual citizen of the United States.

This streamlined economic system is a hybrid of our current economy, and still uses cash and credit to purchase the things you need and want every day. It doesn't change the IRS tax code or create a larger welfare system. It differs from the current system in that it directly affects and regulates four specific industries: energy, healthcare, transportation and housing. These industries represent our highest household currency expenditures per month, and drive the greatest need for jobs in our economy in order to produce the steady stream of income needed by all Americans to survive. This plan is not a one-size-fits-all policy or socialism; nor does it create more government control or less freedom for its citizens. The rest of the economy and all remaining industries would operate normally, exactly as they do today.

This system keeps our existing overhead technologies running normally, so that our energy, healthcare, transportation and housing industries run exactly as they do now. The new system simply changes the rules under which these industries can operate, so that we introduce new survival technology, in the most efficient and cost-effective manner possible for use by the general public, in order to drive down our overhead costs today, before we lose our jobs in the future to low cost overseas labor, robotics and automation.

Every company in these four affected industries would be required to carry a license in order to legally continue its business operations. Under the rules of licensing, those newly licensed companies would become non-profit and non-publicly traded, and patents covering any existing and new technologies in these licensed industries would no longer be enforceable or valid. This new regulation would allow for the open sourcing and cooperative development of technology that we desperately need, not only in the United States to increase our standard of living, but around the world to stop global starvation, debt slavery and poverty.

Workers in these four industries would be heavily incentivized with both quarterly and yearly goals to receive at least 10% more income than their current industry position pays, to ensure that our economy is resilient to the drastic changes we can expect as our human-based labor force slowly and deliberately becomes a machine-based labor force.

Dropping our overhead reduces our reliance on currency, and allows us to work fewer hours per year, while at the same time increasing our standard of living. This tier-based system is to be implemented industry by industry over the next one to two decades of time, starting with just our energy and healthcare industries, to keep our economy as stable as possible; and eventually licenses our transportation and housing industries when we reach a point in time where we have developed sufficient energy and other technologies that we can easily implement into them.

Licensing and regulation changes governing these industries can be enacted through individual state law, through state propositions requiring the direct vote of the people to become law and would not require approval by the federal government. The states, by colluding together in mass force, would be able to override federal patent law governing energy patents, for example, and other laws directly conflicting with the survival rights of citizens.

Propositions could be drafted for public vote by a publicly elected state economic committee, consisting of 12 members. Each committee member would be prohibited from owning stock in any company, and limited to an income of $200,000/year, adjusted for inflation, for up to two, four-year terms, as well as a 15-year cooling-off period, after they leave office. This type of regulation closes the door to improper lawmaking and removes all incentives for golden parachutes for committee members, who would otherwise be incentivized to draft propositions in favor of benefiting corporations, rather than their individual state citizens and the American public as a whole. Each economic committee, in each individual state, would work to draft an Economic Crime proposition that would cover penalties for any type of misconduct or fraud committed by committee members against 100 or more individual citizens. The economic committee would then over time, draft propositions that call for the licensing of our energy, healthcare, transportation and housing industries, which would then become nonprofit, non-publicly traded and patent free. This would allow superior survival technology to be developed in an open, cooperative and transparent manner, with the intention of reducing the cost of each product each industry produces over time to the point where it becomes inconsequential or free. These propositions could be simultaneously voted on through the collusion of perhaps 25 or more states at one time and would force all the companies and corporations in the affected industries to abide by these new regulations.

This system restores equality and access to technology for all Americans, whose human rights are being violated through "at will" employment and outdated, antiquated laws governing our privatized, patent-holding survival technology industries. Technology is being severely restricted in its development or halted altogether by our currency-based for-profit system, in order to perpetuate needless future expenditures by the American public. On a planet approaching a population of 9 billion by 2030, everyone will need open access to low-cost survival technology. This system empowers people who are looking for an answer as to why they continue to work perpetually for their entire lives, yet never see their work hours decrease or their overhead costs drop. This system gives the public the direct power and expertise they need to overturn laws now that threaten their present and future survival.

Author's Note

Dear Reader,

Please be aware that I tried to find several sources corroborating any data or statistics mentioned in this text data, but data and statistics will vary from year to year. So, I urge you to use the internet or any other source of information you can find to get additional answers to questions you might have as you read this book. The purpose of this text is to raise awareness, and the best way to raise your awareness is to ask questions and look for the most extensive answers possible, to satisfy your desire for knowledge. I believe that the more you research you do, towards understanding the workings of our currency-based economy, the more you'll come to the same conclusions that I already have—that our current economic system is only temporary and a means to an end so that we can evolve towards greater accomplishments. Our currency-based economy has come to the end of its useful life. By reading and understanding this text, it is my hope that you'll come to the conclusion that a technology-based economy is the best way for America to build its future.

Sincerely,

Richard Guitar Zen

CHAPTER 1

Forming a Technology-Driven Economy

In order to free ourselves from our current economic problems, we need to look at them from an entirely different direction. The currency-driven economy today causes a mass misdirection of our efforts and time to produce a byproduct called currency, rather than focusing directly on providing us the physical technology that actually brings prosperity into our lives. The idea of a technology-based economy was developed around answering a perennial question on the minds of Americans everywhere: "How do we work less and enjoy a higher standard of living at the same time?" After many years of thought, I came to the conclusion that it would be better for the American economy to shift its focus to distributing technology to its citizens, rather than continuing to distribute currency, which really does not solve any of its long-term problems or survival issues. The overall theme and message of this book is to outline, in a very detailed plan, how we can shift from one idealism to another and eventually create a physically manifested, technology-based economy.

The main factor in determining the price paid for all goods and services in the United States is overhead. We can break down overhead costs for any business or government agency, be they small or large, into two categories:

Operating costs: The overhead of the business itself, its lease or loan payments for its space, equipment expenses, utility expenses, etc. These costs are usually fixed over time and have little variance.

Labor costs: The cost of physical labor, management, executives, accountants, etc. These costs tend to vary over time. The cost of physical labor is also directly driven by the price of each laborer's overhead: the cost of their housing, health care, transportation, etc.

In short, all roads lead to overhead, and if we can reduce the price of overhead, we can essentially reduce the price for all goods and services produced in America today. Our for-profit currency-based system works in a simple three-step process:

Labor = Cash = Survival

Typically Americans spend their entire lives working in order to create a byproduct called currency and, after obtaining currency, they attempt to purchase survival technology to meet their present survival needs or save their currency for the purchase of their future survival needs.

What is survival technology? Anything built by humans for the specific purpose of easing survival is survival technology. Most of our survival technology is created and distributed by four industries: energy, health care, transportation, and housing.

Survival technology includes: planes, trains, automobiles, highway systems, energy producing power plants, power lines, pharmaceutical drugs, medical instruments and surgical tools, anything to do with creating and assembling residential or commercial structures, etc. Survival technology is basically anything ever invented or created that has been used by humans to help them survive more easily or efficiently on this planet.

Let us take a closer look at the three-step process of survival in a currency-based economy:

An exchange of labor for cash: The fundamental ideal of our capitalist system is that everyone in this country exchanges labor for cash and then uses *the majority* of that cash to purchase technology that allows each of them to survive. Each citizen of the United States has no direct control over their survival in this system; instead, they perform a duty based on their skill set and are paid currency, and from that point forward they rely on third parties, corporations, or other private citizens to create their survival technology for them. In other words, their pay period tasks—or the work they do to generate their currency—does not directly affect their survival.

An exchange of cash for survival: The price of all goods and services purchased in this country includes the direct fixed overhead costs for each business operation and the overhead costs for each of its employees. So, any time you purchase a good or service, technically you are helping to pay someone's overhead: their housing, their medical costs, their transportation and their energy costs. Everyone in the United States today is working to pay their own overhead as well as everyone else's overhead each time they purchase a product or service.

This labor, for cash, for survival exchange causes several problems and paradoxes for the population of our country:

1. We are not united to reduce our overhead costs and technically do not take direct action to reduce them through the work we perform each week.

2. We continue to work to pay our overhead costs in the hopes that someday some random person somewhere will invent some great piece of survival technology that will forever change our lives. However, unknown to almost all citizens is the fact that under a currency-based

system, companies will always be incentivized to produce inferior technology—inferior technology that requires our constant repurchase or repair. This system also currently allows any American company to purchase any competing technology that would potentially make its current product extinct and cause it to go out of business. The result of these currency-based incentives catches the American public in a paradox: we end up perpetually working in order to constantly repurchase inferior survival technology, yet our culture or country never sets or achieves any real goals to reduce its cost. No capitalistic system would ever set a goal to make its technology "free" to the American public; yet, with the development of artificial intelligence, automation, and outsourcing, we now have technologies that are directly eliminating labor and human incomes through their ever-increasing development. These advancing technologies, implemented randomly into our economy without a plan, will eventually leave many Americans without incomes and with high overhead costs.

If we can eliminate overhead costs, we can effectively and efficiently reduce the price of all goods and services in this country and decrease the need for the number of human hours worked per week while at the same time increasing our standard of living.

The currency-based for-profit economy—or what we all might like to call good old-fashioned "Capitalism"—runs on basic fundamentals that call for the following actions: randomly creating a business with no specific intention other than to create a profit; following through with eight hours or more per day of human labor over many decades to create more profit; and this earned profit is spent by the business owner on recurring overhead expenses that only increase due to for-profit production incentives over the course of their lifetime. We are fighting a losing battle here—we are just expending effort and spinning our wheels and not creating the technology we need to survive as a means to an end.

The main problem with the currency-based system lies in the purchase (and subsequent constant repurchase) of survival technology that physically manifests in our economy in the form of rents, mortgage payments, home repairs, auto payments, auto repairs, etc., over and over again because the technology is both inferior and expensive. Our currency-based system ensures that the inferior technology we are using today remains inferior and expensive in the future, so that its products do not become extinct and its profits continue to be maximized. The main premise of the system I am proposing is to reduce the constant repurchase of items by creating superior technology that requires very little repurchase or repair. The more items that need to be repurchased by any given individual, the more human hours of labor per year are required to purchase them. By the same token, the more advanced any technology becomes, the longer it lasts and the less repairs are needed, so consequently fewer human working hours per year are required by that same individual while consequently they reap the benefits of a better standard of living.

In summary, as our technology gets better, our standard of living increases, our dependency on currency decreases, and our labor/for cash/ for survival cycle decreases, reducing its impact on our citizens. To put it as a metaphor: We are essentially trying to reduce a big currency wheel into a smaller one. The currency-based system requires massive constant repurchases in order to keep itself alive. Its side effects are causing a giant waste problem and environmental issues for our planet. Our goal should be to advance our survival technology to a point where purchases of survival technology become so infrequent that they become inconsequential, in terms of the number of human hours worked per year. Yet we have no goal as a nation, a people, or a culture to achieve any such type of goal, let alone even contemplate its possibility.

Disposable income is the money you have left over after paying taxes, rent and other bills. This is basically the extra money you have for savings or expenditures. Disposable incomes decline as our survival expenses increase.

In other words, if the available amount of money each person has to spend on extra goods and services not related to their survival declines, there is less demand for these extra goods and services, causing price drops and reducing the revenue of the companies that produce them. Ultimately, this finds any company looking for new ways to drop labor costs again through outsourcing or automation, in an effort to increase its profit margin. Companies and corporations, regardless of the type of product they produce, are always looking to maximize their profit by keeping their labor cost to an absolute minimum. They are incentivized to employ as small a workforce as possible and replace that workforce over time, if possible, through outsourcing or automation. So, the extreme long-term goal of all corporations that follow for-profit incentives is to "not" employ any workforce at all, if possible, in order to maximize their profit. Are you starting to see the big picture here? The goal of corporate America, as it stands, is for its workforce to become machine-based.

On the other side of the coin, the goal of every American worker is to retire: that is, the goal of every American worker is not to work. Almost all citizens will follow this path if possible, and, at present, this goal is mainly achieved by the general public through long-term savings plans. However, in order to obtain long-term savings, at least for almost every citizen, this plan always requires steady employment with opportunities for increased skilled labor positions becoming available over time in a growing human labor-based economy. This goal is based on the economy of the past: throughout most of the past century, our economy required large amounts of human labor and an extended amount of raw capital or natural resources and had no major changes to its technological developments that might replace human labor. Yes, we've had major advances to technology in the past hundred years; however, these major advances in technology have not drastically affected the labor/for cash/for survival cycle. These variables are certainly going to change over the next few decades, rendering a labor-incentivized, cash-based economy inoperable, in which neither side is partial to human labor being the focal point of our economy anymore. Standing in the way of resolution and acceptance of the transition from a human-based workforce to a machine-based workforce are fear, anger, panic, uncertainty, awkwardness, validation of the identity (I am what I do), mass financial insecurity, concern for the survival of family and friends, and so on. In the meantime, labor-replacement technology continues to bore into incomes worldwide and does its best to eliminate labor costs as fast as it can while at the same time giving no credence to helping reduce our overhead, as our real estate, transportation, and medical costs continue to increase decade after decade.

Since it appears to be a foregone conclusion that the labor/for cash/for survival exchange concept will no longer be a viable entity, within the next few decades, the easiest way to resolve this long-term problem would be to come to a common understanding that the best thing we could possibly do as a country is unite to reduce the overhead costs of each and every citizen in the United States. Specifically, we need to reduce overhead in order to combat our future declining incomes, caused by automation and outsourcing, so that our declining labor hours and incomes are balanced with declining overhead (rent, mortgage payments, transportation costs, medical costs, etc.) at a steady pace over the course of the next few decades, until our accepted business practice of labor/for cash/for survival is no longer required by the general public. Unless we all come together and accept this common goal, we can expect our society to become more fractured, people to become indifferent to the plights of one another, massive reductions to our level of abundance and prosperity, our homeless population to grow, our citizens to leave the country for cheaper overhead locations, and essentially a financial crash, as declining incomes get crushed by ever-increasing overhead costs. The basic premise of capitalism is that neither side—the worker or the company—can exist without the other: companies need consumers with cash to buy their products and consumers mainly need their cash for survival. Yet, the ultimate goal of either side is to exist and flourish without the other. One side wants to retire, while the other side wants a fully automated operation requiring no human labor. Essentially, both sides are fighting with each other, rather than cooperating with each other to create mutually beneficial goals. The currency-based economy is a primitive system that we should look to evolve beyond in order to start living the lives that we all deserve.

In order to understand where we are going, we need to have a better understanding of where we are now and make an honest assessment of the present. Right now, we are evolving our survival technology at an unprecedentedly slow pace due to intellectual property laws that allow the direct purchase and shelving of vital new and upcoming technologies we need to survive; that are regulated through patent law. Our current products are built with planned obsolescence and planned repairs to be made a regular intervals by consumers. These planned repairs are built into our for-profit system. Repair services and replacement parts are a goldmine for corporations and shorten the life span any product, forcing consumers to upgrade or replace these products altogether.

Under the currency-based system, no company or person in their right mind would ever design, build, or sell a product that does not do the following:

1. Make a profit.

2. Create any product to last an extended period of time without building in a planned failure of its components, requiring its complete replacement.

3. Protect its inferior technology and brand name through patent or copyright law and purchase any competing technology in order to shelve and not develop that technology. This keeps its inferior product in the public purchasing domain as long as possible, thus drastically slowing the evolving pace of our planet's survival technology development.

In short, we keep recycling slightly upgraded inferior products to the general public decade after decade. If companies ever intended to build products to last hundred years and actually produced them, without any required replacement or maintenance, the forty-hour work week would cease to exist almost completely within the next few decades. **The problem with the current system is that everyone is incentivized to make technology inferior, rather than superior.** We can no longer cling to the past with phrases like, "Well, this is the best we can do." This is 2020, not 1920, and we are not using pencils and pieces of paper to sketch out rudimentary ideas anymore. We possess advanced microcomputers and artificial intelligence to help us design, build, and mass-produce new technologies that should no longer require us to work for cash, for our short-term survival any longer. One hundred years ago, during the time of the Industrial Revolution, we might have accomplished a decent standard of living by haphazardly following these old business models, but based on the rapid pace of technological advancement we currently experience, we are on a collision course between job loss and ever-increasing overhead.

Our goal: The extreme long-term goal of America should be to reduce both its revenues and its expenses to zero. With this goal in mind, it would be better to eliminate all of our expenses first by creating technology to service all of our survival needs, so at the point in our evolution when we no longer need to work for cash, our overhead costs would already have been reduced to zero, thus ensuring that our survival on this planet remains intact. Our human labor should be replaced with more efficient technologies over time and eliminate our need to work altogether, as machines build our homes and grow our food. The plan I am going to outline in this text has one goal, and that goal is to create superior survival technology that the entire planet can use and enjoy.

What is superior technology? It is a portable energy-generating device that would create more energy than it consumes—a superior solar panel hundreds of times more efficient than the ones we use today, with no installation costs, that could easily power all our homes and automobiles with no ongoing monthly cost. A brand-new home costing $25,000 or less: a home that can be built anywhere and does not require hook up to any type of public utility grid, that is completely energy- and water-independent. Finally, virtually any type of technology that does not require repair or replacement for a period of twenty-five years or more.

Our new technology-based economy would be a hybrid of our current economy and still use cash or cards to purchase all the goods and services everyone does today, but it would differ from the current system in that it would regulate four specific industries:

1. Energy

2. Healthcare

3. Transportation

4. Housing

These four industries represent the highest household currency expenditures per month per person and drive the greatest need for jobs, in order to produce income needed by all Americans to survive. The rest of the economy, including all other industries and companies, would operate normally as they do today, autonomous of any of these new rule changes. The Internal Revenue Service tax code, safety rules, and the entire for- profit system would not change and would remain in its current state, as it operates today, outside of these four industries. This system requires no fancy federal tax cuts, infrastructure spending plans, or federal government intervention.

This new system would affect only the energy, health-care, transportation, and housing industries and would keep existing technologies fully in place as they are now: it would simply change the rules under which these industries could operate, so that we could introduce new, superior survival technology in the most efficient and cost-effective manner possible. This would drive down our overhead costs today before we lose our jobs and income to cheap overseas labor and automation tomorrow.

Each company in these four industries would be required to carry a license in order to legally continue its business operations, much the same way that we now require an attorney or physician to be licensed in order to practice their skills and trade with the general public. The sale of their product without a valid license would be a violation of the licensing code and carry extreme penalties, including a lengthy prison sentence. Under the rules of licensing, all companies in these four industries would become non-profit, non-publicly traded, and patents covering all technologies affecting their products and services would no longer be enforceable. Licensing these overheard industries would allow an open sourcing of technology and open cooperative collaboration between companies within each industry, which we desperately need in order to increase our standard of living in America and around the world to help combat starvation, slavery, and poverty.

Workers in these four industries would be heavily incentivized with both quarterly and yearly bonuses based on meeting certain goals, allowing them to make at least 10% or more than they are now and even up to 20% more in our health-care industry, to ensure our economy runs smoothly during the transition from human-based labor to machine-based labor.

Dropping our overhead reduces our reliance on currency and allows us to work fewer hours per year, insulating us from the effects of job and income loss through outsourcing and advancing automation in the long term. This is a tiered system to be implemented over time, starting with just our energy and health-care industries, to keep our economy as stable as possible while undergoing these rule changes. The system is tiered because making these major wholesale changes to the way these industries operate will cause abrupt changes to our currency-based economy, which we shall examine in detail in later chapters. Understand that it is important to plan and implement this new system with patience, temperance, and a clear knowledge of its effects on our currency-based, human labor-driven economy before we actually execute this plan and require any of these four industries to become licensed.

Licensing laws affecting our energy, health-care, transportation, and housing industries would be directly voted on by the citizens of each state through well-drafted state propositions and would not require approval by our federal government to be enacted into law. Collusion would be required by all the participating states enacting licensing propositions. Licensing propositions would need to be voted on and passed by a multitude of states simultaneously, in order for them to be effective and not allow corporations to simply exit any newly licensed state to avoid compliance. I will expand on the practice of collusion between the states in a later chapter in detail, but rest assured this can easily be done.

Propositions would be drafted for public vote by a publicly elected state economic committee, consisting of 12 members. Each committee member would be prohibited from owning stock, or any type of equity position, in any company and limited to an income of $200,00.00 per year (adjusted for inflation) for up to two four-year terms, as well as a fifteen-year cooling off period after they leave office. We simply need to put an end to golden parachutes and multi-million-dollar jobs waiting for those who endorse corporate profits over people. Holding stock in any company while holding a public office is a direct conflict of interest and a criminal act. Each state's publicly elected economic committee would work to draft an economic crime bill to be voted on through state proposition; this proposition would cover: misconduct by any economic committee member (such as violating their income and equites restrictions and fraud crimes committed against a hundred people or more) or by any private company in any given state, as well as cover violations, penalties, and ongoing compliance practices for companies that fall under the new licensing rules. The penalty for an economic crime would be twenty-five years to life in prison, with no possibility of parole. An economic crime bill ensures proper enforcement and compliance of the law covering committee members and all companies requiring licensing. The economic committee would only draft propositions to be voted on by the public and no other branch of their state or federal government, putting the power of survival directly back into the hands of the public. The power over your own survival that has been so blatantly circumvented by our currency-based system would now be directly controlled by you.

A technology-based economy restores the equality of access to technology for all Americans, whose human rights are being violated through "at will" employment conflicted by an old-world system of privatized, patented, and withheld survival technology, technology that is and has been severely restricted in its development or halted altogether by our current system of laws in order to perpetuate needless future expenditures by the American public. On a planet approaching a population of nine billion, it is simply an inevitability that everyone will need open access to low-cost survival technology in order to survive in the future. Billions of people in overseas countries are becoming more educated, representing an ever-increasing low-cost supply of skilled labor that will fiercely compete with an undereducated American workforce. Corporations world-wide are working every day to create technology that replaces human labor. Our aging baby boomer population is slowly becoming lifetime recipients of social security, rather than tax payers, and simultaneously has created an overwhelming amount of national and consumer debt. A technology-based system empowers people who are looking for answers to the questions such as why they continue to work perpetually for their entire lives, yet never see their standard of living increase. This system gives the public the effective expertise and guidance they need to overturn laws that now work against them, laws that threaten their present and future survival. This system provides them the direct power to create a new economy through their direct actions and votes.

We cannot stop using currency today, but we can reduce our dependency on it by taking direct action to reduce the everyday costs to survive comfortably in the United States. Ninety-nine percent of the population spends the majority of their time working to cover survival expenses and paying for inferior technology that requires constant repurchase each month in the form of: rent, mortgage payments, car payments, car repairs, health-care costs etc., which constantly drains their bank accounts. This giant overhead monster, like a six-month-old infant, requires our constant attention in the form of our physical labor, which is converted to cash and spent just as quickly. Our federal government's answer to the problem is to print more money or lower interest rates, giving us greater access to cheap credit, in order to constantly consume a mindlessly produced stream of interior technology. How long can this fiat money system of ours backed by nothing last? Ten years? Twenty? Fifty? How long can we mindlessly print currency without consequences? It is time to eliminate this old game and move forward into a new idealism and, with it, bring about a new physically manifested reality. Let us move away from our fragmented and chaotic currency for survival system in the safest and most efficient manner possible. A country driven by a technology-based economy would unite us all and allow us to move forward with one goal: to provide the highest quality, cutting edge, lowest cost survival technology on the planet so that Americans will welcome the advancement of technology into their lives, rather than fear its inevitability.

Let us take a fictional trip into the past to better understand where we are today. Back in the 1700s, there was a notorious band of pirates whose goal was to plunder all the silver, gold, and jewels they could over the course of their lifetime; after that, they would never have to work again and could live like kings, or so the story goes. After taking over a merchant ship one fateful day, one of the pirates discovered a map in quarters of the ship's captain. The map led to a secret island near Fiji, where, within a hidden sea cave, hundreds of chests lay, holding within them gold doubloons, rubies, emeralds, diamonds, silver chalices, and more riches than they could ever spend over the course of more lifetimes than they could ever live. Miraculously, the pirates were able to use the map, though they faced treacherous obstacles, to find the location of the treasure and boarded the pirate booty onto their ship. Once the treasure was safely hidden away, the pirates could live their lives in a state of bliss, peace, and abundance until their passing. After their haul was safely tucked away, they went to the local tavern, hooped and hollered, jumped up and down, and experienced joy like they never had before. Although they all outwardly expressed their emotions; each one knew the importance of keeping the information and the location of the treasure an absolute secret. The information was never shared with anyone but themselves for the rest of their lives, so they had unlimited access to currency at their disposal, whenever they wished, until their death.

Sounds like a great story, doesn't it? Now what you think actually happened to those pirates? Do you think they lived an incredible life day after day, never experiencing sadness, irritation, or any kind of adversity? Do you think they experienced a truly easy and prosperous life? What do you think they bought with all that treasure? Well, what they were able to specifically purchase and obtain was the most advanced technology available to them in the 1700s. Would they be able to go to a dentist, to have a porcelain crown put in, if one of their teeth failed? No, that technology was not available back then. Could they obtain access to a CAT scan, if they fell and hit their head? How about access to central air conditioning or a refrigerator down in the tropics? No, none of that technology was available to them either. How about the ability to watch movies, make a telephone call, use a smart phone to download music or access to the Internet, to retrieve any information they wanted? Was any of that technology available to the richest men in the world? No: perhaps access to a lot of alcohol and the ability to purchase slaves to do their work for them was their most likely outcome, along with a life span of about thirty-six years, which was the average life expectancy during the seventeenth century.

Wow! So, a thirty-year-old uber-rich pirate could expect to live roughly another six years as an incredibly bored drunk before they died. Gee… Where can I sign up for that life? My point being, *the ease and prosperity of your life is directly related to the technology available to you at the time you are living in on this earth and not to the amount of currency you possess.* The technology is what it is, regardless of the price you pay for it. The richest people in the world could not enjoy air-conditioning in the 1700s; the richest people in the world could not enjoy television or the Internet in the 1800s. Fifty years ago, the richest people in the world could not make a call from a cell phone, and, in the present day, the richest person on the earth cannot not walk through a portal and be instantly transported to another planet. But perhaps, in another hundred years, the poorest person on the planet will be able to do that quite easily and that person will look back on us and laugh and wonder why we thought we had such a great life, when all we had access to was very rudimentary technology. In much the same way, we look back at the richest pirates in the world in the 1700s and would never trade places with them, no matter how much money or treasure would be given to us.

CHAPTER 2

The Currency-Driven Economy of Today

Let us take an in-depth look at the system today so we can better understand why we need to move on to a more efficient system that is going to allow us to work less and create a higher standard of living for everyone.

An economy that distributes currency as its primary focus relies heavily on an uneducated population to do the lion's share of work for a small group of people. This small group of people, those who own the largest amount of currency, will supply debt to the majority of the population in order for them to constantly repurchase its mass-produced inferior technology. The majority of the population keeps on servicing that debt over time through cash, produced through the efforts of their labor. The mass population of any currency-based economy also needs currency to constantly replace and repair its existing survival technology, technology that a currency-based economy gives no incentive to advance, beyond a slightly better substitute, than currently offered by the open market, in order to capture the greatest possible amount of market share. In a currency driven economy, there is a constant need for credit and long-term financing to purchase and repurchase major items pertaining to survival. In this case, two obvious examples would be homes and automobiles and servicing their constant maintenance costs and/ or eventual replacement. The system requires currency constantly flowing through the system and a lot of physical labor in order to keep income flowing to the majority of households within that economy. This type of system is incredibly vulnerable to: changes in technology, changes in weather, changes in the confidence of consumers, changes to the credit system, changes to the tax system, and a myriad of other issues. You can expect life to be very unstable in a currency-based economy, because survival needs are purchased through currency and continued flowing currency, to any citizen, is not a guarantee. A currency-based economy is subject to all sorts of chaos, depending on the whims and fancies of all sorts of fundamentals, one of the major fundamentals being the emotional swings of the major currency holders.

15 Reasons Why the System Is Destined to Fail

There are basically fifteen major reasons why I believe a currency-based system has always been, more or less, a system powered by slaves—either actual human slaves or modern-day debt slaves, depending on the specific time period. History shows us, time and again, a large group of people indenturing themselves to a small group of people in order to purchase evolving technology. The laws driving our past currency-based economies around the world have essentially not changed for thousands of years. Today, as we move into a manufacturing and decision-making system that replaces human labor and even human thought with machines, the current system is destined to fail, because the traditional cycle of labor for cash for survival, will no longer apply. Let us examine fifteen major reasons why a currency-based, for-profit economy has never served the public well, stops the natural evolution of technology, and violates the human rights of almost all the people in any country that voluntarily chooses to participate in it.

Reason 1. The system is so complicated that no one understands it and needs to hire a specialist just to navigate any particular section.

A currency-based economy, in which 100% of the goods and services are purchased with currency, including all survival technology, contains a labyrinth of laws in order to ensure that currency is constantly flowing toward inferior technology. Let us examine the labyrinth of the massive laws associated with our current system: the IRS tax code, monetary and fiscal policies, wills and trusts, federal and state consumer protection and finance laws, the credit system—consisting of mortgages for which, at this time, the FHA single-family policy handbook for FHA loans stretches over 1,000 pages—in addition to auto loans, personal loans, student loans, and credit cards. Do you know of any one person in the entire country who understands all this? There is not one person that I know of who would be versed in all these different types of laws affecting currency. The majority of the population does not even remotely understand any of the laws governing the system and simply gives up, becomes easily manipulated and commits themselves to an endless cycle of income and spending.

Since no one understands the system and its goal—which is only to increase profit, not to increase the abundance and prosperity of our society or its standard of living, so the results of our hard work show highly diminished returns. Where exactly do we need to put our efforts as a society, culture, and people to increase our standard of living, while at the same time working less? Good luck finding an answer to that, making a goal, or navigating this elaborate system of rules. You will need to see an accountant if you want to understand tax law, an attorney if you want a will or a trust to protect your assets, an investment person for long term financial advice, a loan officer if you want a home loan, etc. You need to see a specialist for almost every type of transaction that affects your financial life. So, how can you "directly" affect your survival and your long-term well-being? How can you work fewer hours while simultaneously directly taking action to decrease your overhead?

The only way to do that is to work a job or run a business which produces a single byproduct called currency, which you exchange for your survival, so the actions you take each and every day, week after week, decade after decade, and over the course of your entire lifetime do not directly advance your survival technology, nor contribute directly to your survival, nor do the collective actions of others. The system basically gives most people only one option, which is to solve their survival problems by increasing their income; this is the only power you really have left over your survival since the Constitution was enacted. The system separates survival technology into separate areas and, through a labyrinth of laws, no longer allows the average American citizen direct control over it. The pioneers dug their own wells, built their own homes, and raised a barn with their friends and neighbors. Now you rely on "for-profit" third parties to create your home at an exorbitant price, plus interest, which can take some individuals up to thirty, forty, or even fifty years to pay off! How exactly is that progress? When the pioneer finished their work, their home was done! No mortgage, no property taxes, no insurance premium. Yes, they had to do just about everything to create that home through manual labor, but we have far more advanced technologies now than the pioneer had, and yet we are still working our entire lives and, based on the system we have evolved into, we have absolutely no direct control over our survival anymore. Should we not be working less and enjoying more? Why is this all happening? The laws and beliefs that we currently have in place running our economy that we refuse to change are directly holding us in a state of perpetual servitude to currency. It is only through changes in these laws that we can move forward; trying to solve our problems with more currency or higher incomes will never work, as you will see shortly, because the entire currency system is tied up in so many paradoxes, that it no longer serves the population anymore. Would it not be easier for all of us to work together to reduce our overhead expenses every month, rather always having to chase these ever-increasing expenses, with more work for cash?

Reason 2. Employees and corporations have two different agendas; each is mutually exclusive to the other and each is designed to cause the other harm.

The ultimate goal of any business is to reduce overhead. This means that any chance there is to reduce labor costs through artificial intelligence, robotics, or foreign outsourcing will be acted upon by a business owner or corporation. Contrast this with the goal of every American worker, which is to retire, thus leaving the workforce and no longer working. The hidden goal of everyone is to not work and have machines take care of all our needs, yet we do not acknowledge this publicly. So, if you look at the equation from either side, neither the employer nor the employee is interested in engaging or building any type of long-term beneficial relationship, other than to facilitate the exchange of currency. Further we must ponder the consequence that there will be no one to buy anyone's product in a fully automated economy, where cash for labor no longer exists. If a business reaches its ultimate goal of zero labor costs and 100% automation and each business in the United States follows suit, without the advantage of superior survival technology, chaos results, because there are no longer incomes to be exchanged for survival. The United States, and in fact any country in the world, simply has no idea how to best implement technology into its society for the greatest benefit of its citizens. We are all moving haphazardly forward without a plan, a vision, and an understanding of what we can accomplish together.

Reason 3. Superior technology destroys currency.

Let us pick just one industry of the many in the United States today that use currency as a means of exchange to illustrate how superior technology implemented into our current economy would destroy any currency-based, for-profit economy as we know it, very quickly. The currency-based economy requires a constant circulation of currency, because it is constantly producing inferior technology that requires repair and replacement. Like a giant overhead monster, it constantly has to be fed currency through vast amounts of labor, like a two-year-old child screaming for its dinner. The real estate industry, for example, requires vast amounts of labor to keep the price of real estate constantly increasing. If we were able to eliminate ever increasing real estate lot costs and on-site building costs and perhaps create a home on a half-acre of land for $25,000, that substitute technology or home would be superior to current homes today. All the existing homes based on inferior technology would quickly no longer be relevant consumers. "So, what happens then?" you might ask.

1. The current technology—in other words, the incredibly expensive, existing wooden built homes that we know, love, and dream about today—become virtually worthless. Our new superior home, due to its low purchase price, does not need a mortgage or deed of trust anymore. Consumers could potentially buy a home on their credit card and all the various jobs used to make these home loans possible would no longer exist. The real estate appraiser, loan underwriter, the realtor, loan officer, loan processor, home inspector, pest inspector, and all the executives and supporting positions to these jobs, would no longer be required because you could buy a home with an unsecured credit card or perhaps just the extra money in your savings account.

2. The second thing that would happen is that the financial system would collapse. The collateral securitizing the loans of the outstanding banks of the country would basically become worthless. No one would continue to pay on a thirty-year mortgage, when they could default on their existing home loan and purchase a home on a larger piece of land with superior technology for the fraction of the cost. The irony is, when you collapse the currency of a country, that very moment is the only time when you have true equality across all of its people. In a currency collapse, all the assets of the rich become worthless and all the debt of the poor is no longer is collectible, because all the legal instruments are written for the bearers of the debt to receive income (principal and interest) in US dollars, which is no longer a recognized

form of repayment, so in essence the debt cannot be legally collected under the new denomination of currency issued by the government. Technically, the government has the power to potentially require the repayment of debts under the new currency and keep existing contracts valid; however, this creates a very difficult situation from a legal perspective. I hope this gives you a greater understanding of the currency-based economy: the poor work for the rich in the form of repaying debt and increasing stock prices through their work and make the rich passive income, in other words, income from doing nothing but holding a lot of currency and exploiting the poor. Specifically, this is why there are very serious consequences to introducing superior survival technology into an economy that has adopted a practice of creating jobs and working constantly, doing repetitive tasks over and over again, in order to constantly repurchase inferior technology. This is exactly why I designed the licensing system to be a tiered based system, to be implemented in each of the four survival industries over time, rather than trying to make massive changes all at once, which would certainly cause a strain on incomes, resulting in severe consequences to everyone during the changeover.

Ultimately, our future will be determined by our ability to manage the unstoppable force of "technology" versus the immovable object of "currency." If we develop a high level of technology that is superior and does not require constant maintenance and repair in our energy, health-care, transportation, and housing industries, we will radically transform the way we live and will not need to commit ourselves to service in perpetuity in order to survive. More importantly, we can develop a strong and resilient system of survival, as we lose jobs over the long run to technology.

Reason 4. The for-profit/technology paradox

The current system ensures that we will always make only slightly better technology that is an improvement over the existing technology we have now, only for the sole purpose of getting consumers to buy that product, no other reason. Planned obsolescence and repair costs are built in to the product, no matter how evolved we believe its evolution to be. We will always need currency to cover overhead costs so we all can survive. 100% of everything in our country is purchased through currency, including all our survival needs and survival technology. The problem with the currency system is that the companies that are responsible for reducing your overhead are caught in a "for-profit" paradox. In order to be in the most abundant state possible on this planet, we will need the lowest possible overhead costs. If the companies in the industries that are responsible for producing your survival technology followed this track, they would quickly be put out of business. Ideally, we would want our overhead companies fully automated with almost no labor and the rest of the businesses in America operating business as usual; in order for this to happen, we will need to change the laws affecting the way these companies do business, while at the same time incentivizing the workers to make sure our financial markets do not fail. The irony is, if you created lower overhead, then everyone would not need to make as much money or work as many hours, so it is only with a plan to be able to make the leap toward this new system, transcending away from our high overhead technology, that we will ever reach our goal. What I am simply stating here is that it is time to get the "for-profit paradox" out of our overhead costs (energy, health care, transportation, and housing) and provide these products and services with the idea of offering them to our citizens at the lowest cost possible in the short term and then, in the long-term, continually working on solutions to the point where the cost of these products and services becomes inconsequential and eventually free of charge. No company or group of companies is ever going to follow this plan, because it would put them out of business simultaneously: everyone needs money to survive, hence the paradox and the reason for fundamental changes in the law and ideals. Superior technology kills profits and profits severely delay and even destroy the development of technology, as you will see later on in the text.

The currency-based system incentivizes a mass production of temporary household goods, with a short lifespan that it constantly requires us to repurchase, causing mass waste problems and environmental hazards. The current system incentivizes the supply of all goods and services to be inferior, with short life-spans and built-in repair costs, and the consumer is forced to go into debt because their incomes cannot keep up with the purchasing pace that the suppliers of inferior technology require in order to meet their quarterly sales goals. The result is a constant stream of production on the supply side that requires vast amounts of human labor and the consumer consequently creates and ever-increasing amount of debt. There is absolutely no incentive to create a product that would last for a very long period of time or not require routine repairs in a for-profit, currency-based economy. An internet article by Fastcompany.com stated that as of 2018, "right to repair legislation has been introduced into 18 states."[1] In 2020, 20 states have now either adopted or intend to vote on right to repair legislation. This is in essence the biggest problem we have to overcome today: changing the beliefs, laws and incentives of the aggregate population whose views are outdated and no longer congruent with the current level of technology we have today, in order to create different results for the aggregate population

Basically 99% of the population relies on their labor or passive income from the financial markets and public assistance that is directly supported by the constant repetitive labor of our earning workforce.

Reason 5. Patents

Patents slow down the rate of evolution of technology and cause competition versus cooperation; patents precipitate a cloaking of technology from those that might seek to improve it in the most efficient cost-effective manner possible. Patent law is a fairytale that the American public has falsely believed for thousands of years which simply states that the first person to file for a

---

1   https://www.fastcompany.com/40518779/right-to-repair-legislation-has-now-been-introduced-in-17-states

patent is the owner of that technology for up to twenty years and has exclusive rights to it and can sue anyone who tries to produce similar technology. I am committing a whole chapter of this book to patents and the understanding of patent law and why it is completely and totally unsound. We've simply created a law to allow the monopolization of technology by corporations, while we know in truth that original thought cannot be proven. There have been almost 150 documented cases of simultaneous invention in just this country alone. In other words, multiple people filed a patent for the same exact type of technology within weeks or days of each other, or sometimes even just hours. The law has nothing to do with merit or achievement and automatically perpetuates a state of ever increasing debt by the general public to the inventor for the privilege of access to their technology, a general public that supported the inventor's life by providing them access to food, shelter, and an education, etc., yet the law still states that society needs to pay the inventor for access to their technology. Why, you might ask? Because that is what the law states, and nothing more. This is an antiquated law similar to human slavery. There was no justifiable reason to enslave people, but slave masters stood behind the law, allowing them to own slaves as chattel property, simply because it benefited them. The law had nothing to do with morality, justice, or any type of principle; it was simply an immoral law that should have never been allowed within any society or culture in the first place. Patent law is a misdirected belief held by the collective of our society as acceptable, and this misdirected belief is the cornerstone of our current economic demise. If you can control the technology people need to survive, then you can control an entire planet—it is as simple as that. If you cannot get people to buy into the idea that currency and patents are good for them and that their society cannot evolve without them, then their control over the population simply vanishes! It is all an illusion, please remember that.

Only through sharing ideas and building our country together can we truly lower our survival technology costs. Patents are perhaps the biggest impetus, if not *the* impetus, to creating a technology driven economy. Patents will always drastically reduce the efficient evolution of technology and bring it to a halt, whenever possible, in any industry.

Basically 99% of the population relies on their labor or passive income from the financial markets and public assistance that is directly supported by the constant repetitive labor of our earning workforce. The majority of Americans are indebted and encumbered servants to 1% of our society. An article from *The Guardian* in 2018 cited information from the charity Oxfam that had reported in 2017 that "forty-two of the richest people in the world have the same net worth as approximately half the population of the planet," and that "82% of the wealth generated in 2017 went to the wealthiest 1% of society.[2] By deductive reasoning, this leaves the remaining 18% of the world's wealth to be divided up between 99% of the population of the planet.

I do not know how anyone can look at the system and believe that we should remain in a system of mass inequality, rather than moving forward into a new type of economy that distributes technology rather than currency. Income inequality between rich and poor continues to rise decade after decade, as the average wealth received by the top 1% tripled between 1980 and 2012 in the United States alone. My question to you is: How do you expect a recent college graduate or any young person, for that matter, to get ahead in a currency-based, for-profit economy, when 82% of the world's wealth is already taken off the table before they ever start their first job? 99% of the population fights for 18% of the wealth; the system is set up directly and specifically to be rigged against anyone in the general public from ever attaining any sort of sustainable wealth and prosperity.

Reason 6. The monopoly/technology paradox

In the first draft of my book, I spent a whole chapter covering various types of markets, with all sorts of snappy graphs, charts, and explanations of how

---

2　https://www.theguardian.com/inequality/2018/jan/22/ inequality-gap-widens-as-42-people-hold-same-wealth-as-37bn-poorest

these current markets work, but, quite frankly, my explaining all these mundane details would've lost my readers, so I will try to get to the point of how the American for-profit, currency-based markets really operate, as quickly as I can.

Around the turn of the nineteenth Century, the public could see single companies attempting to take control of certain industries. The people at this time were much wiser and savvier toward the art of fraudulent business practices and public exploitations in order to manipulate humans so that they might sustain their own survival more independently than our population today. Throughout American history, there has always been one company or another looking to control any market and force people to pay hand over fist for its product.

After doing extensive research on the Sherman Anti-Trust Act, a federal law that allowed the American government to force penalties against monopiles and their abuses against the public, my own personal opinion is that honest people in government tried to stop companies from running roughshod over people by creating a law like the Sherman Antitrust Act, but in order to facilitate an actual change of for-profit, currency-based industries, they had to go to court over a long period of time, spend a lot of money and exude infinite patience before any court ever made any type a ruling. We should expect the mass population of country to be ripped off for years, or even decades, simply because they need to survive, before anything can be done through the court system to change current monopoly powers. Would it not make sense to make companies nonprofit, non-publicly traded, and patent free, thus eliminating their incentives to gouge the public over their survival needs, rather than always having to go through long drawn out court battles to get results?

I would like to emphasize a few key points about the incentives for all companies in a currency-based economy:

1. The goal of any company in a for-profit currency-based economy is to create the most profit possible. The goal of advancing technology, protecting the ecosphere, or increasing the standard of living for the general public is simply not part of this directive; slightly better technology is only produced as a byproduct to profit maximization.

2. In order to complete step one and make the most profit possible, any company's goal should be to evolve itself to a state where it can become a true monopoly and control the entire industry and market that it now produces any good or service in. The incentives for the greatest amount of currency flow are definitely present if your company can operate as a monopoly, so all companies under the currency system are incentivized to become monopolies.

3. Monopolies, by definition, can only control markets through the cessation of the advancement of technology in their industry; once they lose their stranglehold on technology and their competitors are able to produce it better, faster, or cheaper than their company can, they are no longer a monopoly or even a market dominator. Therefore, it would be in the best interest of any company, small or large, that wanted to maximize profit, to purchase any potential competing technology by purchasing all patented technology currently threatening it, whether these patents be fully developed or not. If I were the owner of a worldwide corporation with a large market share of any industry, I would certainly go out of my way to purchase any potential competing technology and, if it was not available yet, I would certainly have my research and development department work on patenting even a small portion of the process of any potential undiscovered technology, so that I could bring a patent infringement suit to court against any party that developed this technology. In short, I would do anything and everything I could to stop the development of technology that would actually help people, in order to keep my market share and profit margins as large as possible.

4. What we can safely say based on the incentivized parameters outlined in Steps 1, 2, and 3, is that the goal of every company that operates within the currency-based economy, is evolving itself to a point where it can stop the evolution of technology in any industry! On some level, even the staunchest critic would have to concede this point, to some extent, because the system has blatantly incentivized humans to follow this progression, regardless of the type of market economy their company currently resides in, whether it be small business operators, farmers, airlines, or multinational energy conglomerates. The incentive to control market share is always constant, regardless of the size of the company or the level of control it has over any market's supply and pricing. It seems that only in their failure to become monopolies, companies advance technology at a slowed, misdirected, and chaotic pace directly caused by using currency as their focal point of trade. An oil company is not a monopoly but is certainly part of the very strong oligopoly. Oligopolies have extensive barriers to entry and startup costs and their product is highly differentiated (extremely difficult to produce). Oil companies certainly have the ability to purchase the patents of any potential competing technology, or use their research and development departments to file patents on certain processes that other technologies might piggyback on to produce a competing technology. In either scenario, the general public, by allowing patents to proliferate the energy industry, are basically handing over the "keys to the candy store" to these types of companies, by continuing to support their businesses without questioning the rules governing them. Literally every time you "pay at the pump," you are giving money to a company whose only goal is to stop the development of any technology that would compete with it in its industry. You are actually funding the company with money to purchase the patents it needs to keep itself in a perpetual state of business, selling the same product over and over again. Every time you "pay at the pump," you literally ensure that

you will continue to "pay at the pump" perpetually. Can you see why a carbon tax will never work or ever reduce our consumption of oil? Only the development of alternative technologies that are superior to oil, that are made available to the public at the lowest possible cost, will solve this problem, and the technology we desperately need will never be seen or heard of by anyone within our society, as long as the current laws remain in place, governing our survival industries. Our antitrust laws and supposed "free markets" for energy development here in the United States have not seemed to produce a stellar track record of success over the last fifty years or so. A 2016 article in *The Guardian* by Susan Goldberg stated that Exxon Mobile indeed patented technologies for electric cars, including batteries, as early as 1963, yet never developed them for mass production to the public, while at the same time they urged the government to not research any of these new technologies for public use. Exxon stated they were doing extensive research at the time and there was no need for government intervention.[3]

Patent law opens up myriad of ways companies can stop the evolution of technology by compensating the legal expenses of another aggrieved or potentially aggrieved party in a court trial for rights to a patent. There is simply no end to the different ways in which companies can stop technology, from overtaking their market share, regardless of the strength of the antitrust laws trying to protect "free markets." Would it not be easier to stop infringing on the technology rights of humans and just give technology to people?

If you've been under the assumption that someone is just going to invent an incredible piece of technology and set up a "mom and pop store" to sell it out of that forever changes the face of the planet, my question to you is: If it is so obvious that this scenario could happen, why has it not happened

---

3   https://www.theguardian.com/business/2016/may/20/oil-company-records-exxon-co2-emission-reduction-patents

yet? We've been burning petroleum-based products for over hundred years and went to the moon over fifty years ago: clearly no sane person could come to any other conclusion, other than that the current laws in place running our economy are allowing for a mass manipulation and sequestration of technology, to be held and separated from the general public's use.

Reason 7. The inflation/technology paradox

This paradox simply states that anytime there are economic cycles on the upswing and more cash flows throughout the general public, inflation occurs. What does that mean in simple terms? It means that any time you have more money and you have scarce amount of goods and services; you are going to pay more for the same basket of goods and the same level of technology. The current system is based on scarcity; it is not based on abundance or trying to achieve any sort of goal, betterment, or higher standard of living for the general public. In short, if times are good, you make more currency with the same level of access to scarce technology, so you are going to pay more currency for the same item in good economic times versus bad economic times—the utility or useful value of the product does not come into play or matter. The bottom line is, the vast majority of America lives paycheck to paycheck, and by increasing incomes, we increase the amount of income taxes that Americans are going to pay, because the income tax is a progressive tax—the more you earn, the more you pay—in addition to the fact that inflation is basically going to take over and increase the cost of a limited supply of goods. There are many factors that go into calculating the actual standard of living any person can attain in the United States: location—the general cost of living in their area or when they bought their house—which might determine the level of their mortgage payment, or they may be protected under rent control, their level of property taxes, state sales or income taxes, their local economic job stability, their level of education and profession. The fact that there are so many factors involved in determining the relative standard of living in a currency-based economy, it certainly makes sense to evolve into something better, if possible, because the more factors involved in determining anyone's standard of living, the more vulnerable that standard of living is to negative changes.

According to data from 2018, from the Social Security Administration's website:

About 67.4 percent of wage earners had net compensation less than or equal to the $50,000.44 raw average wage. By definition, 50 percent of wage earners had net compensation less than or equal to the median wage, which is estimated to be $32,838.05 for 2018.[4]

These numbers are not exactly what I would call staggeringly wealthy.

According to a 2017 article from Carrerbuilder.com using data from a national survey:

- Approximately 78% of the United States population lives paycheck to paycheck.

- About 25% of U.S. workers save nothing every month.

- Nearly 75% of all workers believe they will always be in debt.

- More than half the minimum-wage workers in the United States need to work a second job just to pay their monthly bills.[5]

Let us say, for example, that 75% of the population got extremely motivated and decided to make $1 million per year as their goal and, after several years, all of them reached their goal! Guess what would happen in this scenario? The purchasing power of their money would, in the long run, buy them no more technology—housing, automobiles or other goods and services—than the amount of currency they had today, before all these people ever embarked on this journey. Of the population, 75% would continue working perpetually, most likely for the rest of their lives. The results of this

---

4   https://www.ssa.gov/cgi-bin/netcomp.cgi?year=2018
5   http://press.careerbuilder.com/2017-08-24-Living-Paycheck-to-Paycheck-is-a-Way-of-Life-for-Majority-of-U-S-Workers-According-to-New-CareerBuilder-Survey

scenario are caused by inflation and all inflation is: is paying more currency for limited technology. Some critics might argue that there would be some short-term benefits to this increase in income to our economy, but over the long run inflation would kick in and most likely negate all those benefits. Arguing over crumbs does not cease to change the big picture. Increasing the level of our income does not increase the level of our technology; only inventing, creating, and mass distributing technology to the public allows the public a chance to cease their endless forty-hour work week. When the majority of the population makes more money, the Federal Reserve is there to raise interest rates, and this simply translates into the fact that you are going to have to pay a higher interest rate now that times have been good and you can afford a down payment on a home; through these direct efforts, the federal government decreases your access to technology. The system is constantly mitigating any short-term success the public might have at gaining access to technology, to keep the public in a constant state of stagnation. Again, the system is based on scarcity; it is not based on abundance. These are unmitigated facts and cannot be debated, and yet people are willingly going along with the ideals of this currency-based economy and accept its limitations, without ever questioning the origins of its intentions. As an American citizen, I think you should seriously question why the value of the United States dollar has dropped roughly 95% since 1933? To purchase the same level amount of goods and services for $100 in 1933, you would need to spend the equivalent of $1,917.81 in 2020.

Roughly 60% of the people make just enough currency to survive month to month. Is it because they are stupid? Is it because they are lazy? Modern-day Americans have been hypnotized into thinking that currency will solve all their problems, so they do not have to work anymore, when that can never happen—only technology can replace human labor and only technology can make the price of your car, your house or your health care less expensive. Many people are afraid of what might happen to them if they stop working; most likely their beliefs surround family shame and homelessness nightmares, so with the only alternative of suffering major emotional strife, they "willingly" enslave themselves, as growing teenagers into a system that isolates people, divides the population, and provides false hope that one day an inventor of new technology is going to free them from their endless labor.

The system does not work for the aggregate; it is based on survival of the fittest, and it only serves a few that can fight their way to the top. It will never serve the aggregate, because *the aggregate will always lose out to inflation*. All of us suffer under a currency-based system; even the super-rich suffer because they could have access to better technology if patents and profits were not massively slowing down the evolution of technology in this country, or in some cases even halting it all together.

The currency system is based on a hierarchy that propagates separate rights through currency, rights that involve the ability to pay for the use of an express lane for example at a buck a mile in rush house traffic, while other motorists, whose taxes actually help to pay for the building of the road, sit in stop and go traffic. Separate rights to technology, such as purchasing a fast sports car, a mansion with the option of having swimming pool, etc., permeate our way of life. This is a system of inequality, no different from the apartheid system in South Africa. It certainly makes no sense for the general public to continue on suffering endlessly in order to keep for-profit incentives and fairytale patent laws in place.

Reason 8. Investors and executives are disconnected by system fundamentals from the evolution of their technologies.

The first stock markets started in the 1400s, and the East India trading Company was the world's first publicly traded company, shipping spices and silks from Asia. Eventually the New York Stock Exchange was founded in the United States in 1817.

Stocks were historically used as betting capital; in other words, speculators could bet on risky business ventures in the hopes of gaining back many times their initial wager. Stock markets are basically glorified gambling houses that mainly bet "for and against" products, commodities, and developing technologies needed for the survival of humans. Speculation also extends to both the greed and fear of society's social responses—to a lack of or abundance, changing natural resources and labor. Why is it necessary to have a stock market? Why has it ever been necessary to have a stock market, in the history of our country? What fundamentals does the stock market provide the public, in order to decrease their overhead and increase the overall prosperity and well-being of the common person? Financial services now represent 20%, of the gross domestic product of the United States. Basically, 20% of our domestic production is created by moving money around through middlemen, who produce no tangible product to benefit society and only exist to profit off the general public's labor for survival, through their parasitic relationship to currency. A March 2016 *Washington Post* article by Christopher Witko stated the United States finance, insurance and real estate industries now make up about 20% of the United State gross domestic product; this percentage of GDP has nearly doubled since 1947.[6]

Investors in stocks do not just seek a small return on their investment but expect a "gigantic" return on their risky investments. Venture capitalists make the price of developing technology on this planet far more expensive than it would otherwise be if we used alternative forms of financing for the growth of new technologies. Could long-term loans, perhaps at a 1–2% interest rate, be used instead of venture capital money? How about crowdfunding? Yes, of course they could: we should be doing everything in our power as a society to eliminate speculation from the development of our survival technology. Stocks trade on current and future potential earnings; as a general rule, the higher the profits of any company, the higher corresponding share

6   https://www.washingtonpost.com/news/monkey-cage/wp/2016/03/29/how-wall-street-became-a-big-chunk-of-the-u-s-economy-and-when-the-democrats-signed-on/?utm_term=.119b5c685af7

price of the stock. A price-to-earnings ratio is defined as the price of the stock divided by its earnings per share. So, if my company issues 500 shares of stock and my profit is $1,000, my earnings per share will be $2.00. If my stock is trading on the open market at $20 a share and my earnings per share are $2.00, that would mean my price-to-earnings ratio = 10.

A price-to-earnings ratio of 10 used to be a good fundamental barometer used in the decision-making of buying any particular stock; however, today many companies stocks do not trade on this fundamental but rather on sales revenues alone, and many investors ignore the fact a company is not making profit: they simply speculate on the company's ability to generate future sales. In other words, many publicly traded company's stocks trade on pure speculation and no fundamentals whatsoever. If you want examples of this, look no further than the insanely overpriced tech stocks that traded during the boom prior to the September 11 attacks. It is not hard to find examples of *Fortune* 100 companies that were trading at insanely high price-to-earnings ratios, of even 100 or more. My point here is that most stocks basically trade on pure speculation and get heavily overvalued during positive economic cycles, and this overvaluation eventually leads to massive selloffs, which potentially spur job layoffs, recessions, and puts the survival of American citizens in peril. Why should the speculation of a small group of people potentially put the survival of other humans in peril? Why should we allow this to continue as an accepted business practice in the United States? Clearly, it serves a small group of people and puts a large group of people's survival capabilities at risk.

The fundamental mission of the venture capitalist is to receive a massive return on their investment, and that can only be done through the creation of a large sales volume of their company's product in order to push the stock price as high as possible, so the investor can sell their stock and produce the highest currency windfall as possible.

In order to serve the whims of an investor who basically puts up money and expects a massive amount of money back in return, the fundamental intent of any company must change from developing the highest and best use of their product, to developing an inferior repairable and quickly replaceable one. The company no longer just needs to make a profit; it needs to make a massive profit, and it needs to continue increasing its profit year after year in order to satisfy the whims of the investor. The specific return expected by a venture capitalist can vary greatly from company to company and the emerging technology it intends to produce, so in most cases the expected return—which is basically determining the actions of the company and all its employees the first few years it is in business—is determined in many cases by an emotional whim of a third party who has no knowledge of the product rather than a directed plan by the experts on the front lines.

The investor:

1. Invents no technology.

2. Does no physical work whatsoever.

3. Neither manages nor administrates the employees of the company, nor overseas the creation and distribution of its product.

The investor simply gets money for putting up money to start the company, so any time a venture capitalist is involved in the development of technology, the price of that technology skyrockets exponentially and the cost must be borne by the general public. Initially, in the for-profit system, any company needs profit to pay their employee's wages and overhead costs and theoretically can reserve money for times when sales are bad, but when a stock investor is involved, all those fundamentals go out the window. The investor has a sociopathic idealism attached to their expectations; they expect company profits to rise every single year. This is simply unrealistic and insane thinking. We know economic cycles come and go; there are times when economies rise and economies fall; yet, the investor pays no mind to this and literally expects profits to increase during times when the economies of countries are faltering. These unrealistic expectations cause a ripple effect of stress from the executives, who are continually reminded by the Board of Directors that its share price is not rising and on to the frontline employees. This sociopathic expectation continues in its misdirection of price versus quality toward the consumer, to make sure that any potential buyer of the product, will always pay the highest price for it. Therefore, our current system is built on the belief that consumers should initially "always" pay the highest price and overall, the greatest number of consumer dollars for any developing technology in our country. Yes, competition can temporarily bring down prices, but overall but this fundamental works only to a point, as the shareholders of the competitors must also be satisfied, and thus the industry continues to expect rising profits, no matter what the cost to society as a whole. If jobs need to be cut in order to keep profits up, the shareholder demands it, because again the shareholder has no emotional ties to the production and development of the product, only to the return on their investment. For example, laying off 10,000 people from any given company is no big deal to the stock investor or the board of directors, first and foremost, because *they* do not actually look the workers in the eye and lay them off—someone else does—so this type of negative behavior that is incredibly damaging to the economy and puts the survival of humans in peril is left unchecked. This type of detrimental decision-making power is granted to a small percentage of people in society directly through the currency system and will never be counterbalanced by any other means, unless we change the laws affecting the for-profit, currency-based economy.

Let us say company "X" decides it is going to lay off 10,000 people. There is some decision-making in a nice fancy boardroom somewhere, and the decision is made. The information is then sent to the human resources department, who is responsible for delegating this information, to the employees, who will no longer have jobs. The human resources department also has an option to hire an outside agency to complete this dirty work or do it themselves, depending on the amount of currency the executives want to throw at the problem. The executives and board of directors' drive home in their luxury cars to their luxury homes as if it were just another day, because they are not responsible for the consequences of their actions. They are not responsible for looking any of the people, whose survival they have just put in peril, in the eye, seeing their emotional reaction, stating that they have families, or stating that there are ways that they feel they can turn their particular department around to make it more profitable. All this goes unheard by the executives and it is just another day in their world. The fact that the investor or corporate executives can use a proxy or agent to carry out their dirty work absolves the executive or investor of personal responsibility and personal growth. This absence of personal responsibility in the life of the investor causes the investor's life evolution to stagnate from a psychological and emotional perspective. The currency-based, for-profit economy helps to cement a cycle of mental and emotional evolution that is extremely resistant to change, because negative emotional consequences from directly interacting with other humans do not follow the decision-making actions of the investor. In other words, those in power learn no more about life and how to evolve as a human being than a child who plays video games all day. The investor is well padded with survival technology and their ability to purchase it in the future and experiences very little stress relative to their negative decision-making actions, while the vast majority of the country that lives paycheck to paycheck and experiences a job layoff undergoes extreme stress and emotional chaos, because they have almost no access to survival technology, since they are forced to purchase it with currency that mandatorily requires their access to ongoing labor, which has temporarily (or, in some cases, permanently) been denied. According to a March 2018 article by Emmie Martin at cnbc.com, 61% of surveyed Americans said they could not afford a $1,000 emergency expense without using savings or credit.[7] The majority of Americans in this country cannot save for retirement—and again, get nowhere under this plan.

---

7   https://www.cnbc.com/2018/01/18/few-americans-have-enough-savings-to-cover-a-1000-emergency.html

Would it not be better to develop a different system, with a different set of rules so we can avoid these situations from continually happening? Not only does this lack of evolution in the mind of the investor perpetuate programming that is impervious to failure, it additionally affects the programming of the minds of the American public, who aspire to be like the investor, a king, an emperor—never wavering and always set on their goal, regardless of who it hurts. So, in essence, the emotional, psychological, and mental state of our society, taught through currency, is to fight to the top in order to be in a position to emulate role models who rarely, if ever, due to their padded bank accounts, encounter enough emotional trauma to precipitate psychological introspection resulting in psychological growth and, furthermore, to become impervious to the fact that they are wrong about anything! Does this sound like a certain president we have an office today? *Currency allows the elite to hide from the necessary forces that precipitate personal change and blocks them from becoming more aware, conscious, and evolved as human beings.* Can you list some ex-CEOs who are exceptions to this rule? You might, but they are few and far between. Our capitalistic, currency based, economic system dictates a human programming mindset of scarcity and intolerance to others that is perpetuated from generation to generation. These scarcity and intolerance norms are expected from the richest people in our country and accepted as proper human behavior by the general public and taught to them at a very young age, so in the later stages in of most of the population's lives, the mass aggregate of America is totally unaware that they are giving their power away to others, who bear no incentive whatsoever to change the general public's survival concerns, let alone institute any policies or create laws to change their plight. The only way to ever change the current status of our economic programming is to change the laws governing the capitalistic currency-based system, and the only way we can do that is to raise our awareness of the origins to the problems currently affecting our economy. Are you becoming more aware?

Let us look at what happens to any country, as a whole, based on the fundamentals of a currency driven economy during the beginning of a downturn of any economic cycle. In the beginning of the cycle, most companies will lay off workers to keep their stock prices up during slow or declining economic cycles. The worse the downturn of any economic cycle becomes, the more layoffs will occur; as jobs and incomes decrease, there is less money to spend on the products and services that a country produces. When companies lose demand for their products, currency circulation slows, resulting in further decreases in profits for industries and markets within any given country as a whole. Then guess what happens? Our sociopathic investors are there to make sure more employees lose their jobs, in order to keep profits steadily increasing or at least not declining as much, in order to keep their stock prices high. Historically, what we've seen in this country are economic cycles that, in my opinion, are far worse than what they should've been had the majority of companies in the United States not had to answer to the shareholder or investor. Historically, during good economic cycles, there is a tendency for companies to hire more employees than they need and expand new departments that otherwise would not be a part of their core business without fundamentally thinking through the long-term costs of these expansions; again this is to satisfy the whim of the investor to continually increase profits and the price of their stock, rather than stockpiling cash in order to meet payroll requirements during economic downturns that are always sure to come. The gospels of the for-profit, currency-based economy dictate that expansion must always occur during positive economic cycles. Companies tend to over-hire during positive economic cycles and under-hire during contracting cycles, causing mass a misdirection and inefficiencies to the development of technology in order to keep the shareholder happy.

We need to examine stock markets and their true efficiency to developing technology in our society. The bottom line is, they do not efficiently develop technology and venture capital only exists to slow the development of technology through patents or halt it altogether. We also need to differentiate between the effects that venture capital has on the development of technology affecting a "want" item like a lollipop versus using the exact same system to develop technology for medical care that the public "needs" to survive.

Reason 9. The system is based on competition and confusion versus cooperation and peace.

Competition between companies in the same industry is a bad way to develop technology. The book *No Contest: The Case Against Competition,* by Alfie Kohn (1992), cites countless examples where competition loses out over cooperation every single time. The text also states that competition turns our family members, siblings and fellow students at a young age in school, into obstacles in our path that we need to triumph over, rather than allies to our success. The text also cites examples of our current economic system only concentrating on the goal of winning or monopolizing the individual's own market or industry, by causing problems for its competitors, rather than trying to make a better product.[8] Competition is a horrible way to run an economy or actually any system for that matter and precipitates negative emotions in its participants, that further reduces their level of performance. Studies from the book show that had participants in various experiments simply been trying to beat their personal best rather than competing with others, they would've attained better performance results. I strongly suggest you read this book and will find it quite eye-opening.

The currency system is designed for everyone to constantly fight against each other over scarce commodity called currency; in other words, in other words the system creates scarcity from nothing. The harder you compete against others to move up the ladder in your organization, which is designed as a pyramid where there are few jobs at the top that actually pay the big money, the more misdirected you and the general population become from the goal of working as a means to an end, rather than creating

---

8   "No Contest – The Case Against Competition" 1992 by Alfie Kohn p. 2 and p. 77.

and developing very low-cost survival technology that allows everyone to work less and enjoy a higher standard of living.

The currency-based economy represents an incredible labyrinth of laws that govern every product and service we purchase. Let us look again at some of the factors affecting the currency-based economy that directly affect your everyday survival: foreign currency exchanges, the world's banks, the IMF, the Federal Reserve, finance and consumer protection laws, taxation, investments—stocks, bonds, mutual funds, options, futures, home loans, auto loans, credit cards, and insurance. Who can understand all this without a specialist? No one really can, and the point is that the system is specifically designed this way, so that the average human being will give up and not try to change the system or rebel against it, as they cannot recognize one or just a few major deficiencies that need to be changed. **Humans are tricked into thinking that such an elaborate system must have been designed to meet the needs and concerns of all the humans on the planet, when the opposite is actually true.** A currency run economy has no direct intention to increase our standard of living, our level of technology, or protect our ecosphere. Simultaneously, humans, while in constant confusion about where to best place their efforts in order to attain the greatest amount of currency, are misdirected through intense competition for a scarce number of jobs that will supposedly lead them to a better life. The mass majority of the American population that that evolves through this system, spends most of their life trying to attain an extravagant income and then maintain it. The code of ethics of our current economy basically states that competition is better than cooperation, confusion is better than simplicity, and emotional discord is better than peace. Is this really the type of system you want to continue participating in? What has been lost on our human population is the ability to use our collective emotions, instincts, and awareness to solve problems in a simple and relaxed manner; this is the way the universe was designed and the currency-based economy directly conflicts with the natural laws of the universe. The sun does not charge money to shine on your face or grow crops;

it simply provides you the light, heat and plant growing technology you need every day, free of charge, to live your life in peace. The technology rights of all human beings, even the most intelligent on this planet, are being massively violated today; yet the most intelligent never question the motives and results behind the currency-based economy because they are programmed at an early age to be driven solely by competition and consumerism as a means of evolving their purpose and emotional intelligence. Competition is simply the idea of winning out over your competitors and the best way to do that is to never allow them into the competition in the first place by purchasing their technology through patent law before it ever comes to market.

Reason 10. The system relies directly on global slavery and poverty in order to maintain its misdirected cycle of income and spend.

Many of the products you buy at your local department store are made in Asian or African countries where people live in severe poverty. A 2016 article in *The Guardian* by Annie Kelly stated that children in Africa as young as seven years old are currently harvesting cobalt used in the construction of cell phones and other electronic devices for purchase here in the United States.[9] Almost all the clothing purchased America today is imported from Asia, whose workforce consists of debt slaves living in severe poverty. I dedicated the last chapter of this book to removing global poverty and ending global slavery in our world, where you can find more in-depth and sourced information. Please realize that you could not buy the things at the prices you do today at your local retail store without the direct support of slave labor, from workers that are paid a wage so low, they can barely purchase their daily requirement of food, in some cases. Where would our current economic system be today without low-cost imports manufactured by oppressed people? If you tried to produce the same products in our country today, their

---

9   https://www.theguardian.com/global-development/2016/jan/19/children-as-young-as-seven-mining-cobalt-for-use-in-smartphones-says-amnesty

cost would be incredibly expensive and there would be a shortage of those products, due to the fact that our high overhead costs would be built into their manufacturing costs. The world's debt slave labor force has become our labor force though container ships and cargo planes. The for-profit system needs this cheap form of imported labor to prop it up daily. Our current economic system is based on a small number of people directly controlling a large number of people. Look no further than the results of the currency system in America today. A recent article from Action Against Hunger.org stated that over 10% of the world's population lives on less than $1.90 per day, 2.1 billion people live on less than $3.10 per day and 17 million children worldwide suffer from acute malnutrition that results in the deaths of over one thousand children per day and over one million children per year.[10]

Stop thinking things are going to work out! Please stop thinking that over time the global standard of living is going to rise; it is not. Entities like the United States and Europe have been using cheap slave labor to provide their needed goods from the continents of Asia and Africa and importing them for many centuries. This is how the system runs and again; this is how the system was designed. You can *never* have equality in a currency-based economy, in terms of equal access to technology, and the entire world will never seriously advance technology running a currency based, for-profit system. The population of the United States historically has turned a blind eye to global poverty and slavery, under the assumption that it is "okay" because this type of oppression is not practiced within the borders of the United States, when in fact the United States relies on it directly to support its capitalistic driven, for-profit economy every single day.

You cannot fix these types of problems with currency; you can only get technology to oppressed people at the lowest most efficient cost possible. If you want to help those suffering around the world in extreme poverty and slavery, the smartest thing you can do is embrace a system that will reduce

---

10   http://www.actionagainsthunger.org/global-poverty-hunger-facts?gclid=CjwKEAjw1a3KBRCY-9cfsmdmWgQ0SJAATUZ8bgs4jRJu_v8JNcFM9zRcqicVrC4r90jQ83pxp8LCDfRoCLWrw_wcB

your own service in perpetuity, keep you out of debt, and reduce your forty-hour work week. Superior technology that requires little replacement or maintenance can easily be cloned and made available worldwide.

Reason 11. Currency does not meet our long-term emotional and psychological needs.

Let us examine why currency does not fulfill the internal needs and emotions of humankind or allow our species to evolve at its true emotional or intellectual pace. The greatest example of receiving a massive amount of currency, at once, would be winning the lottery. About one third of the people that win the lottery end up broke or declaring bankruptcy. In summation, if you put a ton of currency into the hands of the average American who is pre-programmed to believe that they must work their entire life, they will run this silent mental programming until their reality again matches their thought process. Externally changing our lifestyle through a random act does not change our thought patterns and results in us returning, in the long run, to the same manifested reality. Thoughts do in fact create our reality and the basic life purpose of any human is to evolve their thoughts and consequently their physical reality. At any point in time you are a full statement of your being and your manifested reality is the direct result of your thought process. A 2016 article in *Fortune* by Ric Edelman cited that nearly one-third of all lottery winners declare bankruptcy at some point in their lives after they win the lottery and afterward incur higher bouts of depression, divorce, alcohol and drug abuse and suicide than Americans who do not win the lottery.[11]

Money has nothing to do with the natural thinking process of humankind, the evolution of plants or animal species on the planet, or how the universe was formed. No entity in the entire universe "owns" anything except for humans. Ownership is not a part of the natural order of the universe and was never intended to be a part of the universal law or philosophy. **"Ownership" is a limited thought process expressed through paper.** The currency system

[11] http://fortune.com/2016/01/15/powerball-lottery-winners/

is a temporary system, designed to be a means to an end, to bring us to a point where technology can fulfill all our survival needs and replace all of our daily repetitive tasks; yet, through some well-placed laws enacted by some very greedy and powerful people, we have not yet attained this level of evolution.

These are the values of currency:

1. Confusion

2. Greed

3. Fear

4. Depression

Are these the values you want to base your life on? Are these values necessary for your evolution? The monetary system has so many aspects to it; it is almost unthinkable for one person to understand its internal workings and the most fundamental aspects of currency are often an avoided subject in our schools. The ironic thing about our educational system is that the most important information people need to know—an understanding of the currency-based system—is barely glanced over by our school systems. No one really gets a world-class education on the currency-based system or its fundamental workings until they pursue a higher level of education, and the only way for most people to attain that higher level of education is to incur a massive amount of student loan debt.

Now let us contrast the values of money for the true human values that actually make us feel better, that allow us to emotionally thrive and evolve as a human species. Please note the table of Maslow's hierarchy of needs:

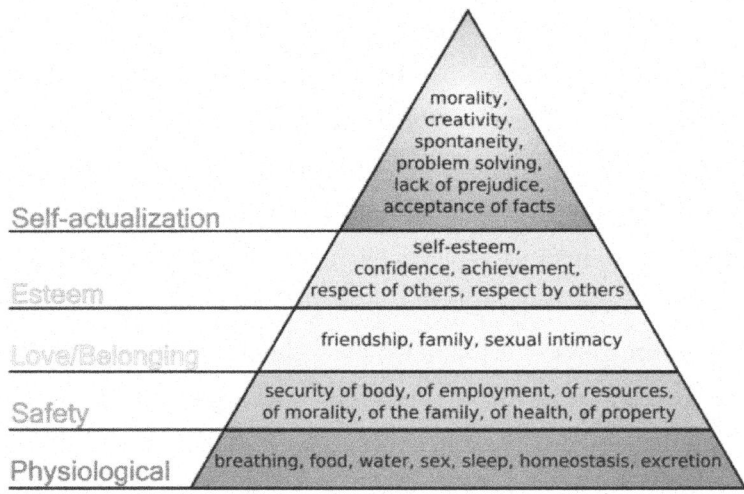

If you read the chart where do you think money comes in to the equation? Money mainly serves the bottom two needs of the pyramid: our safety and psychological needs. True superior technology released to the public would forever satisfy our safety and psychological needs but currency, patents, ownership laws, and governmental restrictions keep us perpetually in the basement of the pyramid. Humans spend most of their time trying to take care of their first two needs their entire life because currency keeps our technology in a constant state of scarcity and inferior development, therefore most Americans are more or less always in a constant state of emotional scarcity, perpetually waiting for their next paycheck to come in order to pay for their overpriced survival technology. This type of insanity leaves humankind with little chance to explore the higher levels of needs as a society and culture, such as love, respect for others, and morality. Is it a wonder the world is always in some constant state of war?

Let us look at the United States specifically. What amount of money do you think a person needs to make a year in order to be happy? According to an article in 2018 by Peter Docrill, published by Science Alert, a study by a world Gallup poll was cited where the income needed to make someone happy is no higher $75,000 per year; however, this could vary based on your location and cost of living, and making more than this amount, for most citizens in the United States, does not propel them to a significantly higher level of happiness![12] We can see from the studies that it does not take a lot of money to be happy. My own personal theory is that once somebody makes enough money to satisfy their short-term survival needs, they no longer look at the long term. Human brains and the consciousness that connects them are not built instinctively to save money. All humans are fixated on their short-term survival, regardless of their education or level of income. Corporate executives at the top of the pyramid never look beyond the next quarter or two as to what their bottom-line profit is going to be, and the 60% of America that potentially cannot cover even a $1,000 unexpected expense never looks beyond next month's bills.

The American worker wants to get to a place called retirement, where they no longer have to work anymore, but the only way to attain this goal, in a currency-based economy, is to do a repetitive set of tasks over and over again for many decades, to the point when their body is worn out and near the end of its useful life. How does this make any sense? This repetitive cycle has two parts that we shall call income, the first half of our circle, and expenditures to inferior technology, the second half of our circle. As you can see, our pathway to retirement is a process of creating and depleting equal amounts of energy over a specific time period. At the end of each monthly cycle or one loop around the circle, each person ends up almost exactly where they started financially, which is supported by fact that the mass majority of Americans are currently living paycheck to paycheck. We will call this plight *intellectual insanity*: the average United States citizen has neither the awareness, the understanding of their connection to consciousness, nor the pure belief in their true self-worth in order to demand what is rightfully theirs—*the same rights to technology that the richest people in the world currently have today*. The American worker is insane and actually wants to work "more" than forty hours a week in the hope of attaining a better life, but never considers the

---

12   https://www.sciencealert.com/how-much-money-you-need-be-happy-according-science-income-satisfaction-well-being

benefits of directly improving their inferior survival technology by means other than income created through the currency-based, for-profit system. Why spend thirty to fifty years paying off a home that requires constant repair, when we can focus as a country on developing technology to build a home for $25,000 or less that is more appealing than the homes we occupy today, a home that can be bought outright for cash or paid off completely, in just a few years on a credit card?

A 2012 article by Faith Hope and Psychology stated the average human has as many as 60,000 thoughts per day; of those thoughts, 80% are negative; and up 95% of those thoughts are repetitive (in other words, the same thoughts the person ran though their head the prior day).[13] If you remove currency from our culture and take a look at the basic actions that the Americans take each and every day, it boils down to this: everyone getting up every day to do a bunch of things that they do not want to do, in order to create and purchase a bunch of inferior technology, entertain themselves for a short period of time and then after the entertainment period ends, bury that technology in a hole. The entire world population is driven by currency for survival, in other words, by the proverbial "carrot and stick." No society or culture trying to advance its technology as a means to an end would ever take these actions or would ever consider implementing this type of thought process into its citizens, because the thoughts that drive these actions are completely counterintuitive to producing superior technology.

Reason 12. The system runs on debt.

What separates the United States from most Third World countries is that our mass consciousness has traditionally believed in giving all of its citizens access to at least some basic form of survival technology; this includes access to decent water and food, electricity from a basic power grid, a basic sewer system, etc. Access to larger forms of survival technology, such as homes

---

13 https://faithhopeandpsychology.wordpress.com/2012/03/02/80-of-thoughts-are-negative-95-are-repetitive/

and autos, have traditionally has been financed through a very robust credit system. It is really through the development of this very open and accessible credit system, predicated on lending everyone money, that has resulted in the people of the United States traditionally having a higher standard of living than most countries around the world. Our system is based the policy of our government issuing bonds and printing money; this borrowed money is spent and then becomes another citizen's income, enabling that citizen to spend money, which becomes someone else's income, and this cycle continues to propagate. The government artificially creates jobs and incomes through the creation of debt, and they must continue to do so endlessly in order for the entire population to continue to buy interior technology; without the constant creation of debt, Americans do not have the ways and means to purchase products with short life spans. The government will continue to issue debt until its debts are so enormous that it can no longer take in tax revenues to pay the interest and then it will devaluate its currency, and this will be followed by a currency collapse as the government will no longer be able to pay the interest on its debts and will issue new currency so it does not have to repay its debt, because those debts are only payable in US dollars and not the new currency. The government, through one quick action, is free to absolve itself of its debts and then restart the game all over again. Every currency in the world is "fiat" currency: this is currency backed by nothing but the promise to pay it back by each individual government. In the history of the world, 100% of the fiat currencies have failed over the last several thousand years. The future of the US dollar is inevitable.

You may be living within your means today, but the people around you are not and your job, standard of living, and the U.S. economy cannot maintain themselves without the constant creation of debt. Americans are forced to comply with long-term debt repayment plans, covering many decades, to pay for the cost of their housing, automobile replacement, health-care premiums, etc. Try running these industries without a credit system and see what happens. Health insurance premiums are a lifetime debt that can never be repaid. Americans make monthly payments toward an unseen balance for health services not rendered, unless they actually use that service and, in that instance, their debt in most cases increases. The constant creation of debt in order to run our economy has reached such an epic proportion that there is simply no way back to a system where the aggregate population can survive *without* debt. The currency-based system requires the constant extension of credit and repayment of debt in order to propagate itself because any given company's earnings per share rely directly on buying products over and over again and the system cannot exist without the constant labor from debtors to support it. The federal government has created a massive debt of near $25 trillion as a result of a failing economic system that it refuses to let go of. Any smart business strategist will tell you that when you are a business entity and constantly going into debt, your business is usually on the brink of failure because you are not selling enough product to stay afloat. Our current debt never stops increasing; therefore, from a financial perspective, we are a failed country. Debt supports the financial solvency in our country the same way a life-support machine maintains the bodily functions of a person in a coma. The credit system is failing us; the evidence is everywhere and all around you in the poor standard of living that so many Americans deal with today. At the same time, our debt is constantly increasing. U.S. credit card debt is now over $1 trillion; student loan debt is now over $1.5 trillion and mortgage debt is over $15 trillion! The aggregate population is going further into debt to purchase inferior survival technology, because its incomes simply cannot keep up with its constantly rising prices. A 2017 article from Leo Sun, published by the Motley Fool through *USA Today*, claimed the average U.S. household now carries $137,063 in debt, with only a medium income of about $60,000 annually to support it, suggesting that Americans are simply living beyond their incomes.[14]

---

14 https://www.usatoday.com/story/money/personalfinance/2017/11/18/a-foolish-take-heres-how-much-debt-the-average-us-household-owes/107651700/

Reason 13. The system directly puts our survival in peril by violating our human rights to technology in order to survive on this planet.

If your paycheck is not guaranteed, then why are our survival technology producing industries like housing, energy and health care privatized and constantly increasing in cost decade over decade? The system neither guarantees nor makes any attempts to make survival technology lower in cost, and forces you to pay for your survival by a non-guaranteed means called labor.

A 2008 article by the National Conference of State Legislatures states that the United States, excluding the state of Montana, follows the law of "at will" employment, which simply means that for any reason your employer can terminate your employment at any time for any reason and without incurring any legal liability; consequently an employee can also quit their job without incurring any legal consequences.[15] The corporation or company you work for is easily able to manipulate you through the fact that you need your job to survive; if you speak out, come in late, or do not give your life to your company, you are fired and you lose access to your ability to survive. This system is one step away from putting actual shackles and chains on your feet. Our survival technology is completely privatized, publicly traded, and patented. There is no incentive to make it low cost and freely available to all citizens. People are simply terrified of losing their jobs because the majority of Americans do not have sufficient reserves to cover their future survival expenses. A de facto state of slavery is created through currency, patents, and "at will" employment laws. People are censoring themselves and living in a state of tyranny from corporate America in order to ensure that they keep their jobs, incomes, and survival intact.

We need to stop giving away our power and realize that we have the same rights to survive on this planet as anyone else does. Privatizing our survival technology through currency, patents, and for-profit ideals forces

---

15   http://www.ncsl.org/research/labor-and-employment/at-will-employment-overview.aspx

us to continually work harder for our survival, with no hope of ever moving beyond our current station, because companies within the currency-based system are directly incentivized to block technology or extensively slow the evolution to technology that would free us to pursue our dreams. We openly and willingly give oil companies the power to purchase any competing substitute technology that might threaten the future purchases of gasoline through patent law and allow that technology to be shelved indefinitely. We pay then for their attorneys through the purchase of their product to argue in court against its development perpetually and fund its research and development departments to patent any potential up-and-coming technologies so that they never can be distributed to the public. Following the law, as we do today, is about as intelligent as purchasing a brand-new Ferrari every morning, driving it to the worst neighborhood you might know of, leaving the keys in it with the doors open, and coming back at the end of the day and wondering why it has been stolen! Over and over again, each day we commit the same insane acts by giving anyone and everyone the incentive to steal from us! It is time we changed the intellectual property laws in this country. Publicly traded, for-profit companies that hold patented survival technology are both illegal and immoral and we need to bring an end to these insane laws.

The United States is a "separate rights through currency country": some have access to toll roads that others do not; some use a bus for transportation, while others enjoy the privilege of automobile ownership; some live-in houses, while others are homeless. The currency-based system produces random results and has no goal of a fixed standard of living. The price you pay for almost any good and service is negotiated and varies based on your location, your level of income, your level of available tax deductions, what health-care plan you have available to purchase, your state, local and property taxes, and so many other variables. No one really understands what they are paying for, nor the true cost to survive in this country, as inflation is constantly changing the cost of all these different variables from year-to-year.

Americans need access to better technology and not more currency to solve their long-term problems.

Reason 14. The currency-based for-profit system is incentivized to never directly address solving our survival issues and its long-term consequences of pollution on our planet; in fact, the system has no goals and is designed to produce no results whatsoever other than to make profit.

This system has no directs goals for society as a whole. The system's only goal is to ensure we keep purchasing inferior goods and services over and over again that are slightly upgraded but still subject to repair and replacement. The currency-based system keeps us walking in a circle of income and spend that never ends. The system has no goal to reduce the forty-hour work week; the system in fact demands that we work as many hours as possible to keep feeding an overhead monster that requires our constant attention. The system has no goal to reduce our massive waste problem as a result of requiring us to repair and throw away constantly produced inferior technology. The system has no goal to reduce environmental waste. The system has no goal to address mass job losses from future technology advancement. The system has no goal to make our children's lives any different than ours are now. The system's goal is to keep us right where we are today, repeating the same actions over and over again, consistently getting the same results, while the public helplessly hopes that some random inventor somewhere will change our lives forever. Simultaneously, the system is directly incentivized to sequester, litigate, or just plain "keep secret" superior technology that would reduce our dependency on currency.

More hours worked by the American public will only cause a small increase in incomes, which will only allow any worker a very small incremental increase in access to inferior technology. Coal miners that supported President Trump were looking to go back to their old coal mining jobs. What might bringing back these coal mining jobs to any local area do? It would only give these people greater access to inferior technology, ignoring their massive overhead costs and most likely creating massive environmental problems at the same time. Do you see the big picture now? We have a system-wide failure due to a for-profit, currency run system. Currency only gives us access to inferior technology, not the full transparent access to superior technology that is innately deserved by all of us. The assumption is that "for profit" will drive us to innovate and create better technology that will lead us all to a point where we never have to work again, but, as you can see from the reasons outlined in this chapter, that will never happen. Our system is a game of illusions that never ends. If we charged an immense amount of money to buy a light bulb, then the majority of the population would live in darkness after the sun went down. If Thomas Edison and his investors decided that the light bulb should only burn for one month and then be replaced with another light bulb, light bulb replacement would represent a mass cost to society and create a mass pollution problem. If you had to pay a dollar for every page on the Internet you accessed daily, how much information do you think people would seek out? It is only through embracing an idealism of making survival no cost that we will enjoy more prosperity and abundance than we have ever known before.

Reason 15. Americans do not directly control their survival, and they cannot vote on economic issues that directly affect their survival.

Americans rely on a proxy to lead them in the form of federal and state government officers who are completely blind to the fact that the general public needs technology to advance in order to increase its citizens' standard of living. In fact, any government proxy is only looking for ways to keep people working. Your government proxy's main goal is to become reelected, and the best way they can accomplish that task is to create more useless jobs and put more systems in place that require more taxes and more hours worked from you in order to pay those taxes. Between the government and your employer, you basically have no direct control over your survival other than to look for new ways to create currency, by means of finding a better paying job or starting a business.

The goal of any government proxy is to be elected just like any corporation's main goal is to maximize profit, and the best way to do that is to create jobs in their district or state. All branches of government, like employers, will always be incentivized to make their decisions based on improving the fundamentals of the currency-based system in order to get themselves reelected. These government proxies have no real concept of what developing technology can do to elevate the standard of living for all Americans. All of their solutions involve increasing taxes to build more inferior technology that requires more work hours from the American public in order to maintain it.

Now that you have an actual breakdown of how the currency system works and how it affects the psyche of not only you, but everyone around you, you may never want to go back to using the same system again. We live in some seriously trying times in a quest for our long-term survival: a fifteen-year-long war in the Middle East, terrorism, constant propaganda on our televisions, and rampant consumerism telling us what to buy to be happy. We are addicted to false idols that misdirect us, causing widespread anxiety, depression, and, as a result, a prescription drug epidemic. We've lost our way and are disconnected from our truth; we have been tricked unanimously into giving our power over to currency and not directly addressing our how we should survive as we occupy this planet. The real issues we need to address are constantly bypassed and circumvented as we forever chase the "carrot" of currency while hoping to outrun the "stick" of survival. We need to get serious about building our future and about how to create together as a country and as a mass consciousness. Today, without a plan, we are firing a gun in the form of creating new income destroying technologies, in random directions, whose effects can only create job loss and poverty; at the same time not decreasing our overhead costs, hoping to hit something...

anything, to change our belief system and get us back on course to creating the technology we desperately desire, to stop us from endlessly working. It's time to get serious about creation and our economy!

CHAPTER 3

Solving Our Real Estate Problem

In order to understand how to change certain laws and regulations, to move forward so we work as a means to an end, we must first have a firm grasp of the workings of the currency-based, for-profit system. This system provides almost no results to the general public in terms of increasing the standard of living over time and has so many negative aspects, that I wanted to take a break with this chapter in order to present some positive aspects of how technology can forever change your life and stop you from perpetually playing the role of a debt slave. Certainly, the biggest monthly expense for anyone over time is their rent or a mortgage payment. Some people rent for their entire lives and, as we shall see in this chapter, sometimes mortgages can take far longer than thirty years to pay off, so let us start tackling our biggest problem first. Our society and culture, like our ancestors, have been raised on the belief that "real estate must always go up." This is the worst goal and idealism that any culture could possibly have. It causes all sorts of problems: it directly threatens our survival issues of needed shelter, causes poverty, creates an endless supply of growing debt, permanently reduces disposable incomes, causes lack of savings and, most importantly, fuels service in perpetuity consisting of decades of work required to pay off a property. It takes decades to pay off the structure you live in. Have you ever considered the fact that the technology surrounding the utility hookups to our residential real estate lots and the on-site building costs are simply not evolved enough to meet our current needs? Can we work at applying our modern methods of developing technology to build structures that are portable, self-sufficient, and a fraction of the cost, resulting in fewer hours worked per year in order to increase our standard of living? Is there any plan to do this at any level by our government, or by any organized group in the United States? If this is not our goal, then how do we expect to reach it? In fact, our goal is just opposite: to keep real estate a scarce commodity with limited availability to the general public.

There are basically two driving forces constantly working to increase the price of real estate over the long term:

1. Ever increasing lot costs: a section of land with access to a power grid, a supply of water, and some sort of waste disposal. In real estate jargon terms, we call this "location, location, location!"

2. The construction costs of the structure itself built on site.

Let us look at some of the current problems that have been caused by rapidly rising real estate prices in the United States over the last hundred years or so.

1. Long-term mortgage debt will at some point no longer be affordable, based on the future projected incomes of the average American family as advancing technology is expected to reduce jobs and incomes.

Real estate financing for the purchase of homes has consisted mainly of first-time homebuyer purchasing a home with an FHA mortgage. Usually the buyer brings in 3.5% down with full expectations of refinancing the property within the first five years to remove the mortgage insurance. FHA charges mortgage insurance on all of its new originations. If you choose a conventional loan, which requires a higher down payment, you have the option of asking your lender to remove your mortgage insurance after twenty-four payments have been made and your property appraises for a higher vale. In either case, the majority of borrowers are basically looking to refinance their loan for another thirty-year term, in order to remove or reduce their mortgage insurance. So right out of the gate, the consumer is already looking to extend their debt another thirty years and resetting the clock, so now a thirty-year mortgage becomes a thirty-three- or thirty-five-year mortgage. Consumers literally purchase homes with the expectation that they will go up and be able to remove the mortgage insurance usually within the first five years of purchase. Is that a realistic expectation? Literally, there could be hundreds of reasons why any homeowner would refinance their property over decades of time, including lowering the interest rate or loan term, home improvements, removing mortgage insurance, incurring a financial hardship by themselves and their extended family, excess medical bills not covered by insurance, etc. As we discussed in Chapter 2, the "For Profit Paradox" requires that we constantly repurchase inferior technology with our monthly earnings. In this case, when it comes to our shelter, we are required under the current laws governing our economy today to take a large portion of our monthly income and spend it on our mortgage payments. The mass majority of the population pays only one 360th of their loan off each month, the bare minimum payment. This type of long-term financing is absolute insanity. Families today are constantly under the threat of long-term unemployment based on outsourcing, staff reductions, changing markets, and changing technology. It is simply unrealistic to expect to work for the same company for twenty-five to thirty years, which most of the population did back in the 1950s and 1960s. Most job changes today have a shelf life of two to three years, with some period of unemployment, at which point long-term savings needs to be used to cover survival needs. Literally almost any small emergency can put the majority of any American family's financial situation into crisis, events like major car repairs, major dental work, accidents causing loss of income or reduction of income before being able to collect permanent disability, having to take care of a family member with a severe illness; the list is endless. It takes almost nothing to destroy the credit and financial affairs of most American households. Our old beliefs and ideals will no longer work; there's too much instability in the human labor force, not only in this country but worldwide; and we can only expect more instability during the next twenty to thirty years due to a massive expansion of automated technology replacing human labor. Let us further understand that any type of superior substitute technology would simply render the price of the current homes on the market that require a mass amount of maintenance and incredibly long financing terms, worthless. There are so many people in the United States today that are already retired and living on fixed incomes that still carrying mortgage loans; the trend seems to be selling these track homes and in moving into manufactured housing or even an RV. The bottom line is the price of tract housing has simply become unaffordable for the average American under the current laws regulating the production of housing, and the industry only intends to push the price of housing higher over the long term.

Can we switch our belief system to the idea that everyone should be able to own a home free and clear, within perhaps its five years—the same time it roughly takes to pay off auto loans today? We can make this possible through the advancement and creation of superior technology, applied to our lot development and on-site building practices.

Housing shortages will continue in the long term, driving the price of real estate up and increasing the amount of debt to be repaid by all Americans. Currently the San Francisco Bay area is going through a mass housing shortage due to the large number of jobs available in a small area surrounding the Silicon Valley and employment not being as plentiful around the rest the United States. There has been a mass migration to this area, causing an increase in housing prices so large it is unaffordable for almost anyone to live there anymore without multiple incomes supporting rents or mortgages. Current homeowners are looking to build small rental units on their properties in order to capture the high rents that are available from these types of structures. According to an article from Rent Café, in 2019 the average rent for a Santa Clara, California county apartment was $2,926, an increase of 2% from 2018, and the average size apartment is 896 square feet.[16] This is a classic example of people being drawn to an area, lured by a high level of income, only to have to turn around and shell out a massive amount of money on survival costs due to the scarcity of housing and find themselves not much better off than before they moved. The currency driven system is simply a tiger that constantly chases its own tail; when any gains are made, they are simply taken away in the long run based on the ever-present scarcity principles that help run the system. This is a classic example of the inflation principle that we discussed in Chapter 2, causing a massive drain on the incomes of highly paid and skilled business professionals. Most business professionals that live in the city of San Francisco have several roommates and perhaps are only occupying a few hundred square feet of space for up to $2,000 per month in rent costs, depending on their location. You might state that if you do not live in Northern California that this problem has nothing to do with you. What I am directly telling you here right now is that this is your future, or at least the future of the aggregate population of America, unless we solve our lot cost problems and our on-site building cost problems. A 2018 article from Freddie Mac stated that "from 1968 to 2008, a span of 40 years, there was only one year in which fewer new housing units were built than in 2017 and this despite rising demand in a growing economy." The corresponding chart also provided in the article readily illustrates this statement.

---

16 https://www.rentcafe.com/average-rent-market-trends/us/ca/santa-clara-county/santa-clara/

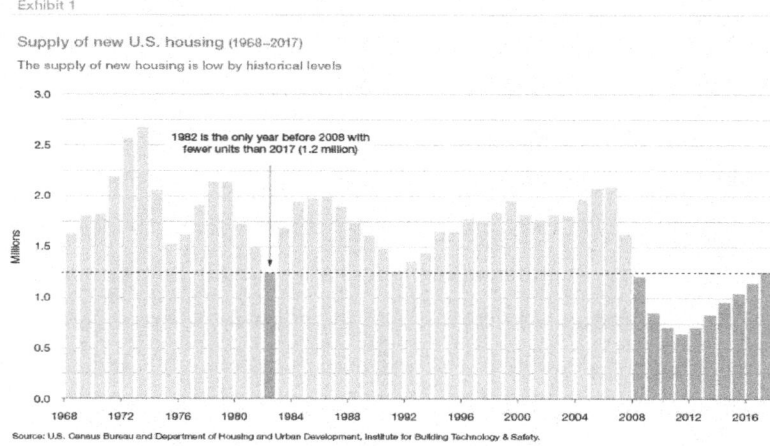

Exhibit 1

Supply of new U.S. housing (1968–2017)
The supply of new housing is low by historical levels

1982 is the only year before 2008 with fewer units than 2017 (1.2 million)

Source: U.S. Census Bureau and Department of Housing and Urban Development, Institute for Building Technology & Safety.

17

Please review the chart carefully and then consider the fact that the population of our country has roughly doubled since the 1960s, and you can see why the price of homes in America constantly keeps rising. There are just not enough homes built, period! You talk to your phone and your phone talks back to you and yet despite having access to all of this grand technology, this is the pace at we produce homes. Everyone needs shelter and any adult is a potential home buyer, not just one that has saved enough money, to put a down payment on a home. The for-profit housing industry, throughout the history of our country, has never supplied us with enough housing to meet our demands. The American housing market is based on home buyers purchasing a limited-edition, scarce, and inferior structure through the longest-term credit instrument they can possibly obtain because American homes simply are not affordable.

The majority of the population can expect in their old age to be living with strangers, relying on boarder income in order to cover their mortgage payment in their retirement years. Why do we want to keep participating in a system that has no direct goal to reduce the price of real estate? The United States can only expect to become more "Third World" as we keep applying

17   http://www.freddiemac.com/research/insight/20181205_major_challenge_to_u.s._housing_supply.page#ResearchChart1

these outdated, for-profit models to our housing structures, and there will be more occupants per structure required in order to cover the monthly costs. I would expect within the next ten years or less, that the banking system will offer fifty year loan terms or longer for home loans, as prices will be so high that banks will have no other choice but to capitulate and issue this type of debt, since without extending loan terms, there will be no other way for the common person to afford home prices at that point in time. An article published by SFGate stated that in 1995, the country of Japan, in response to extremely high real-estate prices and extremely low interest rates, introduced 100-year mortgages to the general public so that housing might be affordable again and the general public would continue to buy housing.[18] It is also a fact that in 2020, 40-year mortgage terms including interest-only options are now again available to the general public in the United States. As I outlined in Chapter 2, the system is based on scarcity and the constant creation of debt and repayment of that debt by the consumer; therefore, we can only expect what is happening in other countries to happen in our country as our population grows and we make no existing rule changes to our for-profit, currency-based system.

If you are reading this, you might be saying that you will never participate in financing like this, but I can assure you that 100 year loan terms will become the status quo in America, unless we apply technology directly to our utility hookup and on-site building costs problems. Current homes are a bad investment due to the long-term financing required and maintenance costs. If you are lucky enough to have 5% down on a $300,000 home and finance a thirty-year loan at 3.50%, which is about the going rate these days, here's what you can expect to pay back over that timeframe: Over the thirty years, assuming you made the minimum payment each month and we know that the vast majority of households will only be able to make the minimum payment if they are lucky, because they live paycheck to paycheck,

---

18 http://homeguides.sfgate.com/longest-mortgage-7677.html

the total pay back over that time will be about: $460,800.00. A 2010 article from The Street by Jeff Brown, noted that experts believe the average cost of home repairs is about 1% of the purchase price per year and you should plan on annual costs greater than 1% per year if the home you purchase is older or poorly maintained. 19 In round figures the average consumer will have paid back almost $550,800, *just in mortgage payments and maintenance costs* for their $300,000 original purchase. So, if the price of this home isn't near double over the next thirty years in this scenario, in round figures you are not even getting the money back you put into it. I did not consider the mortgage interest and property tax deductions, because the true net costs will vary from person to person based on their level income, and it would be impossible to calculate an accurate figure for the mass population. But I also did not consider the property taxes and homeowners insurance that have to be paid yearly as well. The fact that tax deductibility is not included in this scenario was done first and foremost because it is not guaranteed over the next thirty years that the federal government will allow mortgage interest or property taxes, to continue to be deducted from federal income taxes. Other countries have already eliminated such deductions and secondly and this goes into my original point about a currency-based system: it is a game of smoke and mirrors, due to a labyrinth of tax laws and in this case hidden maintenance costs. No one ever really knows where they stand from any perspective with our current system on a year-to-year basis on the true cost of home ownership, and this is exactly the type of confusion that the system I am outlining in this book is looking to eliminate. Property taxes? They also can vary in cost based on the county you live in, whether you have special assessments, etc. Homeowners insurance? That depends on the private carrier you have and your level of coverage, and this could cost you between $500 and $1,500 a year, so the insurance alone might cost another $30,000, over the thirty-year term but again I did not even count it, because it is not necessary to make my point. Why is American real estate a good investment?

---

19   https://www.thestreet.com/story/12806754/1/estimating-annual-home-maintenance-costs.html

American real estate has simply become a horrible investment and the main reason is the lack of technology applied to the development of utility hookups to residential lots, on-site building costs and ongoing maintenance costs. The current system is designed to constantly increase the cost of the shelter where you live. The ending result is a massive number of hours worked over time by any one individual or family in order to live in and maintain a very inferior structure. The cement slab is forming more and more cracks year after year, the electrical wiring is aging, nails and bolts are straining and stressing under the constant year-round heat and cold, carpets are being worn down, paint is peeling, and constant maintenance needs to be performed to revert an aging structure back to its original, inferior state. These constant repair costs are great for currency circulation and the creation of mundane jobs, but they are horrible for the homeowner, because they drain their long-term savings and leave them in a position where they may not be able to retire, as so many cannot retire today once their debt is paid off. An article from *Time. com Money* by Elyssa Kirkham at Go Banking Rates in 2016, stated that about one-third of Americans have no retirement savings and 56% of Americans have less than $10,000 saved for retirement. [20]

5 Steps to Solving a Problem

What I learned going through probably the most trying years of my life is to never get attached to anything material: a house is just four walls and a roof; a car is just four wheels and a steering wheel. Money no longer defines my happiness, validates my self-worth or my ability to feel successful, although I have to admit it has taken years of meditation to get to this level of everyday thinking. In order to get out of some serious financial problems I've had to navigate for years, I've learned to follow five steps to solving any temporary problem, in order to create a permanent solution. They are as follows:

---

20   http://time.com/money/4258451/retirement-savings-survey/

Step 1. **Awareness of the problem**: our biggest oversight today as a population and the reason I wrote this book.

Step 2. **Detaching emotionally from the problem and the outcome**: being ok with the way things are. Getting rid of your negative emotions and reactions.

Step 3. **Creating a plan.**

Step 4. **Following through with action.**

Step 5. **Learning, remembering, and maintaining the process.**

These five basic steps followed slowly by our population over time will create a new economy. The longest time spent on the entire process should be in Steps 1 and 2. Why, you might ask? Because you can never form a sound plan and follow through with action, unless you've already detached yourself from any problem. The problem with today's economy is we are far too attached to the currency-based system and the belief that we can only increase our technology by creating more currency, which comes from our pay period tasks, which has nothing to do with directly developing our technology. So, from the standpoint of labor directly affecting technology, it is a mass misdirection. Do you see the major paradox here? Usually, once someone gets to this point in deductive reasoning, the next statement they might make is, "I am providing income so new companies can exist and create new technologies that will change our economy and allow me to work less with a higher standard of living over the long term." Is that really true? Based on the incentives of the currency-based economy, it definitely is not. So, who exactly is inventing the items we need, so we can work less? Next question, "How many inventors are actually creating viable survival technology in the United States today?" The answers to all these questions are that we have no idea, because our survival technology and all products and services sold in the United States fall under the control of a completely privatized system. Any company working on superior survival technology would not be required to inform the general public, and certainly, since the invention of the automobile, we've seen no real changes to our transportation industry in terms of miles per gallon efficiency, or for that matter any source of power that is directly competitive with an electrical power grid. We are making false assumptions about the biggest problems we are facing as a species in order to survive on this planet. Our goal is to create permanent, long-lasting technology, so we do not have to work anymore; but yet from the consumption perspective, all we do is buy randomly produced, perpetually-inferior technology, created by random people, who have their own interests in mind and not the interests of humanity. What is our result? We continually run around to create short-term crappy products that no one really needs, that provides short-term entertainment for the public, then we bury those products in a hole. What a mess! We are the dumbest most misdirected planet in the entire universe! Let us start reprogramming this insanity right now. This five-step process will help us to begin to build the world that we really need to live in by bringing our attention away from scarcity and toward prosperity, by bringing our attention away from perpetually working, toward perpetually relaxing, by bringing about an end to daily routines that take us nowhere and moving ourselves toward directed activities that bring us permanent results and a means to end. That is all the people on this planet ever wanted who came before us in history: to find a means to an end; to find a means to perpetually stop working, relax, and enjoy their lives and help one another live and love. Isn't it time we stop doing the same thing over and over again expecting a different result? This basic plan is going to help you and it is going to help everyone get focused. We need to spend a long time getting focused before our plan is going to written out the exactly way we need it to be or in order to take the right actions. Over the course of many years, one lesson in business I've learned the hard way is: never get your emotions involved and never get personally attached to any problem or your rate of failure is always going to be very high. It is necessary for us to take a detached view and be okay with the way the system is, without emotionally flaring up or even caring, in order to move on to the planning and action stages. The more emotionally attached you are to any problem, the harder it is for you to solve it and move past it.

Step 1. Awareness of the problem

The purpose of the entire text is to give you awareness of problems we face with a currency-based, for-profit system, and by gaining a broad understanding and awareness, of the currency-based system, we can understand its draw backs and learn to move beyond it. Basically, just by reading this text, you are being given awareness of this problem and if you are not aware of a problem, or what is causing you to not achieve a desired result in anything in life, you will simply never take type of any action to fix it. The basic reason you are not solving any major problem or overcoming any major obstacle in your life is most likely that your thought process is providing constant emotional resistance to solving the problem.

Step 2. Detaching emotionally from the problem and the outcome

In order to accomplish this step, you will need to be okay with the way things are, with the currency-based for-profit economy today, or at least be able to tolerate the hypocrisy of the system to a point where you will have very little emotional reactions to the constant problems created by it. This can be accomplished when you have sufficient information that would lead you to believe that the problems you see associated with the currency-based for-profit system can at least to some point be resolved. Once you see some light at the end of the tunnel in some potential solutions to possibly solve any problem, it is certainly easier to release your negative emotional thinking patterns to it. Your emotions are your key guide to solving the problem; you should attempt to feel, that the problem has already been solved and attempt to feel this way quite a bit, because by feeling this way your mind will introduce you to different thought patterns that will guide you through the problem and your understanding of it. You can apply this action plan to any of the current problems in your life.

What specifically do we need to be aware of, in order to understand how people, develop certain thinking patterns that over time become self-generated habits? Recurring thought patterns definitely generate habits and these habits, in turn, generate recurring thinking patterns. In the book, *The Power of Habit*, Charles Duhigg explains that habits are formed basically through a system of "Cue" – "Routine" – "Reward" in order to create permanent thinking patterns that result in permanent actions over time and that programs like Alcoholics Anonymous force participants to create new routines that create new behaviors.[21] I highly suggest you give this book a read. I personally found it to be very informative and insightful on how humans begin to develop recurring thinking patterns that determine their actions over the course of their lifetimes.

In order to make a technology-based economy a reality, our economy will require a new set of beliefs from all those that participate in it. Our entire population will need to move beyond believing they are a persona who is destined to be working their entire lives until their body no longer becomes useful, to a person that demands technology in order to work less hours with the intent of eventually not working at all. Once we shift our beliefs and consciousness, the system will become a reality.

It is very important to us to examine our beliefs in this era of great lies and speculation. Our media, corporate America, and the Internet are constantly churning out new forms of information toward us daily and it becomes difficult to know specifically what information is truthful and what is simply an exaggerated form of entertainment. We need to follow our inner instincts and let them be our greater guide, but we have lost touch with this talent over a lifetime being manipulated by propaganda. Our current economic system has helped us form bad habits and misguided beliefs surrounding the

---

21   "The Power of Habit" copywrite 2012, 2014 by Charles Duhigg, p. 72

fact the creation of more currency is going to solve our problems and never revels the real truth, which is the fact that our problems can only be solved through increasing our level of technology. In order to achieve our personal life goals, or our economic goals as a society, the first thing we must do is give up our limiting beliefs. So, the first thing we should do is examine our thought patterns openly and honestly to really assess what is going on in our minds and why we keep getting the same results. The reason anyone is getting the same results, in any situation, is because they are thinking the same thoughts and projecting the same emotions toward manifesting a certain outcome. If thoughts are limiting, negative emotions will follow and negative results will follow that, so the philosophy here is simple: if you change your thoughts and then change your emotional patterns, your manifested reality will change. This is very obvious to trained, instinctive minds and not obvious to the average American, whose mind ping-pongs around from one fast food restaurant to another. The concept of "change your thoughts, change your reality" was not invented by me; it has been talked about by many other people. So how do you change your thoughts? You have to examine your core beliefs and constantly question them until you change out your core beliefs for different core beliefs that will produce different results. The problem with our media today is that it is helping to create recurring thought patterns of helplessness and that there are simply no solutions to our problems and that there is no technology potentially available us that can create a better life for our people. We are forever told that there is nothing we can do to change our economy, change our laws, and therefore we default to the only action we have available based on our thought patterns, which is to do nothing as a collective society and wait for a few random individuals to invent some miracle technology to turn things around.

When going through my life's journey to get back to the point of making money again, I realized I was poor because my everyday thoughts were focused on scarcity. I found a quick four-point action plan for eliminating bad thought patterns: ask yourself a series of questions and, based on your answers to those questions, decide whether or not to drop your thought pattern, belief, or emotional attachment toward a particular subject or situation.

Three questions need to be asked in regard to every belief you have right now, and they will help you strengthen the beliefs that are aiding you and eliminate the beliefs that are holding you back.

Question 1: Do you know the belief you are following right now to be 100% true?

Question 2: Do you know the belief you are following right now to be 100% untrue?

Question 3: Is holding on to this belief making you feel bad?

Action Step 4: Now either keep or dismiss your belief.

Here are some examples of misdirected beliefs: I can only get a job in the industry I am working in now. The only person that I will ever love is my current spouse; that is why I cannot leave them, even though I know the relationship is not working anymore. I cannot vote for economic issues on my own; I am not intelligent enough to make those kinds of decisions; I need a proxy. Test any belief you have now or tonight before you go to bed. I am sure you will find the process quite revealing. For example:

Question 1: Do I know the belief that: "I can only get a job in the industry that I am working in now" to be 100% true?

Question 2: Do I know the belief that: "I can only get a job in the industry that I am working in now" to be 100% untrue?

Question 3: Is holding on to: "I can only get a job in the industry that I am working in now" making me feel bad?

Action Step 4: Think whether you should keep or dismiss this belief.

You might need to ask these questions many times in order to keep or dismiss the belief and, in some cases, you may have to simply come back to this line of questioning at another time. Some beliefs may be dismissed very quickly because you may find, even within a few minutes, they are ludicrous to hang onto; still others may take a longer period of time for you to let go of and actually start taking new actions as a result of your new line of thinking. If you need to keep asking these questions over and over again about certain beliefs you have that you cannot make up your mind about, there is no time limit to using this technique; you can keep asking the same questions over days, weeks, months, or years. The point I am trying to make is that I am trying to get you to examine your beliefs, because most of the beliefs that we hold as true today are based on mass assumptions we've carried through our lives, that perhaps formed in our childhood when we had less information about a subject than we do now, that actually, when scrutinized today, are wrong. Going onto the Internet, start talking to a friend, or finding any resource you can to get information confirming or denying your belief are all good ideas. Once you've found a belief to be false, it is pretty easy to drop it.

You can apply this line of questioning to any real belief or thought pattern that you feel is holding you back and give it a test to see if you should keep any belief or not. The point here is that I am trying to get you to question your beliefs because as I noted in Chapter 2, *95% of the average person's thoughts are repeated over again the everyday and 80% of them are negative!* Even if you do not drop the belief right away, you should definitely question it, especially if it is making you feel bad or "off" or you are repeating the same thought patterns over and over again. A repetitive thought process on the same subject is usually a sure sign that you have bad beliefs surrounding it. No person that we recognize today as having accomplished great things in the past ever got anywhere without questioning their beliefs.

Finally, I cannot stress enough that you need to bring your emotions into play here. Your emotions are a major factor in the creation of changes and any new material results you want to bring about into your life. If you do not "feel" on some level you really deserve something, then your mind is still offering resistance to allowing this person or object into your life. If you find something is making you feel bad ultimately get off and stay off that subject while you work on other beliefs. Start working on eliminating the really ridiculous beliefs you have first; if it is a bad day, go general and keep your thought patterns general that day. For example: "The weather is really nice today." "I am grateful for all the technology I have access to now, etc." Feel as if it is already there, as if you already have it; the worst thing that can happen is nothing, so you will be no better off than you are now. What will most likely happen is your mind will create new thought patterns around these feelings in order to bring about the actions you need to create what you want. Dr. Joe Dispenza has some excellent books and videos on this subject you should definitely look into if you want a detailed analysis of how your brain works. I have created a preferred reading list for you at the back of the book to help guide you beyond the bounds of this text.

The idea here is about *receiving*—receiving should be everything to us, yet we've lost sight of our ability to receive technology and our thinking has been massively obscured by money. Our self-worth and ability to create has massively been obscured and misdirected by our continual pursuit of a byproduct called currency, which never seems to give us the end results and feelings that we really want in life. I am talking about a deeper connection here. We've lost our ability to *receive* as a society, not only the technology that we need to develop to stop working, but the love we need from others in order to truly be at peace and be fulfilled. When everyone is in the mindset of receiving abundance, the entire planet will change. Success today in any area of your life, in our currency run system, is mainly a result of repeating a series of mundane actions and thoughts in order to achieve a desired result; this is getting us absolutely nowhere. What we should specifically doing today is creating habits that constantly question our emotions and thought patterns and to become more persistent at implementing solutions, in order to change our thought patterns. Do you think Thomas Edison got stuck after the he failed over and over again, thousands of times? He probably felt like a fool and an idiot at some point after a mass number of failures and was questioning why he should continue trying to create a light bulb with an extended burn period.

Persistence and changing our thought patterns, rather than being persistent at creating more currency, is definitely necessary to achieve our desired result, but, through the course of our persistence, it may be necessary to change our beliefs in order to achieve our desired result in the shortest amount of time. Pure persistence, in its simplest form, will simply not be enough to get us the results we need. Emotionally detaching from a problem allows us to see the problem clearer so that we can make a more specified and detailed plan than we otherwise would have to achieve our goal. Simple things, like asking the three questions I outlined in this chapter, seem child-like but are so very necessary to your own personal success and to increase your ability to receive abundance. The key to everything in life is in your ability to "receive." If you look at all the things you are lacking right now in your life, it is directly related to your ability to innately accept them into your life. Asking questions about why the things you'd like in your life are not there will help you identify the beliefs that are limiting you, and you're on your way!

Probably the biggest focal point of this book is to make the distinction between the thought processes of the mental world and the physical world and the physically manifested results each brings. For thousands of years, people have been caught in the thought processes of the physical world, focusing at "what is" rather than "what could be" in order to survive on this planet, and this line of thinking is coming to an end with the advent of advanced superior technology on our doorstep. If you are lifting weights, for example, there is muscle growth directly derived through pain and suffering, but this type of thinking does not apply in any way shape or form to the creation of money, to the creation of relationships, or the creation of anything in your physical reality outside your physical body. Old ways of thinking, such as believing physical labor and endless suffering produce results, simply are not true. The way you want to think and the beliefs you want to form in order to create a technology-based economy need to be in line with the way universal intelligence creates. I will discuss more about universal intelligence in another chapter, but it is certainly safe to say that physical pain and suffering are not a part of a technology-based economy and physical pain and suffering, outside of increasing muscle mass and perhaps your endurance if you are a runner, do not apply to the mental world of creation. Physical pain, suffering, and relying on someone else to change your life for you need to be put aside and need to be substituted with feelings of being happy, safe, and complete. The American public is incredibly persistent at suffering and needs to become incredibly persistent at feeling happy in order to bring about the lasting changes they so desperately desire.

Meditation is probably the best way to emotionally detach from any problem or any emotional issue in your life, and it is a practice I highly recommend if you want to really get a different perspective on people and the way you interact with everything you come into contact with in the external world. Sitting down for just five minutes a day in total peace, with your phone off and no distractions, when practiced consistently over time, will definitely help to change your thinking patterns and allow you to see your own personal problems, more clearly.

Step 3. Creating a plan

In specifically addressing our problem, building a technology-based economy, I am going to outline a general plan for you in this book, and it is my sincerest hope that you will adapt it and add to it with your own specific subtleties. So, in a way, right now step three, to some extent, is really already done.

Step 4. Following through with action

We will not be able to take action until most of our population completes the first two steps, in order for people to physically vote on certain propositions that are vital to their survival. We will need to come to a state of higher consciousness and most likely many states simultaneously will need to adopt a licensing policy in our energy and health-care industries and force a change through mass collusion on private industry. I've outlined how this scenario will most likely happen later in the text.

Step 5. Learning, remembering, and maintaining the process

This is basically a simple way of affirming that a new habit has been created by our society. This new habit will be to accept the fact that we now create survival technology at the lowest cost possible until it becomes free of charge in the United States, and we can accept the consequences and the benefits of living in a technology-based economy. Once we've formed our new habit by taking part in steps one through four, we are simply going to use our positive emotions of accomplishment to reinforce our beliefs and continue to create new steps and actions to expand our technology-based economy. This is a tier-based system, so as we learn all we need to know from the effects of licensing our energy and health-care systems over the course of perhaps five or ten years, our country will be much better equipped, as a whole, to understand when to license our transportation and housing industries and the effects of their licensing on the economy, consumer confidence, and other variables involved.

Let us move out of the abstract and into a more concrete physical manifestation of what a technology-based economy might look like in regard to real estate development.

Raw land and tract lots are extremely difficult to purchase as the general public simply does not have the cash on hand to afford their high purchase price. When the average citizen attempts to obtain financing to purchase land for building, many lenders may require 30% or more of the purchase price, for the down payment.

Lot cost problems are directly driven by extremely high costs associated with bringing an electrical power supply and water supply to any

intended living site. Only increased development to these specific types of energy technologies will result in lot cost decreases over time. A 2015 article by the U.S Census Bureau tells us that 62.7% of the U.S population lives on only 3.5% of our country's land, and one of the reasons for this statistic is lack of access to available water in rural areas.[22] Now do you understand why the price of real estate always keeps rising? Of the current population, 63% is roughly using only 3-4% of the usable land in the United States! Why? The answer is simple: you live where the power lines run and where you can run sewer lines and water; you cannot live anywhere else unless you have access to a massive amount of cash to gain access to these basic utilities on your proposed living site. You also must live close to your work in order to pay your overhead, which is a classic paradox, because this paradox herds people into small areas of land, which causes further scarcity and further increases in lot prices. The currency-based system incentivizes ever increasing lot costs. Building "up," is the only short-term remedy for most major metropolitan cities today in order to accommodate their ever-expanding populations. The concept of building "up" only provides the intended residents with a very tiny and confined living space, which can precipitate emotional distress and discord in the mass population of people living in these types of structures over decades of time, which further increases health-care premiums. The more humans you have working in a given population, the higher your health-care premiums are going to be; couple that with confining people into small spaces over decades of time, causing all sorts of emotional problems, which creates illness and disease. So, it is safe to say, if we wanted to maximize the cost of our health-care premiums and keep them rising over time, we should employ a mass workforce of human labor and station these humans in crowded and confined living spaces.

I went to a popular utility company's website Pacific Power and input some basic information to get a ballpark estimate to run a power line

---

22   https://www.census.gov/newsroom/press-releases/2015/cb15-33.html

approximately one-half mile, and the ballpark estimates I got were $23,900 to $43,500.[23]

Power lines costs are going to vary from state to state and the generosity of the existing power company; if you are connecting perhaps only 100 additional feet to a particular power company's existing overhead line, you may even be able to get that connection done for free. Certainly, there are going to be mass discrepancies in price, depending on your location and its relative distance to an existing overhead power line, adding a transformer and underground versus above ground lines. The bottom line is to run this old-time utility (which has been in existence for more than 128 years) to any given lot is incredibly expensive. I do not think it would be overstating statistics to say that only a small percentage of this country could afford to build a house virtually anywhere they wanted just to enjoy the benefits of a low-cost lot price. The cost to run utilities to any given location in order to build a home is the problem, not the amount or cost of the land to build on. What we are dealing with is a technology problem, not a land scarcity problem. If you want to live ten or twenty miles away from any given existing power line, you can forget about ever trying to connect to it, because the cost would be so enormous you would never receive any type of return on your investment.

Solar panels are another option as a portable source of power. An article published by Energy Sage stated "in 2019, the average national solar panel cost is $2.99/watt. The average solar panel system size in the U.S is approximately 6 kilowatts (kW), therefore an average solar panel system would cost $12,558 after tax credits. A 10kW solar energy system costs: $20,920," which is more than a 2% drop from 2018.[24] You can probably finance 100% of the expenditure with no money down, but you also have the option of leasing or renting the panels. Solar energy is not going to work everywhere

23   https://www.pacificpower.net/working-with-us/line-extension-estimator.html
24   https://news.energysage.com/how-much-does-the-average-solar-panel-installation-cost-in-the-u-s/

on this planet as efficiently as other areas, simply due to the fact that certain geographical areas have less exposure to sun than others. Solar is somewhere to start, but the cost to purchase a unit and have it professionally installed is still quite hefty. I am not sure that a 5-kW system is enough to meet all the needs of a standard household—depending on your location, and as you can see, just adding a few more kilowatts greatly increases the price of any system. We are definitely on the right track with solar, but we need to get costs down by following the system I've outlined in this book. Let us try to make a goal to completely purchase and install a solar system for $500 a reality. Even with the advent of decreasing solar energy costs in the private sector, we still have to contend with the issue of a portable water system that produces water on site. The bottom line here is we have a lot of development costs driven by utility installation that the average person in this country simply cannot afford. If the average income is roughly only $30,000 per year, we can expect people to become perennial renters and an increase in the number of occupants per unit due to dwindling future incomes and ever-increasing real estate prices. I'd just like to emphasize here that we run a for-profit system, in which companies make a profit in order to provide humans shelter. This is shelter and is not about buying a piece of candy down at the candy store; this is where you *live*. Why should people be exploited under a for-profit currency-based system for their need of shelter?

So, if we cannot use the billions of acres of land that is available to us to build shelters on, due to utility concerns, what we are left with? We are left with the for-profit lots that homebuilders have already provided utility access to and an energy inefficient, above ground structure, to be purchased at some exorbitant price through long-term financing. Ever increasing real estate costs are a direct result of using inefficient energy technology across the United States of America. The fact that the energy industry is allowed to keep its existing technology and jobs in place directly determines the amount of mortgage or rent payments that you are going to pay over the course of your lifetime. What do you think is more important: the energy industry keeping its patents and jobs in order to keep real estate prices high, or increasing your standard of living by allowing new energy technologies to be openly developed, without patents? Why is every new home built hooked up the power grid and not using solar energy or other sources of energy to power it? Why are home buyers not given a choice? A 2017 article by the Los Angeles Times noted that California's lawmakers have been trying to fix the state's housing crisis for 50 years, but have failed to do so for various reasons, including the fact that local communities are required to put forth plans to build affordable housing but are not required to execute them, and that local communities have asked for prison beds and student dormitories to be included into reported low-income housing figures.[25] My personal opinion is that these actions are driven around the fact that most people in crowded communities do not want more housing units added to already crowded areas – which is rightly justified.

A portable source of energy would solve our lot cost problem. What we really need is a self-generating unit with the retail cost of around $500 that is more or less a "plug-and-play" type unit. Imagine a 2' × 3' unit that perhaps sits in your garage, produces power on site, without hook up to any central-ized system or reliance on any type of fuel or other means to power it. These types of self-generating units could be included as an amenity to your new home at the time of their installation, since the cost would be so negligible, so your new home would be equipped with its own lifetime self-generating power supply. The goal of producing this type of portable generating unit should definitely be the highest priority goal in our country. ColdFusion is another option as a portable source of power, and I highly suggest you read more on that subject if you have the opportunity. Wireless power would also solve this problem: a wireless power receiving unit, for retail price of perhaps $500 or less, would also be just as ideal. We currently have wireless Internet, but we cannot seem to get anywhere with wireless power, or can . we? Has this technology been available for decades to us and simply been

---

25   *http://www.latimes.com/projects/la-pol-ca-housing-supply/*

kept under wraps through patent acquisition? We simply have no idea if any technology similar to the ones mentioned above have ever been developed, because the creation of our survival technology is cloaked under private legal nondisclosure agreements and patents. Wireless power could certainly help us on site to transmit energy between a portable, free energy device and any electrical appliances or devices that need to be run in our home. Wireless on-site power would not only alleviate the need for electrical lines, or the dependence on centralized energy to provide power to any residential lot, it would further reduce the construction costs of any home by eliminating expensive electrical installation costs. Can you imagine your dishwasher receiving power wirelessly from a portable free energy device in your garage? Can you see that, by applying the right energy technologies, how quickly we can exponentially reduce the costs of new home construction in America?

The purpose of this book is to define what technology and infrastructure America really needs, in order to best survive on this planet and then provide a means in which research and development can be accomplished in a cooperative manner, where information is shared and outsourced equally with everyone on the planet in order to best optimize the technology, manufacture it, and deliver it to the public, quickly and efficiently, at the lowest possible cost. We already know that, under a currency-based economy, this will never happen because it will destroy the need for currency and result in a mass loss of jobs.

What we want is to be able to live anywhere in our country or anywhere in the world at a very low cost. Can you imagine people being able to travel the world with a portable source of energy and perhaps even a portable shelter and live in different places around the world for basically no cost their entire lives? This would allow people to travel freely and break down their cultural and primitive differences. It would truly be major deterrent to all wars and hostilities, which are based on our rampant system of scarcity, caused by our currency-based system. The more information I give you, the clearer you can see the situation is black and white, between a technology-based economy and a currency-based economy. Either you live under the current system of scarcity with the same laws constantly getting the same results, or you move into a new system and get different results. It does not take hundreds of years to transition between the two economies.

Should we define our source of energy to be developed in more specific terms? Certainly, what I am outlining in this book is a basic structure that would best serve the needs of the public; other comments and concerns should definitely be added on by scientists and engineers. However, we need to start somewhere with basic needs and basic goals to fulfill these needs. If you do not set a goal, you will never meet it; at the time you are reading this chapter, a portable energy device might seem like an outlandish goal, but anything of significance that has ever been invented or created was, prior to its physical manifestation, considered an outlandish goal! So, it is important to use temperance here rather than let our emotions and currency-based, limited thinking run away with us. Think about the three major US highways that travel across the entire length of the United States, the connection of the first national railroads through unchartered territories, or the invention of the light bulb and the electrical lines that were constructed around the country to power them. All these were considered massive stretches by one person or another at the time they were just thought processes in someone's head, since there was nothing like them before their inception, so I am sure there was mass disbelief that these undertakings could not be done or in some instances, or would be a waste of time based on the current information and technology available during that time period.

We need a portable source of water to go along with our portable source of energy. There are several options currently available:

A well would grant our request for on-site water; however, groundwater is not readily accessible everywhere in the United States. Could we use ground penetrating radar from a satellite to find large caches of water across the United States, so that we could build local communities above? I certainly think this technology would help us in that regard, but my question is: Why are we not using this technology today to help spread the population across the country and reduce our lot costs? I believe it would also be a good idea not to privatize well drilling in order to keep these costs as low as possible. We should put a mass emphasis and millions of people on solving the problem of getting water to any area in this country—or any area in the world that requires it—on demand, at any given location, without the use of an aquifer, reservoir, or any type of piping system connected to it. We need to develop technology that will produce our water on site. Are we doing that now? Absolutely not, because there are simply no incentives under the currency-based system to undertake any such actions. A recent article by Cost Helper Home and Garden outlines well-drilling costs. Pricing can vary greatly depending on the type of soil being drilled—for example, rock versus clay. The cost of a fully completed well including a drilling cap would be approximately $1,500 to $3,000 for a 100-foot well, whereas a 400-foot well might cost upwards of $12,000. Adding a pump, storage tank and piping to the home can increase the costs up to $8,000 more, and a well drilled in very difficult terrain could run as high as $50,000.[26]

We should be working constantly to develop a way to create water at any given home site locally. A portable source of water would solve so many problems, not only in our country but around the world. Can you imagine a machine that simply created water from the air around it or through some sort of alchemy system? I am talking about pure H2O here, not some mixture of chemicals. A 2017 article in CNN Business by Kaya Yurieff noted that a team of scientists has already created solar-powered technology to produce drinking water from the air, even in desert climates.[27] We already have Atmospheric Water Generators available for purchase on the Internet; there are in-home units you can buy that will produce twenty-five to thirty liters per day, all the way up to industrial grade, large-scale units, that will

---

26   https://home.costhelper.com/well-drilling.html
27   https://money.cnn.com/2017/04/19/technology/future/solar-powered-device-drinking-water/index.html

produce up to 5,000 liters per day. This technology is expanding and growing as we speak; the relative humidity does need to be very high, perhaps 25%, to produce water, however the efficiency rating will vary from manufactured to manufacturer and you can purchase these units right now over the Internet. The bottom line is their cost is quite expensive, since the evolution of the technology is still basically in its infancy, but this is certainly something we should be incorporating into all our homes nationwide.

Hydroponic tower farming is a system whereby nutrient-rich water is constantly pumped through hanging cylindrical plastic containers directly to each plant's roots. The plants are surrounded and secured by gravel or coconut husks, which replace the anchoring aspect of soil. Some of these systems can use up to 10 times less water than traditional soil farming; they also produce much higher crop yields per square foot and shorten growing cycles. These hydroponic units are usually run in greenhouses indoors, which eliminates the need for pesticides as there are virtually no pests in these indoor farms. We can easily provide all the fresh organic vegetables and herbs that a local comity or family might need at a fraction of our current soil farming costs if we continue to develop this technology, which is now in its infancy. I encourage you to check out online videos on this emerging technology. Would it not make sense to try to implement these technologies across America on a mass scale?

Our traditional method of water distribution keeps being implemented because it keeps lot costs under the control of the currency-based for-profit system, keeps the available lots scarce, and it would ruin the entire existing real-estate structure and collapse the banks if we were to allow new emerging water technologies to be mass-produced and incorporated into our housing industry as a part of our standard business practices.

Why do we want to continue to build reservoirs, pipe water for hundreds of miles, and rely on weather systems to create water for us? If we simply created a law that mandated the use of portable water systems in every home in the United States today, there would be a mass demand for the product and over time the unit costs would drop dramatically; eventually the technology would become so cheap that Third World countries could afford it and their citizens would no longer need to walk many miles per day for water. The currency-based for-profit system will require us to produce this technology on a mass scale in order to reduce its bottom-line unit cost, and that is going to require financing from banks, credit unions, etc., because the public cannot afford to purchase it without the use of credit. This type of technology will never receive that type of financing on a mass scale in a so called "free market" system, because it competes directly with the for-profit housing system and threatens to destroy the value of the collateral, securitizing all home loans today in the United States. A better way to approach the problem, rather than waiting for decades for the currency system to come around and potentially provide an easy source of financing, would be to implement a licensing system in the housing industry, making this type of technology nonprofit, non-publicly traded, and patent free.

The problem with implementing our current survival technology here in the United States into Third World countries, is that it is so expensive and labor-intensive that charitable organizations and government donations cannot cover the costs to bring it to billions of people. The simple reason we cannot implement our technology into Third World countries is because it is bad technology! It simply costs too much, it is not portable, and it is too labor-intensive to build. Our current system of distributing water is based on building reservoirs that rely on rain to fill them and, coincidently, when it does not rain, they do not fill up.

Perhaps there are other technologies we've yet to discover that would be available to us, in an open sourced, nonprofit, and non-publicly traded industry utilizing free and open sourced information between companies. When you open an industry up to just getting the job done, rather than concentrating fully on making money, the possibilities are endless.

Capturing Rainwater and Recycling for Drinking

"Earthships" are types of homes that have already been developed that are fantastic at capturing, storing, and recycling rainwater, not only for drinking and for waste disposal but to water plants grown inside the home as well as outside of the home. We shall discuss "Earthships" in detail later on in the chapter. There are number of systems available for purchase today. The main problem with these systems stems from the fact that if it does not rain and you run out of stored water in your tank, then you will have no access to water. So, this type of the system might be used as a possible water backup system for residential use, or perhaps would be better used for industrial purposes. An atmospheric water generator would be considered superior technology and what we would want to base our platform on for future development.

Sewer and Gray Water Recycling

This technology has been extensively developed, I think, fantastically by "Earthships," including recycling water four times, from its point of collection, by capturing rainwater, then using it for drinking and showering, then it is recycled into indoor plants, through a drip system and finally to its last point of collection, watering plants outside the residence. Graywater is basically 100% reusable and water from toilets is recycled into indoor plants and then outdoor plants, without smell.

We also have the classic "sewer tank" that can be used as a basic form of a portable sewer system. A recent article from Home Advisor states the average cost of a sewer tank is $600 to $1,000 and the average cost of installation is approximately $6,000.[28] This type of technology also requires some sort of centralized collection company to constantly maintain it; whereas on-site recycling does not, so recycling our sewage and gray water should be the main focus of future technology development. The more portable and self-contained a home we can build, that does not rely on any centralized

---

28   https://www.homeadvisor.com/cost/plumbing/install-a-septic-tank/

systems in any manner, the more usable land we open up for living, and the more this newly developed independence will continue to drive down our lot costs.

The goal should be to create homes that fulfill all the needs of the consumer on-site—water, electricity, waste disposal, and even a limited amount of food production in order to restore the individual sovereign power of each citizen, so they no longer have to rely on the whims of corporate America to provide them inferior, disposable survival technology that constantly requires repurchase. *Let's set our production goal for each lot in America to $1,500.00 or less for all portable utilities, including an on-site power unit, on-site water unit and sewer recycling system combined, that do not require repurchase or repair for a period of no less than 25 years.*

Lot Grading and Preparation Issues

We need some sort of driveway access and parking area for vehicles; under the current system. A recent article by Home Advisor stated that most homeowners can expect to shell out between $1,200 and $4,200 just for grading and parking alone.[29] We will need to develop technology through collaboration that is non-patented and can do the job at the lowest possible cost. $200.00 should cover the price for the entire on-site preparation and this should be funded from tax payer money and the technology provided by nonprofit, non-patent holding, non-publicly traded companies. Anyone should be able to live anywhere they want in this country and no one should be made a slave to the inferior technology we use today, which creates incredibly high lot preparation costs that the majority of this country cannot afford and is instead relegated to an endless debt repayment plan, known as rent in order to provide shelter for themselves.

---

29   https://www.homeadvisor.com/cost/landscape/clear-land-or-prepare-a-construction-site/

Getting Rid of the Garbage

Your only real options in a remote area are to burn your garbage, recycle, compost, or bury it. It will be very difficult to make a lot of garbage when you do not have access to a local grocery store if it is perhaps twenty-five or fifty miles away. So, it becomes impossible to create small communities of people that are fully self-contained with grocery stores, shopping, and other amenities that people in modern day small towns and cities require.

Perhaps an autonomously driven vehicle, powered by a free energy device, would be available to pick up your garbage locally, so your physical location again might become less of a factor, with technology applied to autonomously driven vehicles and perhaps an autonomously run recycling center; better yet, the more recycling and waste control that we can apply locally, right at your home, the better. Perhaps we can convert our garbage into some source of energy on-site by applying advanced technology to this problem. It is only going to be through the development of superior technology in our energy, health care, transportation, and housing industries that we will be able to eventually develop these types of seamlessly running technologies to benefit homeowners anywhere that harmonize with each other.

Let Us Do a Quick Add-Up

Basically, we are out perhaps $16,000–$20,000 for the solar, $3,000–$8,000 for the well if we are lucky, another $5,000 for the septic, and another $3,000 for lot preparation. The cost just for the lot utility access and preparation is anywhere between $24,000 and $36,000, without the cost of the land itself, and that is the bare minimum. Depending on where you want to build, these costs could easily double, and there is no available financing for any of these outlined costs other than perhaps a credit card for the first-time home buyer. A first-time home buyer could easily expect to spend $100,000, depending on location, to develop a piece of raw land for the purpose of building a residential home. Based on the fact that 61% of America right now lives paycheck to paycheck and has roughly $1,000 or less in savings, how is the current system going to make homeownership affordable for the general population? Our general population simply does not have the income and financial support to create a customized home on a lot of their choice and, as we've already discussed, increasing the incomes of the general population over time to make homes affordable will never change these results. The Inflation/Technology Paradox kicks in and, since shelter technology is scarce, the prices I showed you in this text would skyrocket, making them just as unaffordable as they are now. It is only going to be through a mass concentrated effort without for-profit ideals, patents, and stockholders that homeownership will ever become affordable for all American citizens. Based on the existing system, you can expect to buy a for-profit track home with a zero-lot line (that is a fancy way of saying you are ten feet away from your neighbor) for an astronomical ever-increasing price, due to the fact that approximately 63% of the population lives on 3.5% of the usable land in this entire country. We need new technology desperately to move our population to rural areas, covering the other 96% of our usable land.

Reducing On-Site Building Costs

A Russian company called Apis Cor can now digitally print homes, and they are also available for purchase on a very small scale in the United States. Summarizing information found on their website, these homes are printed with a polymer material or geo-cement, a building material made from superior technology. The entire structure can be printed in a few days and the polymer set within two to three days. The material is fire resistant, water resistant, creates far less CO_2 emissions than standard building materials during its creation, has insulating properties and is resistant to frost and high heat.[30] You can also do a search and find a video showing the printing of an approximately 400 square feet home, which took less than twenty-four hours to print and the cost is about $10,000. We are looking to build our new

---

30   https://www.apis-cor.com/

economy on exactly this type of price point and technology. A 600 square foot home was also just printed in Austin Texas by another company with a cost of under $4,000. Since this technology is advancing so fast, it is hard to source. I would suggest using a search engine to get a quote on the most recent and most accurate cost. This type of technology no longer requires the excessive human labor it takes to create a cinderblock wall, which requires constant adjustments and results in an uneven wall. Bottom line: The costs are far less, and there is no limit to what can be done with this technology.

Geocement used to print walls, may also be potentially used to print sewer systems, bridges, and roads. **We should seriously consider digital printing as a solution to creating a driveway or parking lot, as well as the basic foundation of any home. Lot preparation costs are a huge expense and barrier to owning a home, and digital printing should bring down these costs exponentially.** I look forward to the development of this technology, and I am really excited about it as I hope you are; we will no longer need to cut down forests in order to create homes.

The concept of digitally printing a home has also caught on in the United States at the University of Southern California. I expect this technology to begin a phase of rapid development throughout the next decade. This technology will definitely have an effect on homebuilding and most likely reduce our workforce as a result of its continued automation. It is important to recognize that as we see technology rapidly advancing that we have a plan to assimilate it properly into our economy, in order to avoid the least amount of destruction to our financial system as possible. We cannot just implement technology into our society that is going to potentially destroy a wide variety of jobs, including: masons, concrete plant workers, quarry workers, construction workers, additional managers and human resources employees who support their efforts and a host of other jobs that currently support the production of cinderblock walls. So, having a plan to move forward should be of paramount importance to our society, as we are guaranteed to lose potentially many jobs to technology and automation in just the next decade.

According to the Pangea Builders website, an "Earthship" is a self-contained, utility independent, off-the-grid type of home that is currently available for purchase and provides the following benefits: thermal and solar heating and cooling, both solar and wind electrical power, self-contained on-site sewage treatment, and on-site water recycling and water harvesting. The problems of energy and water created on site, as well as on-site sewage disposal, seem to have been rudimentarily solved by the systems currently available in an Earthship. The home's walls are built with tires that are crammed with earth to provide a very stable structure and an extreme level of insulation. These homes are powered by solar and wind exclusively and do not, in most cases, require any external power source or to be hooked up to a power grid, although they can be connected to centralized water and electric systems. Rainwater is captured and recycled four times, and is used by plants both in the home and outside. These homes basically operate the same way a conventional home does today; other than the design of the home, you would not notice any difference in the way the toilet flushes or when and how the lights turn on. These homes are different in that they offer the residents the opportunity to grow food inside the structure most of the year, depending on the climate outside of the structure.[31] I urge you to definitely check out the site and this process: the amenities found in these homes are quite elaborate and the idea of having a home like this would certainly help the average American lower their overhead and their number of hours worked per week.

Probably our best option would be to combine a digitally printed home with the excellent on-site utility systems of an Earthship home. These technologies could easily be combined together, if we adopt regulations to our housing industry to remove patents and remove the shareholder and 'for-profit' ideals, communicating and sharing information between companies and openly helping each other to produce a superior product. Partially burying a digitally printed structure, rather than using tires, might be a better option as well, so the natural insulation from the earth, as well as

---

31   https://pangeabuilders.com/buildings/earthships/

vents and windows, could assist with the heating and cooling of the structure. The structure could make use of sheet rock lining for its interior walls, or some similar eco-friendly material, rather than using stucco, and be made to look quite beautiful. We can also apply various types of artistic architectural designs to these types of homes, providing the curb appeal and "wow" factor that most Americans demand when making a home purchase. Again, I cannot stress enough that we have the ability to make this home so beautiful that nearly all Americans would want to move into it immediately and abandon their current inferior home. We can make this type of home a reality if we simply apply our mass consciousness and our advanced technologies toward its construction.

Imagine an autonomously driven flatbed truck with several machines on it driving to a remote location. Once parked, remote operators through the Internet back machines off the trailer. The first machine grades your lot, the second machine that backs off the trailer is a digital printer that basically follows behind the first machine and prints your road; still another digital printer backs off the trailer in order to print your home, three car garage, pool, and in-ground sewer tank. Your home is powered by a free energy device and sends power wirelessly to all your appliances, so no electrical wiring is required to be placed anywhere in your residence. An atmospheric water generator provides all the water you need on site from the air, and that water is recycled four times through your home. Basically, your entire home is built by machines in a matter of a few days, that can run 24×7, do not take coffee breaks, and do not make mistakes; everything is sited in through the GPS. Once your home is completed, there's no need to hook up to any type of centralized unit and, once you pay for the structure, unless you have property taxes assessed or you decide to get some sort of renter's type of insurance policy, there are no further monthly costs required. Imagine that you can purchase this home for $25,000 and potentially not have to put any more money in it for the next twenty-five years. Does this sound like technology that would change your life forever?

Most of the technology I just described has already been built by a handful of people trying their best to make things better in order to make our proposed construction site completely independent of any centralized systems that result in long-term financing for the customer. What do you think we could do if we took the existing technology and improved upon it? Sending out millions to work on the task, rather than just a few random, brave souls? Our biggest monthly expense is the cost of shelter; yet why does no one ever acknowledge that we should apply technology towards lowering its cost?

Limitations

Cost: According to an article on website Archinia, the cost of building an Earthship home is roughly $225 per square foot, which equates to about $400,000 for an 1,800-square-foot home. However, this only a ballpark estimate; costs will vary dramatically depending on the size, location and intricacies of the home.[32] I expect the cost for these homes, like any other emerging technology, to drop over time. However, the pace at which the costs drop in the free market will never compete with cost of building a conventional home. The basic cost of one of these homes does not fit within the budget constraints of the aggregate public, so this type of technology would not be practical for widespread production at this point. If the design, construction, and on-site assembly of these homes, were to be overseen through a nonprofit, non-publicly traded, and non-patented process, I would expect the cost to be far less. About 50% of the country makes $30,000 a year. Our goal should be a price tag of $25,000 for the entire structure, to build it brand-new, that includes the lot grading, creation insulation of all the on-site and self-contained utilities, and the complete creation of the structure, including all appliances that should be "built-in" and allow our home to be ready to move into, without further expenses. The only way—and I really mean to say the "only way"—that we will ever create a ready to live in structure for this type of price, that still has the curb appeal that all Americans want, is to

---

32   https://archinia.com/earthships/earthship-pros-cons

create it through a fully automated system. Really, 99% of this home should be built by machines that are considered "superior" technology, and the "only way" that we will ever create superior technology like this is through a serious coordinated effort of human beings on this planet, openly sharing their information and technology through a nonprofit, non-publicly traded, and non-patented industry.

Financing

This represents the major sticking point to applying superior technology to our housing problem. Housing represents the largest expense; most anyone will purchase throughout their entire lives. The currency-based, for-profit system will always be incentivized to create any type of housing that is the most expensive to the consumer, simply because it makes the most profit by using this method. A digitally printed, energy independent home that costs $200,000–$300,000 will never compete with the current wooden frame structures of today, because buyers cannot obtain secured financing If we tried to find financing for these digitally printed, utility independent homes built in remote locations that are off the county or city grids and do not have standard utility hookups, they are not unlikely to be financed under any type of known loan programs. The general public does not understand the operating nature of these homes, the workings of their portable utility systems, etc., so they would have a difficult time being resold to the public in the event of foreclosure. Financing for these homes at this time would be almost impossible, as the structure does not meet government loan guidelines as approved collateral for a government backed loan. The structures would be considered a geodesic or a yurt type of home and would most likely not be acceptable collateral under any federal loan programs. So, getting a loan to cover the purchase of a property like this is simply not going to be attainable, hence the reason for the $25,000 price, or at least having that price as a goal, so the home can be financed through unsecured debt, like a credit card, or just paid for in cash. Banks, savings and loans, and credit unions have absolutely no incentive to finance these types of homes, because they are a substitute for the high priced, site built wooden homes they lend on now, and replacing these homes with a superior substitute would directly threaten the value of their collateral and the performance of their existing real estate debt. Financing for these homes might become available through other sources like credit cards and unsecured loans, if the general public accepted these types of homes as an accepted and safe structure to live in; in addition to that, these new digitally printed, energy independent homes would have to appear desirable for the average family, from a utility, beauty, and comfort perspective, for them to want to purchase immediately. The major problem is that if you do not have financing for these types of structures, you cannot drive the volume you need to keep driving production costs down, year after year, under the currency-based system. We will need to drastically reduce the price tag of these homes in order to finance them as unsecured debt, and the only way to do that is through a non-profit, non-publicly traded, non-patented industry openly sharing information; otherwise the industry will never be able to get the price near the $25,000–$50,000 range.! Let us always remember that the economy runs on consumer confidence and the ideals of the people in any economy directly drive the products and services that the people of that country are willing to consume. So, the economy is as much emotional and psychological as it is functional and material; even if people fall in love with these homes, if they cannot get financing for them, this type of technology will never find its way into the mainstream of our society.

Utility limitations

After doing some research and reading several articles, it is uncertain whether these homes can be built, in any type of climate, because they run on solar energy. The amount of sun they receive is also a concern, as well as the efficiency of the solar or wind systems powering the residence. Will these home's heating and cooling systems work just as well in the desert, as in the frozen north? Based on the solar and wind technology, these homes use today I do not believe, at this time, they can be considered completely energy independent in any climate not requiring any type of assistance from a centralized energy or water system. Furthermore, there is the fear by many Americans that not being connected to any type of centralized energy and water systems, could leave them potentially stranded in an emergency situation. If our home were connected to a free energy device, this device could provide an unlimited amount of energy for the home, and many of these geographical and emotional concerns might be alleviated. There might also be concerns that rainwater would not be consistent enough, to meet the water needs for any given family, but combining rain water capture for outside plants and garden needs, coupled with clean H2O provided by an Atmospheric Water Generator, might greatly alleviate that concern as well. A combination of different technologies is what an open sourced system is all about, creating and adding to our self-sustaining home. Add in a satellite dish for Internet and television and you have a completely sustainable and self-contained home that does not require any physical attachment to a centralized system. These technologies need to be developed further, but certainly the basic building blocks are already in place. We are definitely on the right track to create a completely energy, water, and waste independent structure; if you combine these processes with a very low-cost construction procedure like digital printing, we would be well on our way to solving all of the real estate problems currently facing America.

If our culture accepts creating and owning these homes as part of the American dream rather than the traditional colonial home, which is powered by an electrical grid, centralized water, and sewer systems, a mass demand for these homes would allow for a price drop, due to the mass volume of homes that would be produced. You would find a large number of industries being able to streamline their costs, to manufacture such homes and a mass volume of parts that would be produced as well, such as: electrical systems, water tanks, batteries, and solar systems. Again, more demand for these types of products drives volume and lowers the cost for them, as do technological innovations like digital printing. Certainly, Third World countries who do not have a mass population with access to obtainable credit or consistent employment and not nearly the same manufacturing capacities as the United States, could make great use of these types of homes and their implementation would massively increase the world's standard of living. Having and achieving a goal of creating this technology at the lowest possible cost here in the United States will allow us to implement and clone it worldwide. Can you imagine local sustainable communities using these types of homes? At one time, the entire Internet was pushed through a phone line and anywhere a phone line did not go, people did not have access to the Internet. There is a great demand for portability now; with smart phones, we have that portability, and just about anyone can access the Internet from almost anywhere in the United States or across the world through a satellite dish. It is time to implement the same ideology of portability and independence, currently in our phones and computers, toward the design, manufacture and distribution of homes in this country, making them completely self-contained in regard to their generation of energy, water, and disposal of sewage, where food can be grown and eaten on site. Most of these ideas and technologies have already been developed; it is simply a matter of expanding and refining these basic technologies in order to create a desired price point and eliminate decades, of endless mortgage and rent payments.

Being close to work creates higher lot costs and the need for more hours worked and thus more cash to pay a bigger mortgage. Real estate values are based on location, location, and location. Factors that drive high real estate prices higher include the following:

1. Location due to the beauty and desirability of an area, including weather and climate

We would be better served by living in the country, either telecommuting from home or driving a short distance, to a local office a few days a week located in a rural area, surrounded by a low cost and abundant amount of land for development, rather than continuing to build tiny structures, vertically, purchased through long-term financing. If people move from the city to rural areas, it will be important to designated areas for people to meet and converse. I am certainly not eliminating the choice to live in a densely populated area for those that seek it as a life experience: a technology-based economy is built around the idea of giving humans more options rather than fewer about where and how to live. I know most people live in the city for its varied lifestyle and diversified sources of entertainment that are not available in our current rural areas. Consider the fact that city real estate will also become cheaper if a relative substitute is available at a fraction of the cost. Some people might be able to own more than one home in both the country and the city, and spend time in each location for a more balanced existence. Owning two homes free and clear is certainly almost an impossible feat for most people under the currency-based system; also consider the fact that hotels and short-term rental units would also become exponentially cheaper, if we develop our real estate under shared and nonprofit regulation.

2. Location relative to place of work—commute

Those that choose to live in cities and densely populated areas suffer from an income/expense paradox. People in big cities will tend to make more money and there will tend to be more job opportunities available; however, the downside is the fact that the cost of living is far higher than rural areas and continues to increase over time, as the population of these areas increases due to a constant shortage of usable living space. People living in highly populated areas do not enjoy a high standard of living, as they are usually forced into a very small square footage of living area without access to any type of backyard, let alone acreage, commuting on highly populated public transportation to work, and then occupying a small cubicle for the rest of their day, rather than enjoying their time outside. Living this type of existence is not a natural state for any human to endure for a long period of time, let alone their entire life. I believe a "caged" style of living (moving from tiny apartment to crowded subway or roads to a cubicle) creates anxiety, depression, and general mental health issues for the vast majority of our population. These early mental health issues can lead to serious and even chronic or lethal physical health issues over time. If we want to reduce our health-care costs, I believe it would be better to spread our population out, where they have access to nature daily, or least provide that "option" to the public where none exists now. I seriously believe that we would see far less need for prescription drugs if people were working less hours and spending more time outdoors.

3. Location relative to the designated schools in the area and educational concerns

Sustainable local communities would be a huge draw for young families, due to their desirability of peace and safety for their children. I would expect the development of schools to flourish in these types of communities, once they become relatively established. It would certainly be easy enough to digitally print a school, grocery store, shopping mall, and other amenities once any community was fairly established, as they could be built for a fraction of the cost, as compared to creating them in a currency-based, for-profit system.

4. Location relative to existing family members and friends

There are other factors that come into play, as far as the desirability of a certain location for private residence, but if you look at the fact that you could build a sustainable local community that relied on on-site energy to power it and never ran out, it would be quite easy to build businesses around this type of infrastructure. There would also be a vast decrease in the number of hours needed to be worked over time, so over the long run most people would migrate to such communities, knowing that they did not need to create a lot of cash flow, living in energy efficient low-cost communities versus the incredibly high overhead costs associated with for-profit driven locations.

Schools would eventually open, and if culturally people began looking to move to communities like these, friends and family would begin to relocate as well and a cultural trend would become a part of our new belief system. Portable sources of energy that are self-sustaining and would lend greatly to the development of food growth in greenhouses, so that food could be grown year-round for the local community and restaurants.

Imagine for a moment a beautiful little town that is completely quiet as cars and even leaf blowers run on self-generating or wirelessly receiving energy devices that make no sound. Every home has a greenhouse next to it, which is heated and cooled geothermically by simply burying PVC corrugated piping in the ground eight feet deep over a mathematically determined distance based on each unit's square footage. Each unit is heated and cooled solely by a fan blowing air at a constant ground temperature of 56 degrees into the unit, which costs the owner pennies a day to heat and cool in any climate. Hydroponic tower farming centers, supplied by atmospheric water generators at the center of town, supply local restaurants with fresh produce. Satellites beam in high-bandwidth television and Internet, so everyone has constant access to entertainment and information. Mothers and fathers work their fifteen-to-twenty-hour work weeks and spend the rest of their time having fun with and educating their children. Some of the parents might have extra time to volunteer at their digitally printed, energy independent school, creating a free source of guidance for young children, not only to elevate their education in traditional areas of history and math, but also in creative areas of music and other arts. Massive overhead, no longer being fed by currency, would no longer be a concern for the local townspeople, because everything, including the local grocery store, has no mortgage on it and runs virtually free of operating costs, resulting in extra disposable income to purchase musical instruments, sports equipment, science equipment, and other highly sought after educational tools for students to explore. School becomes fun and is no longer a chore; people spend time together; people volunteer their time or spend their time writing books, working on projects, or helping others with their emotional and psychological problems, meditating and evolving themselves toward a greater standard of being and setting an example for others to follow. A domino effect of positive emotional states becomes the baseline of our culture. America, in any given community, would experience lower crime rates, less need for government interference, less dependence on prescription drugs for balance, etc. Are you starting to see how incredibly time-consuming and repetitive it is to keep our currency-based economy supported today?

Personally, I see the development of these digital communities starting initially with retirees who have a fixed level of income and are desperately looking to lower their high fixed overhead costs. Retirees would certainly be the first demographic of customers to inhabit these types of communities, should they become available for occupancy. Artists and other entrepreneurs who seek low overhead while they pursue the things they love to do would also be drawn to these areas. Once these types of communities become established, virtually everyone will want to live in them, as they now have the option to avoid the endless drudgery of a constant forty-hour work week, just by changing their location.

Technology Destroys Currency

The true reality is that there is no shortage of land in the United States. We've only lacked in ways over the centuries to be able to live on it in a low cost, comfortable, and environmentally sound way. Today, with the advent of high-speed computers and highly developed technologies, in almost every facet of our lives including the Internet, where over three billion people are connected worldwide and share information, we have more opportunities than ever to move beyond the currency system, in order to truly enjoy the abundance that we deserve. Why should 63% of the population continued to live on 3.5% of the usable land in this country? The banks want higher real estate prices based on the simple fact that they can issue higher loans to borrowers, making more interest and thus more profit; banks will never finance superior technology-based homes, because they are a direct threat to the value of their current collateral! Realtors want higher home prices so their commissions are higher for the same amount of work; the entire industry and everyone connected to it is geared with the incentive of making everyone into a debt slave. This is a form of insanity that has to end. Thus, we will never see this technology produced on a mass scale in order to bring costs down, hence the reason for the regulation of the housing industry outlined in my plan.

Let us look at some other scenarios, facing our potential very near future. Corporations continue to automate themselves at an unprecedented and unregulated pace, and the demand for human labor worldwide drops 75% over the next two decades. There are food shortages, massive problems with incomes, keeping a job for any length of time, runs on the banks, constant shutdowns of the government, constant problems with supplies of all products, and repairs needed to existing technologies. In short, we would encounter what I would call "a period of waiting"—this is simply a time when you have expensive overhead, as we do today, contrasted by a mass shortage of jobs due to automation and outsourcing, and a vast majority of our population might end up living homeless, on welfare, or some type guaranteed basic income just to survive through it. Understanding that job elimination through technology is all but a forgone conclusion will help us to plan better for its inevitability.

Let us try to better understand our current economic scenario right here in the United States. In 2017, there were roughly 125 million people working in the United States: this includes both full-time and part-time workers. If you take the roughly two billion hours that were worked in 2017 by those people as a ballpark figure, my question to you is: What did we accomplish by working those two billion hours, as a collective society? To pay off $1/360^{th}$ of a house? To keep paying rent, a debt which has a balance that can never be paid? Even though we have jobs, why do we want to stay in the same system we are in now, even if we have access to plentiful employment? We are basically just walking in circles under this system and not creating access to the technology that we need in order to reduce our forty-hour work week. A 2017 *Forbes* article by Jessica Lutz stated that one-third of our workforce between the ages of 22 and 65 is "underemployed," and this level of "underemployment" has been the same now for about the last three decades.[33] What I am trying to articulate to you is that there are simply not enough jobs available to meet the advanced skill sets that many people in this country possess and there really have not been for a long, long time. Underemployment is getting worse for young people. The statistics show that there are never going to be enough jobs available for people to match their skill set, let alone going to approach their income requirements, regardless of the amount of education or work experience possessed by the candidate. Our population is growing, and we simply cannot expect to wave a magic wand to create jobs for the future billions of people that are expected to inhabit this planet over the next few decades. I seriously believe that the only option for most young people today is to keep living with their parents, renting a room with friends, or just relying directly on government aid to pay their rent and mortgage or random donations from their parents in order to meet the ever-increasing survival costs associated with a currency-based for-profit system. Unfortunately, for young children, I see no other long-term solutions or pathways to homeownership ever becoming available to them as an aggregate population, based on the current regulations and incentives of the currency-based system.

The system has always failed us and will continue to fail us as an aggregate population, and it is time to evolve out of it into a new, more efficient system. Either our current system will die from a lack of income caused by technology and outsourcing, or it will die from decreasing overhead costs if we implement a licensing system. Would you prefer to be in control of your future, rather than a victim of it through non-action? This book will help you become a master of your destiny, in order to give you a plan and method of

---

33   https://www.forbes.com/sites/payout/2017/07/21/the-underemployment-phenome-non-no-one-is-talking-about/#12e7fc1a5a01

thinking to potentially control your future, bringing you into a mindset of prosperity you've never contemplated before.

CHAPTER 4

Understanding Patents, Confiscated Technology and State Secrets

In order to better understand the solutions that we need to solve our economic problems, we first need to understand our current problems from a different point of view. We know that "awareness" of any problem, or finding out what the problem really is all about, is the biggest obstacle to solving the problem. In order for you to better understand why I've outlined the specific solutions for the four industries that represent our greatest monthly expenditures, we first need to gain a better understanding of how some of our current laws affect our overhead industries and the entire economy.

Specifically, the laws that create the biggest obstacles to the evolution of technology are patents and state secrets. There are a lot of assumptions surrounding patents and technologies that are kept classified under our current federal laws. Our technology has advanced so much in the last hundred years that there's simply no point in adhering to old laws that block precious survival technology from the public, that have run our currency-based for-profit system for so long. We can only form a new economy by breaking down our old assumptions about how our current economic laws work, before we can create new laws that produce different results.

In order for our country to create true equality between our citizens, we must first demand a universal belief in equality—and the best place to look for a working example of equality is the universe. The inner workings of the universe are all based on equality, and if we can better understand physically how the universe works and the universal laws that govern it, we can better understand how to build a new economy—based on equality and efficiency, working towards a means to an end rather than perpetually working with no specific goals for our aggregate population.

Let's try to rationalize for a moment some conceptual understanding of our current knowledge of the universe versus the consciousness, beliefs and assumptions that currently drive our economy. The universe doesn't operate on a system of debt; the universe doesn't deprive power to 99% of itself and concentrate all of its power into 1% of itself; the universe doesn't compete against itself for egotistical gratification; and the universe doesn't exploit or enslave parts of itself for the benefit of other parts of itself. The universe shares information openly, freely and transparently and gives equal importance to each atom, which creates its mass, in a cooperative and loving manner. If the universe shares information, freely and openly, in a cooperative manner, with the understanding that no one part of it is more important than the other, in order to have created the physical world that we know today, wouldn't it make sense to create an economy based on the rules that follow this system of intelligence—a system of intelligence that has proven itself over billions of years of time—rather than trying to create a new system, based on the illusion of separation from that intelligence, that constantly creates debt, concentrated ownership and competition?

Quantum physics is basically teaching us today that everything is connected, that atoms represent intelligent life, without the use of a brain or body and can respond telepathically to our thoughts. Let's call, for purposes of our discussion today, the physical space we occupy, which most scientists call "time-space," a *smart field*. All of the atoms in this smart field are interconnected with each other. I believe Nassim Haramein, a brilliant physicist, has solved the unified field theory, giving us a basic understanding of how the universe divides itself and proves a direct relationship between mass and frequency that is scalable across all parts of itself. He has also mathematically proven that there is a tiny black hole at the center of every atom, potentially from which unlimited energy can be pulled from a parallel dimension. You may want to check out some of his videos on the internet; his work is currently being peer-reviewed.

We have certainly come to a place where technology is over going to advance at a rate that we cannot imagine over the next hundred years and obliterate our past fears, idealisms and beliefs that have been running our planet now for thousands of years. If we can understand that as a society and culture, we're all connected, then we can begin to resolve one of the biggest problems our economy faces today, which is the illusion of separation. Humans fundamentally believe that they are separate from everything else in the universe and have no innate connection to it. Most believe that our planet is a random creation based on chance, as well as our moon and the humans on planet Earth, and that humans are the only form of intelligent life that exists in the universe. We also fundamentally believe that there is nothing more intelligent than us in the universe and therefore it is our divine right to rule this planet and do with it whatever we would like to do, at any given time, regardless of the consequences of our actions.

This belief system is also based on the belief that all intelligence lies in the human brain and that because everything else is physically dumber than us: plants, animals and certainly atoms—they have no innate intelligence and are our pawns to rule over. Currency drives separation between humans by relegating people into classes, based on how much money they make, allowing humans with more currency to exploit humans with less currency, through their need to purchase survival technology. If our planet distributed water the same way our economy distributed currency, there would be a hole the size of a doughnut running through the entire planet filled with water and a few droplets of water scattered throughout the rest of the surface of the planet. It's safe to say this type of water distribution system would not be a good way to distribute life throughout our planet, as we would find only a fraction of the creatures on our planet that we do today, rather than utilizing the current "everywhere" water distribution system governed by universal intelligence.

Another huge law that affects society is patent law. Providing discovery evidence in court to prove original thought is basically impossible, yet we give over our power to this illusion every day. Ownership of property is another giant illusion that humans have; ownership is a concept held by humans, and no other species in the universe practices the concept of ownership. In summary, we have quite an "illusion of separation" going on, on this planet. In order to build an economy of true abundance, we need to understand that we are innately connected to everything. If we can understand that everything, in our current universe, is physically connected and therefore connected to us, then we can better understand what our innate rights are as humans, as individuals and what each of us, as human beings on the planet today, deserves to receive.

Are you familiar with the placebo effect? An article from Medicine Net by William Shield, Jr. states that a false treatment—whereby a patient is given an inactive substance like sugar, distilled water or saline solution—can sometimes improve a patient's condition simply because they believe the treatment will be helpful.[34] This theory basically states that our thoughts can directly control our health and cause sporadic healing. When we firmly stand behind a positive idealism or belief emotionally, already seeing ourselves as healed, these thoughts and emotions precipitate immediate healing. The placebo effect also supports interconnectivity and equality among atoms. When we examine the placebo effect, we can witness that our conscious thoughts

---

34   https://www.medicinenet.com/script/main/art.asp?articlekey=31481

have an effect on our physical health. All prescription drugs have to be field-tested, which is basically measuring the level of each candidate's healing effect, by taking a newly developed drug versus the placebo—our thoughts, conscious state, emotions and beliefs affecting the movement of atoms in our body in order to heal ourselves, as a result of ingesting something similar to a harmless sugar pill. If the newly developed drug performs better than the sugar pill, in most cases it's brought to market for consumption by the public. I find it funny that the entire pharmaceutical industry works tirelessly to provide drugs they can sell for money, that only slightly heal us better than what our own bodies do, rather than trying to develop a better understanding and application of the free-of-charge placebo effect on humans, given the fact that most of the people who participate in these experiments have no training in meditation, creative visualization or any general idea of how to heal themselves at all, through their thought process. Since the placebo effect shows that all humans have a vetted and documented ability to heal themselves without drugs, wouldn't it be better for our medical industry to focus solely on training our minds to become better at healing ourselves? This focus would actually reduce the cost of our healthcare, because a well-trained mind, with the ability to heal the body connected to it, would basically result in little to no profits for the healthcare industry; so, we can see first-hand how for-profit incentives run counter-intuitive to universal intelligence. Wouldn't it be better for us to model our economy after the universe, which is vastly more intelligent than we can ever imagine, rather than trying to believe that we can reinvent the wheel and do things in our own unique and separate way?

Our bodies, in other words the atoms that make up our bodies, follow our expectations, when we firmly believe in them and support them with an emotional response, as if what we believe can happened, has already happened. This is a scientifically proven fact. "So how do the atoms in our body understand what our conscious mind is telling it?" Let's look at one of the ways the universe allows particles of light to cooperate and share information between each other. There has been a concept in science for some time now, called *quantum entanglement,* which simply means that atoms are pieces of the universe, that can talk to each other intuitively, without any formal system of communication that humankind can understand—there is no language, no sound. This communication seems to be instantaneous, with absolutely no lag time between each entity. A 1997 *New York Times* article by Malcolm W. Brown reports on a scientific experiment that was performed where a particle of light was split in two. Each new half of the original particle, now known as "twin" particles, was placed a total of 14 miles apart, connected by a fiber-optic cable. The scientists performing the experiment moved one of the twin particles in a particular direction, and when they did, the other twin particle moved simultaneously as they had intended the first particle to do.[35] In other words, the twin particle, which wasn't intended to be part of the experiment at that time, somehow telepathically picked up the mental intent of movement from the scientists or its twin and decided to move on its own accord and grant their specific request.

The point I am trying to make to you is that, the more our knowledge about the universe advances, scientists seem to be proving—through vetted experiments—that all atoms including photons of light have intelligence and are able to communicate with one another. All the pieces of the *smart field* are connected and can potentially form themselves into usable matter and technology.

In 2017, the Mind Unleashed reported an article by Crystalline Nutrients YouTube channel stating that human beings are made of photons of light and that there are about 1,000 photons of light in a strand of DNA. These photons are essential to the basic health and function of DNA and allow DNA to communicate with other strands of DNA in the body.[36] Since there are literally many trillions of strands of DNA in the human body, deductive reasoning would tell us that since photons of light are a part of DNA and

---

35   http://www.nytimes.com/1997/07/22/science/far-apart-2-particles-respond-faster-than-light.html
36   http://themindunleashed.com/2017/01/new-science-dna-begins-quantum-wave.html

since photons can communicate instantaneously back and forth with one another regardless of distance, that human beings must be connected to other human beings in some innate and universal way. Perhaps we're not ready to make the jump to telepathy yet in a conscious way, any more than a pilgrim would conceptualize the thought of inventing a cell phone, but it seems that the more we experiment with the universe, the more we see that "it" seems to be much more intelligent than the conscious minds of humans, and perhaps mimicking it would be a good idea, especially if we want to repair the mess that we're in right now.

Let's take a step back for a moment and try to understand the incredible intelligence that it takes to form our own human body. An article from Science Focus by Hanna Ashworth stated that one strand of your DNA, if unraveled, would stretch about two meters, and if all the strands of DNA in your body were unraveled and linked together, they would reach about twice the diameter of the solar system in length.[37]

When we read this kind of vetted scientific information, it's almost unimaginable to comprehend let alone believe it's true. The creation of DNA, its division and replication, certainly had to come from an intelligent force far greater than our own and that we can comprehend, through our five senses. Did you create the DNA in your body? Did your brain create the DNA? If DNA created your brain, then don't all patents belong to DNA? The idea behind patent law is simply looking at things in a vacuum and stating that a human or a human brain created something, in this case some sort of original thought. It's interesting to note that the device called the human brain, that an inventor believed they used to create an original thought, that spawned an invention, was not created by the inventor!

About 5 billion new people have been created on this earth since 1950, all through the magic and wonder of DNA run by an unseen force

---

37   https://www.sciencefocus.com/the-human-body/how-long-is-your-dna/

that continues to replace cells, while we grow into adults, replacing various blood and tissues in our body throughout the course of our lifetime. Can your conscious mind do that? Yet this is done automatically time and time again, by a force unseen that assists DNA in doing so. We should therefore conclude that this unseen force is vastly more intelligent than us. This unseen force has the ability to create on a mass scale the planets, the sun, the stars, all humans, all plant and animal life on this planet, all oceans and all ocean life. Wouldn't it be easy enough for this unseen force to telepathically transfer an idea for a new technology into our rudimentary human brain? After all that creating, it sounds like a cakewalk to me!

If human beings are really interconnected in any sort of way, is there any evidence to support this assumption? Can the thought process of one human, or a group of humans, have an effect on the mass consciousness of a local set of people or geographical area? The *Maharishi Effect* is basically a term, used to describe the physical results that a small group of people, about 1% of the population in a given geographical area, have on a local population and immediate surrounding geographical area, through repeated performances and practices of transcendental meditation.

I'm not here to state that pie-in-the-sky, cult practices or that wishful thinking is a guaranteed and vetted practice for changing our world—but undeniably, there are verified effects of this practice historically, that have affected the behavior of local populations on our planet. Transcendental meditation actually does not only have an effect on humans who are meditating but on others simply located within a certain distance of the meditators. There was a definite drop in the number of factors affecting local communities, where transcendental meditation was taking place on a daily basis. The Transcendental Meditation website reports the result of case study seven, done in a war zone in Lebanon beginning in 1980. It took approximately three years to teach and get 1% of a population of about 10,000 to mediate regularly. By the spring of 1983, when the 1% threshold was reached, for the prior two years there were no bombings, not one death in the village and no reports of property damage. When the practitioners stopped transcendental meditation, the escalation of violence increased.[38]

If you would like to learn more about the Maharishi Effect or transcendental meditation, I would certainly encourage you to do further research online, where you will find quite a bit of data supporting the correlation between meditation and its effects on human behavior in the immediate surrounding geographical area. I believe the Maharishi Effect shows that what we hold in our minds has a direct influence on the minds of other individuals living on this planet—so pay close attention to what you're thinking of, every day!

Imagine the negative effects that the daily news has on the mass consciousness of our society. I actually cringe when I think about it, and it's one of the reasons why I never watch the news because it's just negative information that keeps repeating itself and feeding back negative ideas to our communities. I think we should be aware that the negative images and negative stories portrayed by the mass media of our country not only have a direct effect on the physical actions people take every day, by constantly perpetrating negativity; but as we can see from the study below, the negativity held by those who are consistently hypnotized by the media may very well have an extremely negative effect on the mass consciousness of our society and its daily actions! At the very least, we can say that the negative thoughts and images, constantly projected at our mass population, have a direct effect on our emotions and the overall plans and actions we will take, over the course of our lifetimes.

Further transcendental meditation studies found a decrease in the level of long-term crime in 24 cities in the United States where the transcendental meditation practice was used in those local geographical areas. Does our thought process have an effect on our environment? Yes, absolutely. Look around the room or area that you're currently sitting in. Everything created

---

38   https://tmnepal.org/study-7-prospective-1-effect-study-in-lebanon/

in that room started as a thought first, so nothing can be created without thought behind it. And with the Maharishi effect, we can definitely say that our thought process also may have a direct effect on other people in our local area. Just the thought process alone, without any physical action taken, by the creator of those thoughts, may be able to change the actions of others, especially when those thoughts are loving and in harmony with the well-being of others. If we want to change the fundamental concept of ownership, it would seem one of the best ways to do so would be to have large masses of people meditating on the highest and best use of the concept of ownership, as it relates to our technology and information today.

Together we can create a new economy. We simply need to change the thoughts that we are thinking and organize new thought processes, in a very specific manner; and as this movement will spread like a virus into the minds of others, we'll see that the concept of carrying these ideals in our minds may actually have a direct effect on other people's interpretations of ownership, in our own communities. Contemplate the fact that now, as you're reading this book and forming an idea of what you would like to see the economy become in your mind, you're actually helping to change the mass consciousness of our country. Furthermore, if you physically discuss this book with others and share your thoughts, you're having a mass effect on their consciousness as well, because you're influencing those people's current beliefs and assumptions. This type of behavior eventually creates a domino effect, where the mass consciousness on certain subjects and laws changes and precipitates a permanent change, to the physical existing written laws restricting us today, and allows for the creation of the physical manifestation of a new economy.

If you want to create anything in life, you're going to have to fall in love with the process, and that means having a consistent thought process. Consistent physical actions can only be created by a consistent thought process and consistent emotions backing them. If you want to change our economy, fall in love with the new ideals of sharing, service to others and unselfishness, you will find these concepts easy to hold in your mind, because they are harmonious with the nature of the universe; and as you hold them in your mind, others will too. This new idealism of oneness and interconnectivity between atoms as well as humans is the most important process to be aware of in order to create anything you desire in your life.

In order to build another economy that is going to be based on something other than the currency and scarcity beliefs that dominate our minds today, we're going to have to get rid of some of the dogmas that we absolutely, completely and totally hold firmly. Everything in our physical world resulted from our thought process. If we can find new information that allows us to change our beliefs, then we can change the physical manifestations of our environment around us. Until we change our thought process, nothing else will ever change; we will continue to take the same actions over and over again, regardless of time.

The idea of the automobile developed itself because someone was interested in a faster and more efficient way to get from place to place rather than riding a horse. But if the general public did not accept that riding in automobiles was a better way to travel than horseback, we would still be riding horses. I'm sure there were negative emotions and major doubts that people back in the early part of the 19th century had to overcome, because at the time the automobile was first available for sale, there were really no roads at all to drive on. So the idea of getting around from place to place, came with the caveat of having to build a massive number of roads, at great expense to the public, in order to enjoy the benefits of automobile ownership, rather than bouncing around over bumpy dirt, getting stuck in the mud or not being able to cross rivers.

Most of humankind has historically believed that by exploiting its own species, through slavery and now modern-day debt slavery, we have plateaued at the highest state of evolution attainable to humans and that there is no greater system other than the currency-based for-profit system available to humans. The pyramid-like structure of our economy today that forms the basis of capitalism consists mainly of a small group of incredibly wealthy people controlling drone workers who tirelessly take continuous actions to support the top of the pyramid. This belief system is actually a major detour away from universal consciousness and the knowledge and actions used to create our physical world in the first place. If we want simplicity and peace in our lives, we need to mimic universal intelligence; and so far, we've found out that the universe treats everything equally and intelligence is found in all things and not just in the brain of the human species or the top of the pyramid.

It's well known that DNA evidence has been used to identify a specific perpetrator of a crime. Prior to the invention of DNA evidence being used by the current legal system, there were people wrongly accused of crimes as heinous as murder and sent to prison for life, for something they never did. An awareness of a new technology made it much easier to catch the perpetrator of the crime, because if the DNA evidence at the crime scene did match the DNA sample taken from a suspect, this very strong evidence would provide a link to the crime scene and the suspect and a high conviction rate. If we specifically apply what we know about the universe today, it would seem that there are number of laws that are antiquated and outdated, which directly conflict with universal intelligence and the physical laws of the universe. These laws create massive discrepancies, inequalities and suffering throughout the world, similar to the poor conviction results our legal system had prior to using DNA evidence. When we crucially examine our economic laws, based on the knowledge and technology available to us today, it becomes obvious that many of the laws and beliefs currently surrounding our for-profit, currency-based system should be changed immediately. Let's start eliminating these old steadfast beliefs in order to take specific actions we're not taking now, to build our new economy.

One of the most steadfast laws, governing our entire economy today, which needs a radical overhaul, is patent law. Patents allow modern-day companies to directly control the advancement of technology on this planet.

The concept behind patent law is that the first human who is able to document the creation of something, is the sole owner of it and the controller of it for decades, and that all humans who wish to participate in the use of this technology must pay the owner of the patent in currency—currency that they obtain through their labor. On a planet of seven billion people, at this point in time, we can no longer afford to abide by a law that was created thousands of years ago, in order to keep our future world population healthy and in relative state of abundance. A patent is the most potent and deadliest piece of paper on this planet, whose basis was formed on the same ideals that created human slavery. The laws of human slavery, when created, basically had no validation, other than to state that certain humans could hold other humans as slaves indefinitely. The idea behind a patent is that one human can hold back knowledge from other humans for decades and through the court system, indefinitely.

What gives certain humans these rights? The law does. Whether the law is correct, moral, just or wise is not relevant. A small group of humans are allowed to control technology on this planet, only because patent law allows them to do so. Patent law, is simply a law of false ownership in perpetuity, which increases our homeless population and the propagation of debt slavery throughout our country. Patent law stops access to technology that is rightly everyone's, to our entire population. It innately "belongs" to all of us, but this law forces all technology on our planet into a system of false scarcity, where long hours of labor need to be performed in order to create a byproduct—called currency—in order to receive access to any modern technology on the planet, rather than just receiving it at an extremely low cost or even for free. Sooner or later people are going to realize that their technology rights are being violated. When this country was founded, we did not have access to any of the technology that we have now, and our laws have not been updated, to allow for the free flow of technology to people, to better their lives and reduce their time working. The people of this country have been forced into a monopoly of sorts for their survival, as technology directly affecting their survival has been patented. The internet shows the benefit of shared information, and the more we share information and the less we hoard it, the more our technology seems to be advancing, at least in certain industries, However, when it comes to our overhead, the cost isn't dropping the way we would expect it would, relative to the advanced level of technology we possess in our country today. I believe patent law is the major cause of this problem.

Let's take a serious look at patents and how this law massively affects the standard of living and the survival abilities of everyone in the United States. Patent law was enforced by the ancient Greeks as far back as 500 BC. Patents were granted for only a year back in ancient times, but now most patents cover a period of 20 years. Let's understand that about the same time that patent law was conceptualized, the Law of the 12 tables was created in ancient Rome. An article from Tribunes and Triumphs explains that under the Law of the 12 tables, which was the law of ancient Roman times about 450 BC and formed the centerpiece for the Constitution of the Roman Republic, a father could imprison, enslave or kill his children with no consequences, and from the time of their birth they were considered his property.[39]

Do we have laws like this today? Today we have organizations like child services, and if even a fraction of this behavior went on, the children of this irresponsible parent would be removed from that household. The reason behind these actions is because we have conceptualized a different understanding of the concept of "ownership" than in ancient times. Our consciousness has adjusted as an aggregate population, with the understanding that there is more equality between people and certainly over the last 150 years, our consciousness is expanding as an aggregate population, toward the understanding that there is intelligence and interconnectivity between everything. In other words, it is most likely that the currency-based, for-profit system will be eliminated at the point when our aggregate population comes

---

39   http://www.tribunesandtriumphs.org/roman-life/twelve-tables.htm

to the understanding that there can only be true equality between humans, when humans no longer see a mass separation between themselves.

The Romans had a very centralized rule over what humans could or could not do. When you restrict the basic human rights of people, violence and ignorance are required to ensure that these restrictions are continually enforced for the benefit of a small group of people. Violence and ignorance walk hand-in-hand, so it would seem that the more ignorant a society is as a whole, the more restrictive the rights are of the population. An ignorant society does not recognize equality between its different points of view, from its different citizens. The currency-based for-profit system is based on ignorance, because it does not recognize equality between humans, based on the fact that it continually violates the technology rights of the mass population of the country.

The United States transcended slavery with the Emancipation Proclamation, and in the early 1920s gave women the right to vote. In 1974, the Equal Credit Opportunity Act allowed women for the first time to borrow money without their husband acting as a co-signer; women until 1974 had a very difficult time living on their own without the assistance of a male figure. From a historical perspective, you can see that our world is trending in the long run towards giving its aggregate population equal rights, but we still have a long way to go at this particular point in time. We are in what I would call the second stage of slavery. The first stage of slavery was attained through physical force, and the second stage of slavery—our present state—is enforced psychologically, through currency for survival. In examining our conscious evolution, it seems logical that we will at some point evolve out of a currency-based, for-profit system, into a system where our laws allow all humans equal access to technology.

"What is a patent?" According to the *Encyclopedia Britannica,* a segment on patent law written by William Weston Fisher states that a patent is formally recognized as property and has the attributes of property. The patent stops the general public from using, manufacturing or selling the invention without paying royalties or other compensation to the patent holder. The patent holder may take legal action against anyone infringing on their idea or process and the patent may be inherited by the heirs of a deceased inventor.[40]

That definition states that a patent is recognized as actual property. A thought process, something completely abstract, that no one can see, touch, smell or hear, under patent law, becomes a physical, intangible piece of property that someone can own, just by the federal patent office waving their seal of approval over it, so to speak.

What is property? According to the *Encyclopedia Britannica,* a segment written by editor's states that property is "an object of legal rights, with strong connotations of individual ownership." Property consists of the "tangible, such as land or goods, or the intangible, such as stocks and bonds, patents or a copyrights"[41]

Notice the intangible elements such as stocks, bonds, patents and copyrights are all creations in the minds of the human species and cannot be measured or verified physically, yet through the magic of law they become real property. When humankind stretched the illusion of ownership beyond physical land itself and tangible goods into the realm of abstract thought, humankind made a fundamental mistake and we should work as a collective species to correct that mistake in order to create a stronger economy. Let's keep in mind that patents historically were granted by kings and emperors who had the power to take someone's life, without a court trial, any physical evidence or any justifiable reason whatsoever. Kings or leaders simply made up laws that suited them, impromptu. Patent law most likely originated by someone who decided, in an instant, in a childlike egotistical state, that a King or Emperor had dominion over an abstract thought process. Throughout history, humans have tried to abuse patent law to the fullest extent, so they could line their pockets with coin. World history tells us that in the sixteenth

---

40   https://www.britannica.com/topic/patent
41   https://www.britannica.com/topic/property-legal-concept

century patents were secured on intangible elements like salt, and others were made to pay the patent holder for the privilege of using it, until society evolved enough to a point where justice prevailed and patent law was amended to cover only new inventions and not things that already exited. My question to you, dear reader, is since the law has no merit, why didn't we just eliminate patent law altogether at that time?

Patent law was carried forward into the British colonies and colonial America. This may have been a good idea at the time, based on the fact that we knew nothing about DNA, quantum entanglement, the placebo effect, light-speed financial transactions, videoconferencing or even computers. The fact that humans believe that they can could take abstract thought and force others to pay for it, is the main driver behind our concept of modern-day debt slavery, for without access to technology on a planet of seven billion people, it is certainly impossible for our mass population to ever survive without severe hardship. A patent can usually run for a term up to 20 years. The state of technology in the year 1600 basically pales in comparison to the rate with which we're advancing our technology today. Back then, 20 years was a lifetime. Today, most jobs don't last more than three years, yet we're staying with the tried-and-true 20-year patent term. Why are we still carrying the same 20-year term for a patent today, in the age of light-speed financial transactions? Do you think patent law was deemed by the courts to be completely beneficial to the entire public, in a transparent and open manner, where everyone in society, including the working population, had a chance to express their opinion, at the time it was decreed? Over and over again as we examine this law, we can see how ridiculous it is for our country to allow its continued existence.

Patent law, it turns out, is actually a part of the Constitution; however, at the time the Constitution was written we didn't have access to any advanced technology. Homes were built with a pic, a shovel, an ax or saw from natural resources; water was taken from nearby streams or lakes; there was no electricity or power grid; so perhaps it seemed like patent law was a good idea, a long time ago, to include as part of the laws of the United States, so businesses and people could develop technology slowly over time, to sell to the general public. The idea of patent law covering new inventions that were considered during colonial times by many to be luxury items, that provided mainly entertainment value, were not seen as any type of threat to the survival of the human population. There is quite a difference between filing for a patent on a device like a phonograph (record player), which represents entertainment value, versus filing a patent on a free energy device that can single-handedly change the way the entire structure of our economy runs.

Our founding fathers made a grave error when they allowed survival technology to fall under the dominion of patent law. I think it's safe to say that poor people historically neither had the time nor the money to understand the complexity of patents or their enforceability, and they were simply too busy trying to ensure their own survival, mainly by working tirelessly, gathering and processing their nearby natural resources, to ever be concerned with its long term consequences. Patent law, covering survival technology, is completely outdated today because we rely on advanced technologies to help us survive. Patent law in modern-day terms creates a stranglehold or monopoly on any given technology, in order to create the most profit and currency flow to the person or company possessing it. Do you think it's time for the law to be amended, when it applies to patents on survival technology? Let's step back from this primitive idealism for a moment and try to bring things up to date for a second. Let's ask ourselves a couple of questions:

1. Where do thoughts come from?

2. Can anyone really own them?

First of all, we have no idea where thoughts come from, nor do we have any data or tangible scientific way to quantify or prove their existence. Secondly, even though we cannot prove they physically exist, it seems under the law that someone does own thoughts, it's the patent holder. The patent holder owns the patent and can stop anyone from using this advancement in technology by suing them in court, because a government, king or emperor decreed it and everyone went along with what they said and continues to do so, century after century, never questioning whether at its origination the law was fair or not, or should have excluded certain technologies from ever being patented. Humankind, for thousands of years, has been ruled by a small percentage of its society. The Egyptians had their pharaohs, the Europeans had their kings, the United States has its 1%, but the bottom line is that the rich have always held power over the poor, through currency. I find it ironic that almost all U. S. citizens feel they're part of a democracy when 1% of our population has had their wealth increasing for the past 50 years and currently hold 40% of all the wealth in America. Clearly the devil is in the details, and from my perspective, the details concern currency and patents, these are knights and swords of the modern-day kings, to keep the majority of the population in a state of perpetual servitude.

Patent law, a law that governs intellectual thought, simply states you must pay someone for up to 20 years, because they've invented something, even though they could never prove they had or created an original thought, if pressed to do so, by presenting discovery evidence, in court. Modern-day patent law is exactly the same as ancient human slavery law, in the fact that the law pays no respect to individual merit or reason whatsoever; the law itself simply creates "chattel" ownership over technology, the exact same way, that slavery laws created "chattel" ownership over certain humans, where none existed before. The continued enforcement of patent law on our planet creates a scarcity of technology, by continually withholding it from the mass population. This leaves us fighting over limited natural resources, with most of the planet living in poverty and endless wars between governments. The only way for 7 billion people to survive on this planet, continuing forward into the future, is to stop enforcing patent law where survival technology is concerned. Until that time, the technology rights of humans on this planet will continually be violated on a daily basis, because all humans have the right to survive and coexist on this planet, no more or no less than any other human being does. We can expect our standard of living to change little or not at all and watch our overhead costs continuously rise, as they have always historically done until this law is eliminated.

Let's examine patent law more closely and scrutinize it, with the advanced consciousness and freedom of information we enjoy today. Let's say you and I are inventing a free energy device and you live on one side of the country and I live on the other. We both invent the devices at the same time; you file for a patent, and I don't. I decide a week later to file for a patent, but my patent is denied, because you filed your patent earlier than I did. How is that giving credit to the inventor? I invented something and can take no credit for it; I can't make any money from my invention, because my invention now belongs to someone I've never seen or heard of, through the magic of patent law. Does this law sound insane to you? Does it sound like something that might have happened before, in the history of our country or the history of our world?

People filing patents within days or even hours of each other in some cases has actually happened many times, especially concerning breakthrough technologies: calculus, the microscope the telescope, the steamboat and the telephone just to name a few. An article from Alder IP cites "in a writing for *Political Science Quarterly* in 1922, William F. Osborn and Dorothy Thomas compiled a list of 148 well-known and more obscure examples of simultane-ous invention." There were five patents filed for the steamboat from 1802 to 1807, three patents filed for the microscope around 1610 and another patent was filed just four hours after Alexander Graham Bell file his patent in 1876 for the telephone.[42]

Historically, 148 well-known inventions, where multiple patents were filed very close to one another in terms of their timeline, were documented back in 1922! The concept of multiple people coming up with the same idea, at basically the same time or multiple patents being filed, within a very short

---

42   http://www.alderip.com.au/blog/uncategorized/simultaneous-invention-and-the-race-to-the-pat-ent-office/

time, even as little as a day, is called "the multiples affect." This is another way of describing multiple discovery from individuals with specific ideas, concepts or inventions. Keep in mind that at the time when many of these patents were being filed, there was no internet or telephone; some of these patents were even mailed in once completed to the patent office for validation. Filing was simply a matter of the inventor or the attorney, who represented the inventor, getting to the patent office first, by means of horseback, train or foot.

So how did all these inventors get the same idea at the same time, if they most likely had absolutely no way of communicating with one another? My supposition here is simple: They didn't get the idea independently, they received it from consciousness. Their brains simply received an idea, which was transmitted by the field of consciousness, or what I like to call our "smart field" at a particular point in time. These inventors "received" new information through consciousness and were emotionally driven, by receiving this new information, to create some sort of plans and a rudimentary physical manifestation of the information that they received. I believe this is strong evidence against the fact that human brains are capable of original thought; rather, I think humankind is transmitted information by consciousness, when humans are deemed ready to evolve and receive new information. I've come to my conclusion based on 148 cases of verified evidence of multiple cases of discovery. I'm sure additional information could be provided and updated since 1922, but I see little point in doing so, as the internet and other forms of communication between humans has become more prevalent and might precipitate the ease of theft or leaks of information, through modern-day information technology. If you disagree with this theory, perhaps you have a theory, backed by discovery evidence, that could contradict it? This book is about raising awareness, to promote greater participation in the formation of our economy. So please feel free to chime in with your ideas and communicate them to me.

I think if you look into a history of patents and the inventors who filed them, you would find that a large portion of our most useful technologies were an improvement on some basic idea that somebody else had already developed. In the case of the radio, Tesla improved upon the idea of UHF transmissions from a German inventor. Edison did not invent the lightbulb, but did vastly improve the length of time and the consistent brightness that it burned. We desperately need open-sourced collaboration, in order to develop the technology that we need to survive on this planet, over the next hundred years. It's absolutely imperative that we abolish the concept of patents, when it comes to developing technology for the advancement of our survival on this planet. It's simply better to work as a "mind hive," openly sharing information, in a directed and coordinated effort, towards a common goal, rather than through a few stand-alone brains, haphazardly trying to file patents, subject to for-profit and monopoly paradoxes.

Humans need to come to the understanding that they don't really "create" anything. The creation phase of our universe has already been completed. The universe has intended all humans to share equally in all its technologies, love, emotions and wonders. The purpose of humankind is to create, by rearranging matter and frequencies already provided by the universe; therefore, humans play a false role, when they take ownership over the rearrangement of anything that has already been created. The concept of ownership by humankind remains its greatest downfall and its greatest sticking point, to the evolution of its consciousness. The concept of ownership is destroying our planet and our people, and we must come to a greater understanding of what ownership really means, and realize that by distributing ownership equally, across the population of the planet, we will work less, stop polluting our environment and enjoy greater peace and harmony together.

If humankind can understand that consciousness runs the universe and is a vastly more intelligent entity than the human mind and freely gives knowledge to humans, who "receive" it as a gift, it's far easier for the human ego, to resign itself to sharing technology, with other humans. We have to understand that intelligence is nonlocal, and that all intelligence is dispersed equally, throughout the universe from the smallest photon to the largest galaxy, consciousness allows equal access to universal intelligence. If we somehow can come to this understanding, as a species on this planet, the evolution of our technology is going to accelerate at an incredibly rapid rate.

When it comes to the concept of original thought in the conscious mind of humans, we can further speculate what percentage of our thoughts are actually coming from our conscious mind and what percentage of our thoughts are coming from our unconscious mind, whether we believe them to be original or not. Furthermore, what controls our unconscious mind? What form of intelligence is responsible for our heartbeat, respiration, cell replication, nutrient absorption and waste elimination? It's certainly not our conscious mind, concerned about fast food or what TV show it's going to watch tonight. How can someone prove they invented something, if they can't even prove they're responsible for their own creation or basic bodily functions? An article from Simplifying Interfaces in 2008 noted that neuroscientists have conducted studies revealing that the 95% of our cognitive functions—meaning our decisions, emotions, actions and behavior—emanate from our unconscious mind, and that some scientists believe 5%, or even as little as 1%, of our brain function is conscious function and as much as 99% may be from unconscious function. Think about the constant focusing of your eye pupils it takes just to read this page, look at a computer screen or recall your learning of the English language as you read it.[43]

I don't know how people can look at verified scientific evidence and still deny the existence of consciousness and an unseen creative force that runs the universe. I'm not making a case for any religion ruling the world; as a matter fact I prefer we leave religion altogether out of the discussion. What I'm seriously trying to point out here is that we need to come to an understanding whereby we can all agree on some universal truths, as a culture

---

43   http://www.simplifyinginterfaces.com/2008/08/01/95-percent-of-brain-activity-is-beyond-our-conscious-awareness/

and as a country, in order to change certain laws for the benefit of the most people. If we can all agree together on some universal truths, these may be enough to move us forward, so that we can build our new economy. The ideals, beliefs and thought processes we'll need to carry us forward need to be based on vetted facts and in the best interests of our long-term survival; in parallel to our emotions and inspirations about who we are and how we intend on evolving and what we intend on creating, as a species. Once we understand that consciousness is doing the vast majority of the work in creating everything we desire, it's much easier for us to get out of the way and let things happen as opposed to fighting amongst ourselves.

No one can explain why a white blood cell is created by our bodies in order to ingest pathogens that can potentially cause disease in our body; it seems this nonlocal universal intelligence works independently and beyond the level of comprehension of our conscious mind in order to keep us healthy and alive. Let's take a look at another example of nonlocal, independent intelligence found in our own body, commonly known as the heart. An article from the Heart Math Institute cites that scientists have discovered that brain neurons exist in the heart, and that the heart has the ability to learn, remember and make decisions independently of the human brain and that the structure of the heart's ganglia, *neurotransmitters* and support cells is exactly the same as those found in the human brain.[44] Perhaps we can say that on some level, two brains exist within the human body.

Heart transplant patients report all sorts of strange behaviors they pick up from their donor's hearts. The Namah Journal article published in 2001 noted that food cravings, artistic tendencies and all sorts of desires that seem to be a part of the donor's life somehow constantly seem to be on the mind of the new recipient. If a donor liked a certain type of food or music, the new recipient would find themselves constantly craving that specific type of food or music. If a recipient, for example, receives a heart from a vegan donor, they suddenly can't stand meat. Case three cited a murder mystery being solved

---

44   https://www.heartmath.org/research/science-of-the-heart/heart-brain-communication/

by the donor recipient. An eight-year-old girl received a donor heart and began getting nightmares of the murder of her donor; after consultation with a psychologist, it was deemed she was witnessing a real murder, the police were called and her insights led to the eventual capture and confession of the murderer.[45] These cases represent the results of actual scientific studies and not fictional movies. The fact that a new heart transplanted into your body can independently send its stored information to your brain in a manner that your brain can comprehend and understand, is a very real phenomenon. Cellular memory is most likely the explanation, and as our science and medical studies advance, we find more evidence to prove that intelligence is nonlocal to the human brain.

If you would like more information on "the heart brain," you may want to check out the preferred reading list at the back of the book as well as videos and books by Gregg Braden. On a personal note, I would just like to say that sometimes when I look at the sun, I wonder how a massive source of energy can burn with such consistent regulation, never too hot, or never too cold, never flaring or singeing our atmosphere. How does molten hot lava keep burning in the icy cold of space for billions of years and not burn out or blow up? I personally believe that the sun is a conscious entity and is instructed by the same intelligence that assists in the creation of DNA.

Understanding what we know today about the universe and how it communicates to every part of itself including us, based on the technological advances we've made in even just the last decade or so, proves that intelligence is everywhere and not just confined to the human brain or even just one particular human who happens to file a patent. Can you understand why patent law, regarding survival technology has no place in our society anymore? Patent law is simply an outdated law, like slavery, that we need to move on from, at least in terms of removing its dominion from new inventions that are going to dictate the future ease of our survival on this planet, in order for

---

45   http://www.namahjournal.com/doc/Actual/Memory-transference-in-organ-transplant-recipients-vol-19-iss-1.html

us to enjoy a more harmonious existence, so that everyone can receive the technology and abundance they deserve.

Let's look at four reasons why patent law overall is unsound in its concept and should not apply to our energy, healthcare, transportation and housing industries. The idea of removing patent law entirely from our society is not something that I'm trying to press for here, but again let's differentiate from the fact that there is quite a difference between patenting something that someone might "want" versus something that everyone on this planet "needs" in order to survive. Our licensing plan only covers our four "need" industries and allows all other industries, most of which produce "want" items, to run business as usual as they do today.

1. Proving original thought from one human mind is impossible. Does an idea come from you or the space around you and then is received by your brain? Where do ideas specifically come from? If an idea can be originated in one human brain, then certainly any another human brain that was created by DNA, which was created by a force unseen, would be capable of generating the same idea, would it not? Thoughts are intangible; they cannot be proven as originated by the filer of any patent, nor can they be time stamped. If you went to the Supreme Court today, to prove that the case, that you had original thought, what discovery evidence would you provide? If none can be provided, then we should ask ourselves why are we still awarding individuals patents? Perhaps we feel it's the only way any company will develop technology, because it needs exclusive rights to it in order to make a profit and recoup its original investment from its development costs. But as we've already seen, as outlined in previous chapters, this strategy includes currency and must involve the for-profit and monopoly paradoxes, which only leads to a slowing down or blocking of that particular technology.

Are there other ways to finance the development of new technologies? Of course there are, and we will outline them in later chapters. Now back to our "original thought" hypothesis: let's just cut to the chase and award patents to DNA, which continually creates and asks for nothing in return. Since no one can physically prove or distinguish original thought coming from an individual human brain, or a human brain receiving information, transmitted by consciousness, the argument for an individual to establish dominion over any thought process should be invalid. The idea that original thought comes from the human mind should be challenged. Medical evidence shows people have lived without brains, or very small portions of their original brains, and still operated with some level of intelligence. An article from *The Lancet* tells of a 44-year-old French male who went to the doctor claiming weakness in his legs. As a child, the man had a shunt inserted into his brain as he had trouble draining fluid from his brain; this fluid is necessary to maintain actual ongoing brain material. At age 14, the shunt was removed, assuming everything was back to normal, but it wasn't. The fluid continued to build up in this man's brain over the course of his life, resulting in very little brain material inside his skull. Scans showed he had almost no brain material, despite having an IQ of 75, which is below normal but he maintained a normal lifestyle, married and fathered two children.[46] So to assume that thought comes from the brain directly, and that intelligence is nonlocal; or the hypothesis that only one human brain is capable of original thought while other brains are not capable of the same original thought, idea or invention; is something that can certainly be challenged through past medical case studies. If I have the same DNA that you do, then why is my brain not capable of creating the same technology that any other brain can? I might need some time, more education or exposure to different groups of people, but in the end, any human brain should be able to come up with the same idea, concept or invention, as any other human brain.

2. Multiple people have invented various technologies at virtually the same time. There are a multitude of examples of multiple people inventing the same technology at roughly the same time. Some 148 inventions were documented

---

46 https://www.thelancet.com/journals/lancet/article/PIIS0140-6736(07)61127-1/fulltext

by 1922, all with multiple discovery; in other words, multiple patents were filed for the same technology within a very small period of time, as you read earlier in this chapter. The patent for the telephone was filed within hours by different people on the same day. This would be direct physical evidence to support that thought of an original nature is not created in the human brain but is rather received by it, similar to the way a computer interfaces with a wireless internet network. I see no other concrete explanation to explain why multiple people have received the same idea at virtually the same time over and over again, regardless of the type of technology they attempted to patent or the language or country of origin of the inventor.

3. The law allows the inventor to resell their patent. Society assumes that the inventor should be given credit for all their hard work, so that's why they're awarded a patent. If you are the holder of a patent, a corporation or individual can also buy your technology and assume the rights to it. They can also buy competing patents from individual inventors, to keep their inferior technology, their predominating or monopolistic product on the market. Any company or corporation under United States patent law may purchase your patent, take your idea, throw out the bulk of it and slightly upgrade their inferior product, which gives the consumer the appearance that company "X" is trying to make things better for you, when they're simply trying to gain market share over their competitors, while raising profits to their maximum level.

Let's use a concrete example, so you can better understand this concept fully. If petroleum company "X" hears or sees of an emerging technology that would put it out of business in six months, it may pay an exorbitant price for such a technology and then shelve it in order to keep itself in business. So that every time you go to the gas pump, you are literally paying money to ensure that you continue to use petroleum-based products forever and ever. You're directly funding your own demise, by providing the currency these companies need, in order to continue to purchase any competing technology. Another example of patent abuse is the process of "Evergreening" (which I will cover in depth in a later chapter), which is used by the pharmaceutical industry. This process involves a labyrinth of techniques used by pharmaceutical companies to sell their patented products to the general public, at the highest possible price, for as long as they possibly can, even after their patents expire. Let's keep in mind that people are looking to technology with hope, in order to extend their own lives, and yet in this pursuit, they are shamelessly ripped off! This is a massive exploitation and manipulation of humankind, of the worst order. We, as a human population, should no longer allow this to continue. I believe taking actions for personal gain, in order to exploit someone trying stave off physical death, is both illegal and immoral—and at the same time you, the consumer, through patent law, are funding all of this! You, the consumer, are enslaving yourself voluntarily to a system that you are not even aware of, whose laws are outdated. Large corporations with large market shares of their particular industries are highly incentivized to shelve new technology and pass the cost of purchasing rival technology on to their consumers through the sale of their existing products. So, my sincerest question to you, dear reader, is why are you allowing this to happen? Moreover, why is the federal government aiding a few entities—corporations—in keeping new emerging technologies from the aggregate population of the United States? The bottom line here is money, the second reason is power, and as long as everyone is paying into the system and can't see through this illusion, it continues forward.

Centralizing power and giving complete dominion over our entire country's technology development to the patent office, creates huge incentives for fraud and crime. Who decides what patent arrives first? Could someone be bribed, in order to deny one person's patent and approve another's? If you think about it, the office of patents basically has control over our entire survival, because it's going to dictate what technology gets assimilated into our society and what does not. This is too great a power to leave under the control of one government office.

If you work in your corporation's research and development department for decades, trying to invent something of worth, and finally make a breakthrough…guess what? You get nothing. The patent belongs to the corporation that provided you with a paycheck. Time and again the aggregate losses their dominion over technology to the rich individual or corporation, who then turns around and uses patent law against society, by withholding a less expensive and more efficient technology from the general public.

Let me use another analogy, so that you can better understand. Patent law gives too great an incentive to buy up competing technology and too many incentives for businesses to take advantage of consumers. Prior to the Emancipation Proclamation, it was easy to understand the problem of slavery in our country. Certain people were seen as chattel property and were put into chains. It was much easier to see them as fellow humans and remove their chains, making them free people, than it is at this time to unburden all races and sexes in the United States from debt slavery, which is a far more complicated scheme, requiring a greater understanding of the currency-based system and the laws that govern it.

4. Patent law states that society should pay the inventor for up to 20 years, and that the inventor owes no debt to society at any point during their lifetime. *If you believe adamantly that consciousness does not run the universe, or that intelligence is nonlocal, and perhaps also you don't believe that only a small percentage of brains can come up with inventions, and that everything I've said to this point is completely and totally false, you may want to seriously consider this point, because it's going to be almost impossible to refute.* According to existing patent law, society's contribution to the inventor's existence should not be given credit towards having helped the inventor create their technology. The collective people of any given country, who work to pay its taxes, giving the country infrastructure, including the inventor's education, roads, housing and the laws that were passed that kept the inventor safe; the inventor's parents or those that supported the inventor with food and housing growing up; the sun; the atmosphere of the planet itself—all those people,

entities and events that allowed the inventor to survive up until the point of when their great idea took place—are all discounted to zero! It's assumed the inventor created something from nothing and right at that moment, they're God and society should bow down to them and pay them money for their idea and everything that society and the mass culture did for them in the past, that allowed them to live in their body on this planet, in order to have this idea, counts for nothing. The entire population of this country, DNA and our smart field owes the inventor a debt, according to the law. Yet without all these actions and support from our holographic universe and all its people, this so-called original idea or patented process would have never happened.

In our modern-day society, we should come to the understanding that nothing can be created without the help of the aggregate. We're all in this together. We seem to live in a world where acts of kindness are considered worthless and acts of selfishness are considered valuable. In summation, when someone files a patent that is accepted by the patent office as being valid, society instantaneously owes them the debt for the use of their technology. My question to you, dear reader, is…Why? Why are all the actions of others, in a country, that allowed the inventor to live, in a somewhat prosperous and abundant manner, in order to come up with their idea, *not* taken into account as part of patent law? If all inventions were patent free and given to people, at the lowest cost possible, then every American would have the lowest overhead possible and the inventor would not need a lot of money in the first place, nor follow a delusion of grandeur to exploit others needs for technology, through currency. Currency and patents cause nothing but distraction and chaos, from attaining the goal of creating and distributing superior survival technology to all Americans. Isn't it time we made this goal public, in a structured and definitive plan?

The United States government has the right to keep secrets from you. These are secrets that if revealed, would supposedly cause irreparable damage to our financial system and to members of our military or undercover agents. *The State Secrets Protection Act* is a national law that states that during an civil court trial, the government has the privilege of refusing to provide information or to prevent another person from giving information, if the government shows that in revealing this information it would cause harm to the national defense or foreign relations of the United States.

This law comes into play mainly in cases where families wish to civilly sue the government, when a government employee was on a secret mission, task or had access to government secrets that might be revealed, during a civil trial. You need to question this law. Would the United States government use the power of withholding information in order to better a few people's lives? If I'm the manager of a parking garage, I'm going to give myself the best parking space in the entire parking garage, 100% of the time. In order to get a better understanding of your place in our current society, I suggest you ask the following questions to yourself, perhaps over a period of weeks or even months, to get a better understanding of how technology is sequestered from the general public: Are government officials somehow committing illegal acts, by keeping information from the American public? Are government officials withholding information that is beneficial to the survival and freedoms of the American public? Are government officials withholding technology that is beneficial to the survival of the American public? Is restricting information a violation of human rights, because certain classes of humans are not granted equal access to the same information? Should we add another amendment to the Constitution stating that all Americans should have equal access to government information? The biggest question in all this is: Why is the secrecy necessary in the first place?

The answer seems to point to the fact that information must be withheld in order to suppress the development of our survival technology, in order to keep our financial system intact. Let's look at the information restriction issue from a different perspective. If we didn't have a highly developed financial system, which forced restricted access to technology, through currency, then why would we need all these state secrets? If technology were provided freely to people without patents, there would be no probability of a large currency payoff, since anyone could create new forms of technology and the information needed to create it would be shared freely. So why the need to keep secrets? We wouldn't need to keep them—it's as simple as that. Secrecy, information restrictions and patents walk hand-in-hand. Please make no mistake about it: Your access to information is restricted in this country. Why else would the government create huge metadata centers in order to surveil the American population? Are these metadata centers still active today? The simple answer is we just don't know; we'll have to take the government's word for it—the same government that was surveilling us illegally in the first place. We've now come to the point in time where secrecy is not going to matter anymore; the amount of data available on the internet to people and the free exchange of information brought about by advancing technology are crushing the ability of the government and influential parties to keep secrets and restricted information under wraps.

We've crossed over into a time when there is certainly no going back, and in our future, currency is going to be eliminated altogether as a medium of exchange, at least at some point. The old paradigms that held true for thousands of years are going to come crashing down. It's only a matter of time. The information given to you outlined throughout this book, will allow you to make the transition from a for-profit, currency-based economy to a technology-based economy, in the easiest, smoothest and most efficient manner possible. We are entering into a time when most likely, over the next hundred years, all goods and services will be provided to us at no cost, due to the advancements of technology directly replacing human labor. If we have no labor, under the current system, we cannot exchange it for cash and then exchange that cash to purchase our survival technology.

So how do we get to there from here? The best way to solve the problem initially is to have the best possible understanding of the current situation, from a detached perspective. I urge you to keep reading this text with a detached perspective, so that you can better understand how the current game of thrones really works. Once you see that the current system holds no promise to you or anyone you know, it will be much easier to change your beliefs in order to produce different results.

The specific reason I have outlined so many negative aspects of our currency-driven economy is that I need you to understand that it is time for you to make a change, because as long as you see an option to stay with the current system, you'll never take any action to change it. Also, you must realize that it is *not* necessary for you to be emotionally attached to any of the current problems in this country, in order to solve them. As a matter fact, it is better if you do not get attached to any of them at all. People make better plans and are better at following through with action when they put their emotions aside.

Another government law that has been around for decades is the Invention Secrecy Act of 1951. This law actually allows the government to confiscate patents. Any patent currently filed as part of standard operating procedure, will undergo a under review by several government agencies, and if it is determined *for any reason* that this patent is a threat to national security, that patent will be sequestered, or in layman's terms, confiscated. Have you ever wondered why any newly developed energy technology never competes directly with oil or gas or precipitates the need to move away from the electrical grid? If a newly invented solar system could be installed on a house for perhaps $1000 or less, everyone would move to solar power over-night, especially if you could purchase the entire system, including hardware, for just a few thousand dollars or less and eliminate your current electric bill potentially for decades. If a system like this were to be invented and a patent filed on this technology today, it would be immediately confiscated, under the Invention Secrecy Act of 1951. I can assure you this law is very real and affects all technology that has ever been distributed to the American public since 1951.

Let's look at this issue from the highest perspective. If a free-energy device, an invention that produces more power than it uses to operate itself, is invented, and that inventor files for a patent of that technology, it's pretty obvious that this would destroy jobs in several key industries in the United States, as we know that only 3.5% of the usable land is occupied by 63% of the population, so the ability for U.S. citizens to move anywhere off the power grid would result in the mass defaults of real-estate loans and precipitate a currency collapse. The major problem with a currency-based society is that Americans are paying massively over-inflated prices for outdated and inferior technology though a very-well-developed credit system. If a superior substitute technology became readily available for purchase, which represented a massive upgrade to the existing technology, the existing inferior technology would simply become worthless—expressed in terms of currency. Therefore, any developing technology that might cause this chain reaction would be a threat to national security. The law doesn't define what a "threat" specifically is, but in any case, under the law, this patent would be confiscated by the government and the technology ordered to be kept secret by the inventor.

What about other countries like China? Don't they clone any new technology they can get their hands on and mass produce it? China runs the same currency-based economy that we do and enforces more restrictive rights upon their citizens, so the chances of technology breakthroughs happening there are even less than in a more open country like the United States, which has a more benevolent attitude towards providing some level of basic survival technology to everyone. If the people of the United States have such incredibly restrictive laws, when it comes to the advancement of technology, I personally believe any inventor, living in any country, throughout the rest of the world, would have a more difficult time getting their patent approved in another country than in the United States. If it were obvious that an inventor in the United States could simply move to a foreign country and file their patent there and get their invention out to the general public for consumption, my serious question is why hasn't this happened yet? There are no examples of it happening in the past with breakthrough technologies.

In subsequent chapters, we will examine numerous examples of how many of our basic survival technologies have not moved forward at all, in terms of the benefits they offer their customers, for many, many decades or even a over century of time. The internal combustion engine was invented almost 160 years ago and is still used in 90% of the vehicles in the world today. The price of housing continues to rise decade after decade, for the past century. Contrast these industries with other industries like the computer industry, which doesn't seem to have a history of its information and patents being regularly kept secret and consequently its technology is accelerating at a pace today that far exceeds consumer expectations: Cell phones and computers talk back to us and give us detailed information we need in order to more effectively and efficiently run our lives. It would also be reasonable to assume that if the United States government is willing to confiscate a patent that is in the process of being filed openly and notoriously, they would be willing to confiscate any developing technology if knowledge of such a developing technology, came to their attention, regardless of whether a patent was filed or not.

What specifically happens after the 20 years have passed regarding technology that has been shelved by corporate America? If it's a threat to national security, the government, under an open and vetted law, would confiscate the patent at that time. A large corporation that had a large market share of any given industry and was holding a patent to keep its inferior technology on the market could simply contact the government and make them aware that the patent they own is expiring and ask that the government review it for confiscation, under the Invention Secrecy Act of 1951. A subcomponent or subprocess needed to make vital new survival technology can also be patented by a competing entity, purchased through an overseas bank account or confiscated by the government, thereby never allowing the main process or function of a new technology to evolve or be created. The 20-year expiration of an existing patent really has no relevance when it comes to the creation of new survival technology that according to our government would disrupt or destroy the current financial system, as that would be considered a threat to national security. New technology can be kept under wraps through a myriad of various lawsuits and forms of government confiscation, virtually forever. The Invention Secrecy Act of 1951 is quite real, I can assure you, and you may use any reliable source of information you wish in order to confirm its validity.

I'm not going to delve into conspiracy theories in this book, SWAT teams showing up at the residences of inventors, threats of violence, extortion, the removal of children into state custody or the threat of death itself towards past inventors. There are other books you can read on those subjects. If this only helps to strengthen your paranoia, then I see no reason to keep pursuing these negative aspects of the government, because they will only force you back into one de facto state, which is to keep doing nothing, so the problem will never be solved. The point of this text is about understanding, becoming aware of and finding positive ways for you to take action, without attachment, to resolving this issue once and for all.

Priority one is to develop hardware that reduces overhead. You can see that one of the major reasons why we're headed towards disaster is because the government indirectly aids in perpetually increasing the average American's overhead and consequently keeps the average American in a continuous state of scarcity, by limiting their access to purchase and enjoy superior survival technology. In the long run, robots and software will continue to hammer away at reducing American labor, labor needed to produce currency to purchase all goods and services, representing quite a paradox. I would personally expect in the next 50 years that 50% to 75% of all-American labor will be completed by digital printers, highly automated machines, robots and supercomputers. This is just my personal speculation; but certainly 50 years ago, if you would've said that in 50 years you would be able to talk to your phone and your phone would talk back to you and provide you answers to questions such as directions to any destination you want to go, flight information, your bank account balance and purchasing virtually anything you desire, and have it sent to your door, including groceries—you would've said I was watching too many episodes of Star Trek and that we were 300 to 400 years away from that actually happening.

We should expect technology to increase at an exponential rate in the next 20 years. Conceivably we could evolve further in the next 20 years, in terms of technological development, than we have in the last several hundred years, so it's important to prioritize what technology should be built first and what we should concentrate our full efforts on, in order to give our economy a smooth landing and an easy transition into a world that weans its dependency off currency and relies very little on human labor to survive.

The first thing you need to understand about the world you live in now, in order to create the world you want to live in, is that you have the same rights to technology that everyone else does on this planet, no matter how much land they own or the amount of currency they possess. We all have same innate rights. A homeless person also has the same innate rights that everyone else does, as they are a U.S. citizen just like you. I've outlined many ways in this chapter that our existence comes from a force unseen; it does not come from our conscious mind; and we must use the understanding of this force in order to battle the current illusions of our time. Currency, ownership and patents are the main creators of power by the elite.

Do you see yourself as elite? Do you see yourself as having the ability to receive the same amount of abundance as any billionaire on the planet? Are you emotionally ready to accept a massive amount of abundance and technology coming into your life that would cause you right now to stop your 40-hour work week and only work 5 to 6 hours a week for the rest of your life? You will need to envision yourself receiving superior technology that vastly reduces your work week and come to a new understanding of what new role you might play in a technology-based economy, your daily activities in this new economy, what your emotional well-being and overall mindset will be, and finally you need to see yourself enjoying the life you truly deserve. The best way to solve any problem is to truly raise your consciousness and detach from the problem, before you take any action—and this book is designed specifically to help you do just that. Some fundamental questions to be asked at this point are: Does the invention of technology come from a simple prospective, a mindset that anyone can tap into, and thus can anything be invented by anyone? Is newly created information local to the brain, or are our ideas innately part of every atom, in the smart field that we call the universe?

Let's ask some more questions to gain a better understanding:

1. Can new and unknown information to create new technology be accessed by multiple people at the same time? The answer is "Yes." Look no further than the 148 documented cases of multiple discovery of the same inventions prior to 1922.

2. Does the intelligence to invent anything exist locally within the human brain? The answer is most likely "No." The heart brain, white blood cells and even chemical bonding would all represent examples of intelligence existing outside of the human brain. The fact that people have actually lived without brains, or with only a very small portion of their brains, for long periods of time and yet were still functioning humans, also lends support to the fact that intelligence is nonlocal to the human brain.

3. Do we live in a smart field? The answer to that question is also most likely "Yes." Quantum entanglement proves that when you split a photon of light, the two split pieces have established some sort of rudimentary communication system between them. There are many other vetted scientific studies to support interconnectivity between all things, which you can find in the preferred reading list at the back of the book. My personal, innate conclusion is that we do, in fact, live in a "smart field," and I have no reason to doubt it. Waiting for peer-reviewed science to come to this vetted conclusion,

in order for us to start taking action before the earth is completely destroyed, from constant repurchases of inferior technology, is not something we should hold out for, before attempting to take action.

Every scientist to some extent is influenced by currency, as every scientist can be manipulated or influenced through the loss of their job or their ongoing project funding, like any employee in America. Corporations don't act as a matter of policy to assign scientists to work on projects or come up with vetted evidence through studies to support conclusions that don't support for-profit interests. I'm not openly saying that all scientists or scientific studies are faked or fraudulent, or manipulated to produce a desired set of results. I'm simply stating that the influence of currency over scientists and scientific studies cannot be ignored because scientists are paid salaries or require funding in order to survive, mainly from our government and corporations, which are undeniably for-profit supportive.

Patent law is thousands of years old. At the time the concept of patent law was invented, Roman fathers could enslave or kill their children without consequence, and human slavery was an accepted business practice. Our technology barely developed at all from century to century, so there was no real consequence felt by the public, when the population allowed patent law to govern all technologies, including survival technologies, even up to the point of colonial times in the United States, we strayed off track. America is still running on antiquated and outdated laws that serve the rich and leave the mass population of the United States in a constant state of scarcity. Technology that replaces human labor, threatens the survival of all humans on the planet, as our future population will no longer be able to exchange labor for cash. Our 244-year-old proxy government has absolutely no incentive or intention whatsoever to allow survival technology to be produced at the lowest cost possible, for all Americans. Insane laws like patents, covering survival technology, are still in force today and almost all of our society believes the laws running the currency-based economy cannot be changed and that if they were changed, we would be worse off than we are now!

As our own technology and understanding of our environment broadens, we seem to be evolving toward the idea that intelligence is nonlocal and located everywhere around us rather than just in our skull. This intelligence, consciousness or "smart field," as I like to call it, created everything on this planet, including us, and does so with such incredible discipline in its constant creation that its existence seems to be undeniably true; it's only in the denial of this consciousness or this unseen creative force that we falter. We humans believe that we are separate from everything else and essentially, we are separate at the moment we create something that we deem is "new or original," and then created a fake law behind this mass misperception. There is nothing new to the intelligence that created us and keeps re-creating us; we're simply discovering what's already there. If you look at the world from the perspective that consciousness or an unseen creative force is coaxing and guiding us in the right direction and we're simply coming along for the ride, we start to feel better. Our minds and emotional states open up to the idea that sharing technology allows us to feel more connected, grateful and peaceful by cooperating with one another. If we live in a world where in our constant perspective, we feel we're separate from the universe, that original thought and new technologies only come from a small number of unique human brains and that that endlessly working 40-hour weeks is good for us, we start to feel alone and depressed. Which state of mind would you rather live in?

Our currency-based economy creates the illusion that our investment in the development of the technology of today will allow us access to technology that we've never had before, tomorrow. This assumption is actually, completely and totally untrue, when it comes to implementing specific new technologies into our country that will interfere with or destroy our currency-based economy. For-profit ideals, currency, patents and restrictive laws in our country, only block vital survival technology from coming to us in a simpler, transparent and more efficient manner. The purpose of this book is to change the way survival technology is created, assimilated and distributed into the mass consciousness of our society, by reducing the deterrents and paradoxes that the laws of currency, patents and lack of information constantly block, to impede our progress. Abiding by ancient business practices will simply no longer work anymore; we're going to experience massive economic scarcity and collapse if we keep looking to a currency-based, for-profit and patent-riddled system to solve our problems. The labor-for-cash economy has already cycled through its useful life and needs to be overhauled and replaced by a technology-based economy, an economy that produces and distributes survival technology, at the lowest possible cost to all humans. Now that we have come to a new understanding that our past actions only keep us walking in the circles of income and spend, let's begin creating our new economy.

CHAPTER 5

Reforming Our Energy Industry

How can we get to a point where we're no longer required to work anymore but at the same time can enjoy an extremely high standard of living?

In order to accomplish this task, we'll need to implement superior technology in the four survival industries that represent the highest monthly cost to the average citizen. We know that through the currency-based economy, companies are not incentivized to create superior technology, in any way shape or form. In order to extract the justice we deserve from the currency-based system, we as consumers using the current rules of the system would have to fight our federal government and state legislatures, corporations, the 1% of society, our own fellow citizens whose jobs might be eliminated as a result of major changes to the currency-based system, the Federal Reserve Bank and the entire banking system in general, all the stock markets or equity markets across the globe and the entire credit system. Trying to gain equality through the currency-based, for-profit system is a battle we can never win by conventional means. Our current system can only provide us with more currency, which just creates inflation and evolves our technology at an incredibly slow pace, only providing slightly better technology, year-over-year, yet always building in planned obsolescence and repair costs to every product to ensure profit.

Wouldn't it be easier to implement a licensing system upon the energy and healthcare industries, initially, by direct vote through state proposition, carefully crafted by an economic committee that can't receive large payoffs or stock options and under the law and has the best interests and benefits of our people in mind?

It is no longer necessary to run our economy based on old, outdated ways, now that our technology has advanced to a point where we no longer need to rely on human labor as the primary driving force of our economy. Can technology replace currency and at the same time, increase our standard of living? I personally believe it is the only thing that can, but in order to replace our labor-for-currency-for-survival economy, we must follow a very strategic plan, one that is tiered, implemented in stages and taken in small steps over time to ensure that we do not rush the process, because this misdirected haste might cause what I would call a "period of waiting."

A Period of Waiting results when labor replacing technology causes a major financial collapse in the existing system, creating a permanent reduction in flow of currency to citizens of our country, who rely on currency for their basic survival needs. Our citizens are now left waiting for new technology to lower their overhead with very little savings and monthly income to meet their continued survival needs. Technically we are in a period of waiting now.

The system should be built on cooperation and getting to the bottom line, which is prosperity for everyone; and this starts with reducing overhead costs before reducing incomes. We're only going to achieve prosperity through advanced technology, which is going to cost us very little in terms of human hours worked per year, in order to purchase it. Consequently, we'll need less income to maintain the same or better standard of living. In order to evolve our technology efficiently, we'll need transparency in our survival industries. Simply put, this means no patents, no secrets and complete transparent communications of its development to the public. What could be more important?

The focus of our primary plan would be to reduce overhead slowly, as the world's supply of available jobs dwindles due to automation and an increase in the available number of humans per job. As our world population increases by another two to three billion in 2050, there will be fewer jobs and fewer human labor hours available to our world population. If we can reduce overhead first, as a priority over reducing labor, we can avoid a "period of waiting" for the general population, which at some point, unless we make massive wholesale changes to our overhead costs, will become stranded without enough income to cover their survival expenses.

Please keep in mind that the IRS tax code currently runs to thousands of pages. If I spelled out every explicit detail of this plan, which I'm sure you may have questions about, this book would extend to over 1000 pages and would be so boring and trivial that no one would be able to read it. Building a technology-based economy is about Us! It requires input from everyone: scientists, economists, business owners and our entire population, including all of our industries—but mainly it needs input from You. You and others like you, who believe they're going to feel better, be more productive and be more artistic, creative and evolved by participating in this change. We need those who have the vision, foresight and discipline in order to make this happen. I'm merely providing a large overview of this plan, so that the rest of the members of our society can fill in the details, in order to draft the right propositions for each state to vote on.

This is about us working together. So, let's begin reviewing a general plan of how we might best implement a technology-based economy in the United States of America.

Step 1. Requiring a license for all energy-based companies.

The idea behind licensing is a simple one: Requiring an energy-based company to hold a license in any given state in order to sell any energy-related goods or services, holds all companies within the industry to a certain standard of conduct regarding minimum standard of production quality, subsequent repair costs or reuse costs, and through lawful restrictions removes for-profit incentives and forces innovation within the industry. It would be illegal for a licensed energy company to produce or sell energy on the wholesale or retail level without the use of a license. Selling or producing energy without the use of a license would result in direct criminal fraud, prison time and heavy fines. I would propose that these fines may be up to 1 million dollars per person and be paid, if necessary, over the life of the perpetrator; they cannot be plea bargained, nor deferred through any other means by the court. I would also propose a mandatory 10-year minimum federal prison sentence that also could not be plea bargained. Each state would adopt its own licensing agency, and this entity would be responsible for licensing of all energy companies within that state and monitoring ongoing company practices, to ensure that each company remains current and up-to-date and acts in accordance with all laws, codes or rules governing their industry, their individual company and their employees.

The best way to implement this plan into action would not be at the federal level initially but at the state level, through the sovereign power of each of the states and the crushing collusion effect that would be forced on the federal government to comply, should all 50 states or perhaps even as few as 25 states band together simultaneously, in collusion on uniform agreement on licensing laws affecting the energy industry. I have dedicated an entire chapter later in the book, to covering how each state can originate licensing laws and multiple states can come together in collusion, to make national licensing a reality.

Any company that produces any type of energy—whether electrical, nuclear, coal, petroleum-based or any new emerging energy technology—would require a specific license to operate, produce and sell energy to the general public. This would include holding companies, limited liability companies, partnerships and sole proprietorships as well as any corporate entity, even if the sole purpose of the company was to act as a holding company and redistribute any energy-related product or service at no cost. Licensing would be required for any company that originates any type of raw materials used for the purpose of energy consumption and/or refines said raw materials for the purposes of energy consumption, as well as buys, sells, holds or redistributes any energy product or raw material to be used by any consumer, regardless of the size of the market. In short, any company within the entire energy industry, including developing energy technology companies, would require a license and would be required to abide by the laws and guidelines set up by each individual state, in order to maintain a valid and current license, within the energy industry.

All officers and executives of any company within the industry would be required to go through a criminal background check as well as a credit check, to serve as second-layer risk management, to expose any possible past criminal violations or inappropriate behavior and to ascertain whether a court filed a lien or judgment, criminally or civilly, against the potential candidate for employment. No one could ever be employed at an energy company who had ever committed any type of past fraud in any state. The background check would also include a complete verification of a 10-year history of employment. The licensing system would require a vetting process for officers and executives of energy companies; if they failed the prescreening employment check, they would not be a viable candidate for a job interview.

Annually, the officers, executives and even the employees of all licensed companies would require mandatory training of up to 20 hours, that would cover morals and ethics, safety and the understanding and review of the existing energy codes and laws, as required by each individual state's licensing agency. Failure to complete required ongoing training would result in termination of their employment. A complete criminal background check and credit report would be required every three years, as part of ongoing licensing requirements, for all executives and officers, of any licensed energy company.

Any violations of these codes and ethics, by any executive or company employee within the industry, regarding licensing could be considered an Economic Crime.

An Economic Crime: Committing a monetary fraud, or fraud for profit, against over 100 or more citizens of the general public. If charged with an Economic Crime against the people, any individual state would have the right to disallow bail for the accused party, prior to trial. The penalty for an Economic Crime would be 25 years to life in prison and a minimum fine of $1 million, if the perpetrator was found guilty.

The law would allow for a mandatory statute of limitations of 10 years, which simply means that if there was evidence that surfaced regarding a potential Economic Crime for up to 10 years after any initial fraud incident essentially took place, charges could be filed against the perpetrators. I would also seriously suggest that the states work with the federal government and our foreign policy heavily, to create Economic Crime law throughout the world, and if any person committed an Economic Crime and sought asylum in another country, fleeing to other countries would no longer be an option in this particular case and that person would simply be extradited back to the United States or the country where their Economic Crime originated.

It's time the people on Wall Street, who keep getting away with Economic Crimes, be put in their place. In the energy industry, greed is not going to be a factor for personal gain anymore, so establishing a code of ethics and consequences for violating that code must be first and foremost put into the minds of everyone employed in the energy industry.

About the middle of the 20th century, electrical utility companies were actually seen as monopolies, even though one could actually state that they are strong oligopolies. An oligopoly is an industry with a small number of competitors that has massive startup costs and large barriers to entry. Examples of oligopolies would be the airline industry or the electrical utility industry. Oligopolies have ability to capture and maintain market share with little competition, and historically this was seen as very dangerous to the developing economy of America; therefore, oligopolies were strictly regulated and limited by the federal government in their pricing and business dealings

In December 2000, a bill was put through Congress that allowed energy futures contracts (contracts for units of electricity to be purchased at certain prices, to be bought and sold, by traders and investors) to be traded through an organized system and no longer be subject to government regulation. This allowed Enron Online to be formed.

Enron simply had its traders sell contracts back and forth to fake shell companies, to artificially skyrocket the price of electrical power. What resulted was a disaster for the American public, particularly in the State of California, as the residents saw their bills skyrocket in just a few months. Later an investigation into Enron found that the company was guilty of illegal trading and the company was shut down. Employees lost their pensions, investors lost fortunes and the consumers in the many states that were forced to pay exorbitant prices for their power were never reimbursed for their losses. The reasons these events happened are simple: Our entire country was exploited by private companies over their need for energy, and our government allowed these private companies to operate completely unrestricted under the rules of for-profit and at the whims of financial executives who were all heavily incentivized to charge as much for their privatized product as they possibly could.

Energy is needed for survival, and the rules need to be different governing products of need versus products of want. When mass scandals arise like those with Enron, the public is powerless to recoup their lost currency, except through futile exercises such as a long, drawn-out court cases that can take years of time to be settled. Let's end this ridiculous form of greed in our energy industry now, and never see it happen again, bypassing these old federal laws, by creating new laws in our states—requiring licensing, a code of ethics and severe penalties for not abiding by them, including major prison sentences. Better still, let's remove all the incentives for greed, by making the entire industry nonprofit, non-publicly traded and patent free.

Step 2. Removing the shareholder.

Any time you have venture capital involved in the development of any technology, that technology is not going to be created and implemented to the general public, without the need for repair and replacement; otherwise it would lower company revenues, earnings and the shareholders' stock price. When you have a shareholder involved, you can expect with 100% certainty that any developing energy technology is only going to be created on the basis of how many units can be sold, how high a price can be obtained for each unit sold, how much market share this new technology will capture and how much market share can be maintained by gobbling up any and all competing patents. No shareholder in any company wants "free energy," because the price of the shareholder's stock is going to drop; therefore, if we want to move our society forward and lower overhead through advanced technology, the logical conclusion here would be to remove any stockholder from the equation. The only way energy is going to be directly consumed by the public in a for-profit industry is with the direct expectation that this energy will need to be provided on a temporary basis and constantly purchased over and over again by the public. In a for-profit system, more importantly, all energy must be transported through a power grid, which must be distributed from a centralized source. The for-profit energy industry would never allow portable energy sources to be utilized by the public. If they did, we already know this would allow anyone to build anywhere and destroy the price of real-estate lot costs. Centralized power limits areas to build homes to only those pieces of land where power lines run; this silent collusion between energy companies and banks keeps banks from collapsing by keeping the value of their real-estate collateral high, by keeping lot costs scarce due to the exorbitant cost it takes to run power lines across long distances to new potential building sites.

You can expect any new emerging energy technology to be severely dummied down, cannibalized or reshaped, in every conceivable way, in order to create the most profit by any company acquiring a patent to such a new technology, therefore allowing the most capital gains to the shareholder. Most initial public stock offerings are structured in a manner where a massive amount of insider stock is given to a few individuals, at almost no cost or practically free to those insiders, who take a ride on the general public that purchases the stock as an investment, at a high open-market price with the hopes of future gains. The fact that people actually invest their pensions into a piece of air backed by nothing, that can easily become worthless, I find to be absolutely amazing!

In order to develop true technology, which does not require any new forms of energy development, to be pushed through a centralized power grid and monopolized, we will first have to eliminate the shareholders of all energy companies, whose only goal is profit, which diametrically opposes our goal, which to create a portable a free energy device that produces free power—electrical power provided at the lowest possible cost, combined with a long-term goal of reducing that cost to zero.

The issuance of stock, options or warrants would be prohibited by companies within the energy industry, as a requirement of their state licensing. It would also be illegal to create or trade any type of investment that speculated on the supply or distribution of the commodity of energy to the general public; this would include any futures and options contracts and you can forget about exotic investments like derivatives. The goal here is to eliminate all the incentives, to take advantage of the general public, through any type of fraud, for profit.

The existing outstanding stock of any companies now producing and distributing energy, or any energy product, would be purchased by the state in which the company did business, at a price equal to 5% of the average of the last three years' daily market closing prices. States enacting licensing could split the shareholder buyout cost for companies producing energy on a nationwide basis—such as oil companies, between themselves, taking the number of states (for example, 25 states), and dividing the buyout price for national companies by 25. There wouldn't be any last-minute golden parachute buyouts for overly inflated trading prices; this is why I chose a three-year average, of the stock price. The repurchase price of the stock and therefore the monies that would compensate the existing shareholders could be debated endlessly. My simple supposition here is that people who invest money in the stock market can afford to lose it, so why should the mass majority of the population that cannot afford to lose money and work endlessly worry about the excess losses of money of people who can in fact afford it?

My greater concern would be how the buyout price affected the liquidity, overall safety and consumer confidence of the general public. The contrasting argument is that basically the shareholder is being bailed out with public money, similar to the banking crisis of 2008, and the resulting debt would have to be paid off at some point. Theoretically, if over decades of time we were able to move beyond using currency at all, the outstanding debt carried from the stock buyout would simply cease to matter. Currently, the federal government has no plan to pay off the principal balance of our ever expanding $25-trillion federal debt, and the current system is most likely doomed to failure anyway due to defaulting interest payments. Our system runs on debt, and all the world's currencies are backed by nothing; every day we borrow from our future selves to run our economy today, so in the long run it appears we're on a collision course with bankruptcy no matter what angle or method we take to preserve our survival.

My concern for the shareholders only goes as far as the effect it will have on the "consumer confidence" of any particular state or region. Certainly, the dollar buyout of these shareholders needs to be debated as well as if the current shareholders will receive any money at all. Shareholder compensation could be a hotly contested topic, for the general public, should this plan move forward into action. The shareholders could also be compensated by changing the tax laws, in order to allow them to write off a portion of the loss, on a deferred basis many years forward, rather than just a one-time capital loss for the current tax year. This tax loophole actually might create a source of future income for the shareholder, by allowing them to pay less in taxes year over year. My specific purpose here is to outline a basic plan. Let me say to you again, dear reader, that it's up to you to decide where you want this plan to go and how you want to implement it. Without your input the plan dies right here on these pages.

We also face another "conundrum" by offering any type of money at all to existing shareholders. If one individual state adopts licensing regulations for its energy industry and foots the bill for a stock buyout through state-issued debt, that particular state is going to need to issue a massive amount of bonds in order to do so. It may be a better idea for that state not to compensate energy shareholders at all and rather defer their compensation to tax incentives. This is again why it is incredibly important to have licensing regulations adopted by as many states as possible, simultaneously. This type of "collusion effect," with perhaps 25 states passing licensing laws simultaneously, on the energy industry, would allow these 25 states to pool their monies together, through various means, in order to compensate the shareholders, to help make these policies work effectively, rather than just one individual state going through massive trials and tribulations trying to enact a licensing system on its own. This system will require the unified cooperation of many states in order for it to be implemented, and your participation as well the participation of everyone in your home state, your community and other states across the nation. This is a group effort—nothing less.

Step 3. Removing all patents from the industry.

In order to hold an energy license through a given state's licensing agency, any corporation or company entity would be required to release all of its patents to the general public and would not be able to hold, buy, sell or redistribute any type of patent regarding energy technology. Patents for energy technology within a given state undertaking the plan would no longer be enforceable. In other words, patent laws would no longer apply to any type of energy technology. Any existing energy technology currently held by any company undergoing licensing would be required to be turned over to the state's licensing agency, which would make it available to the general public. The term "Energy Technology" would be defined under an incredibly broad spectrum, to include all existing and past energy technology known to our planet, as well as any energy technology that could be used by a consumer as a form of energy technology in the future, and should be broadly defined enough to close any future loopholes of exploitation. All patents, both past and present, would be released to the general public and distributed to all licensed companies within the industry, through a centralized database, for potential further development.

If any given state enacted this type of licensing regulation, anyone in the world could go to that state, start a company, create and distribute energy technology, under the licensing laws and restrictions of that state and never have to worry about anyone suing them for patent infringement. The law would be all-encompassing regarding energy patents; they would no longer be enforceable within the borders of that state. State law, or the lack of federal patent enforceability, would now conflict with federal patent law. Human slavery at one time in this country was enforced from state to state, where "free" states existed alongside "slave" states; so if enacted, this would certainly not be the first time in the history of our country that the laws of one state conflicted with the laws of another state or the laws of the federal government. Same-sex marriage, through state collusion, was eventually adopted into federal law. Looking to the federal government to pass a plan like this would simply never happen, as the goal of any proxy is only to be reelected and the greatest means to be reelected, in today's economy, is to create jobs. In reality, the irony of that situation is that neither the federal nor the state government is physically capable of directly creating any jobs in the private sector, through the for-profit, currency-based system, unless it taxes the public directly or issues debt to create government jobs. Even if the federal or state governments were capable of creating permanent long-lasting jobs, creating jobs changes neither our standard of living nor the level of our country's current technology.

A policy of "safe rooms" should be adopted where technology can be transparently developed, in labs of licensed companies, on live streaming video to the public, at state-run facilities. The public should see and hear everything when it comes to the development of their survival technology, and be able to ask questions and get answers from on-site customer support people, through chat and e-mail response teams, whenever anyone in the general public requests it. Adopting a policy of a "no-patent" industry would allow anyone to produce energy technology without the concern for filing a patent or being sued in court for producing or developing their current energy technology or invention. A transparent industry would allow any new technology to be created and distributed as quickly as possible, keeping planned obsolescence and maintenance concerns to a minimum. All trademarks and copyrights currently held by existing licensed energy companies would expire two years from each company's initial licensing date.

It is important to note that, in order to calm the fears of any extremists, controlled substances such as radioactive materials would be classified as banned substances. Banned substances that are environmentally hazardous would be banned as an ingredient or byproduct from the development of any type of energy technology being used in the future. I fail to see the point of how nuclear energy is going to help our planet. It's centralized energy that is pushed through a power grid, creates high real-estate prices and creates limited electrical access to buildable lots, in addition to creating potentially disastrous environmental hazards. Let's not forget the past nuclear accidents that occurred at Fukushima and Chernobyl. These past examples should be enough for the public to realize that the cost of this type of technology far outweighs the benefits to the public. Our licensing plan should call for the closing of all nuclear plants in any given state, within 25 years after its adoption. Simply by changing our goal to create a portable source of power, provided at the lowest possible cost to the consumer, and making it a reality, nuclear power would become an inferior substitute technology and quickly eliminated from our future economic vision. Since we're not going to be using any hazardous materials for the creation of our new energy devices, we need not worry about future environmental pollution and cleanup costs that are passed on to the general public as the currently technologies like oil, coal and nuclear energies are creating today.

Any new and previously patented technology could be accessed through a central database, overseen by each state's licensing agency, for the benefit of all the licensed companies within the energy industry. The central idea is for the companies to cooperate together and create the longest-lasting, most efficient energy-producing products possible. As I've cited in past examples, cooperation has basically proven to beat out competition in many scientific studies, virtually every time. Allowing companies to share knowledge and build on that knowledge together is the quickest way to create superior technology. A free-energy device or any type of superior energy technology, whether it be superior wind power or a superior solar panel, that can charge a home and run electric cars indefinitely, is going to be quite a stretch goal and in order to complete this goal, we are going to require more than just one person, working for a private company attempting to come up with a single idea and hiding it from everyone else in fear of losing future income. We will need to use all of our existing energy engineers throughout the entire industry, collaborating and cooperating together. These types of actions would be considered insanity, under a currency-based, for-profit model, as it would directly undermine the ability for any company to grab a greater market share and maintain an advantage over its competitors.

A mind-hive type of environment, using supercomputers and artificial intelligence, is certainly a better way to develop technology than using small, random groups of people, working in secrecy, against each other, whose only goal is to maximize profit. If you look back into our country's history, cooperation and collaboration—although rarely used in a currency-based economy—have yielded great results in the development of our past technologies. The text *Smarter, Faster, Better,* by Charles Duhigg (2016) noted that many of Thomas Edison's inventions were the result of importing ideas from existing types of developing technologies and then expanding, complementing or extending the useful life of these rudimentary technologies in the lighting, telephone, phonograph, railway and mining industries, to make them more usable by the consumer. In 1997, a consumer design firm IDEO found that most of the company's biggest successes originated from combining the knowledge of products from different industries. The firm came up with the idea of an innovative water bottle that sold well by "combining a standard water carafe with a leak-proof nozzle from a shampoo bottle."[47]

Most inventions were improvements on already existing technologies that the inventor did not create. This is the type of intellectual environment that we would like to foster, so that our service in perpetuity can finally come to an end. Cooperation and sharing information would be the new goals of the industry. In essence, the industry would be looking to cannibalize its existing beliefs and revenue-producing structures, in order to create energy-producing devices so efficient that the amount of human labor and intelligence needed to oversee the mass creation and distribution of these products worldwide would perhaps only require a very small percentage of the existing industry workforce currently being used accomplish the same results. Obviously, the major concern here again is bringing down overhead

---

47   "*Smarter, Faster, Better*" by Charles Duhigg 2016, p. 214

costs "prior to" removing incomes or labor for cash, from the system. If our overhead technology is cheap enough, being out of work or even experiencing a time of a massively reduced income for whatever reason, would be of less concern to the population of the entire American workforce, since survival technology would be so cheap it would be easy to live a very prosperous life on a massively reduced income compared to today's standards. Either way, I believe we are going to go through a crisis, where at some point there will be a lack of access to technology through currency. I can sum up our future in one of two scenarios:

> Scenario 1: We keep our existing beliefs about overhead technology changing in small increments, over many decades of time. We continue to keep patent laws and government sequestration in place and leave artificial intelligence development and human simulated labor and robotics to run unfettered, exactly as we're doing today. Let me explain to you in military terms exactly the effect artificial intelligence is going to have on the economy, over the next few decades. Technology is like a 50-caliber machine gun, blasting away constantly 24 hours a day and shredding labor for cash, in its path. We need to use our existing technology and resources, to create superior survival technology first, to help our society ween off its dependency from currency, because if we don't aim our gun correctly, we're going to see massive financial casualties by continuing to randomly fire it in all directions, at all industries—killing labor for cash, as we're doing now. Let's look at a real-life example today, where computers and robotics are going to taking the place of not only unskilled but skilled human labor. A 2017 article in Macro Economic by Mike Shedlock stated that a Japanese company, Fukoku Mutual Life Insurance, was going to replace 34 of its insurance claim workers with one IBM Watson Explorer computer. The initial cost of $1.7 million and $128,000 in annual maintenance

will save the company roughly \$1.1 million per year in salaries.[48] If the numbers are right, whether they be blue-collar or white-collar jobs, companies will follow for-profit incentives and cut labor costs any way they can; they are simply following for-profit incentives set up by the current economic system.

I would also urge you to go online and check out the ASIMO robot from Honda. This humanoid-type robot has the ability to not only walk, open doors and carry objects but also understand human gestures, recognize facial features and spoken commands. The Atlas robot from Boston Dynamics is being developed to aid in wilderness rescues and can walk over snow and uneven surfaces. It's very obvious that in just a few short decades or less, the majority of human labor will be eliminated from our country through robots, advanced supercomputers and other forms of artificial intelligence.

What happens in a scenario of vanishing labor for cash is that gradually the population relies more and more on public assistance, because they can no longer find work due to a massively increasing population—that is, more workers are available globally for jobs but fewer jobs are available due to elimination of those jobs by various forms of technology. The short-term savings of Americans will quickly be exhausted, based on what we know already about short-term savings of Americans; the period that most people can survive in this country without a job is most likely just a few months. After that time, I would expect defaults on mortgages and credit cards from lack of income, to begin causing a massive financial crisis. The economy of today is incredibly fragile and relies solely on the fact that the general population constantly feeds the overhead monster monthly, and when this practice stops, the forecasted earnings of companies will dramatically drop along with their stock prices and in a short period of time, the financial markets

48 https://macro.economicblogs.org/uncategorized/2017/01/shedlock-insurance-adjusters-ibm-watson-explorer/

will completely implode. When credit defaults rise—or in other words, people stop paying on their loans—there is normally a tightening of credit or a lack of willingness by banks to lend more money when they are already losing money from defaulted loans. As we saw in 2008, as more loans default, credit gets tighter; as credit gets tighter, the purchases of future goods and services will be more difficult to obtain, especially when it comes to high-ticket items like homes and autos.

Again, I think it's interesting to note here that bulk of wealthy people today are making mass assumptions that our current overhead technology will only change slightly over time, that the incomes of the general public will not change much at all over the next few decades and that the general public will maintain its constant spending on inferior overhead technology. If you're not repurchasing a car every 5 or 10 years, automobile manufacturers will die. If people are able to build on land outside of the 3.5% of the land that 63% of the population is currently crammed into, existing real-estate prices will plummet. These companies and industries rely on your having to constantly repurchase their inferior technology over and over again. In the case of housing, the entire industry relies solely on the fact that the power grid will remain the only method for distributing energy in our country, forever and ever. Our entire economy and financial markets run on the mass assumptions that our economic variables will remain constant and that no new superior technology ever will be introduced that will forever change the habits of consumer spending. The financial markets are betting on the slow progression of inferior overhead technology—but at the same time, these forecasters have not accounted for the fact that all our companies cannot be supported without cash for labor propping them up; as we automate our labor, there won't be cash to purchase their products. The financial markets are actually funding emerging artificial intelligence technologies to replace human labor, with seed money in the form of private equity placements and initial public stock offerings—so in essence the financial markets are guaranteeing the destruction of their own markets in the long run, through their greed for currency in the short run. The only long-term logical conclusion based on these facts is to start reducing our reliance upon our currency-based economy and to begin to attempt to build a technology-based economy, as we know that the long-term path of the current system is destined to end in failure.

Pensions are also heavily invested in the stock market, which most Americans are relying on for retirement income. Many government and corporate pensions throughout the United States are currently underfunded and will not be able to meet their future obligations. What happens to those retirees? Should we allow a mass portion of our public to suffer, so that a small percentage can enjoy an obscene amount of currency, that studies show does not seem to change the general emotional or psychological well-being of any person who earns over $75,000/year? One way or another, it seems we're headed on a collision course towards some sort of financial collapse or crisis, and we need to intervene now in order to make sure the general public can better survive it, by implementing a plan to reduce overhead. The public has time now to better prepare, cope and deal with the future consequences of losing their cash for the constant repurchase of their future survival technology during their retirement. If we stand by and do nothing, retirees will be saddled with a crashed stock market, vastly reduced monthly pension income, few job prospects, incredibly tight credit standards and no new survival technology on the horizon to lower their overhead. The technology needed to free them from this prison would still be held captive under the iron rule of patents, currency and government confiscation. This would represent a classic example of what I would call a period of waiting for reduced survival technology costs.

It is this "period of waiting" that should be the greatest concern of the general public today. If we follow the plan outlined in this book, we can avoid a long period of scarcity waiting for advanced low-cost overhead technology to be freely used by society. If a certain state or even the federal government imposed a buyout of stocks on the energy industry, vetted statistics show that 1% of the country controls 90% of the assets; so if you look at this massive loss to wealthy shareholders on a grand scale, only a very small percentage of the United States would feel this change financially.

Scenario 2:

If we remove patents from our energy, healthcare, transportation and housing industries and follow the plan outlined in this chapter, then it is far more likely that advanced technology will be created and dis-tributed faster than if we wait for an economic collapse to happen and try to bring about wholesale changes to the currency-based economy through violence, anger and fear. If we purposefully intervene and disrupt the ongoing business practices of the for-profit system, we can avoid a "period of waiting" or a period of scarcity, waiting for better survival technology to be utilized by our planet. If we actually pay the shareholders 5% of the average stock price, over a three-year period of time, they would actually be left with some money, and this money could be used to purchase current and future goods and services or become available to loan to the general public, helping to support the existing economy, rather than facing the consequences of scenario 1, where capital is tied up over the long term, waiting for stocks to rise, as artificial intelligence and automation tirelessly work to destroy the future earnings of companies and their stock prices.

Currency is an illusion, a shared and accepted illusion, designed to create action within the population of planet, in order to manifest the current and future reality of its people. People every day work tirelessly toward making ends meet, having some extra money to take a vacation once in a while and save the bulk of their money over the course of their entire lifetime for an unknown event called retirement, incurring an unknown amount of future survival expenses that continue to rise decade after decade. It's time to put certainty back into the lives of people again through the creation and distribution of superior technology that would eliminate these primitive uncertainties.

The central idea here is to stop creating products that constantly need to be created again. Every time you need to purchase a product "again," you need cash, which means you need to expend labor, in order to receive it, or draw from savings created by your labor—so labor becomes perpetual, based on the incentivized outcome of constantly creating inferior technology in order to maximize profits. The idea of creating permanent products, with an extremely long utility life, would help to eliminate or greatly reduce the need to constantly repurchase things like housing (in the form of rent and mortgage payments), car payments, medical expenses, insurance premiums and so forth that seem to only be increasing over time; while incomes at present are not keeping up with rising overhead costs, caused by a scarcity-based system, resulting in an ever-increasing rise in the level of consumer debt to make up the difference, in order to survive.

Rather than bemoan the situation we are in, we should first attempt to solve this problem by placing ourselves in a higher state of awareness and consider all the possibilities available to us, so that our transition can be as smooth as possible from a currency-based society to a technology-based one. It would be of paramount importance to anticipate any unforeseen economic consequences by simulating different scenarios and their effect on consumer confidence and by getting expert advice that is not motivated by greed or personal gain. I have outlined measures later in the text that will directly address these concerns.

Step 4. Requiring all energy-based companies become nonprofit, in order to maintain a valid license.

As part of the licensing requirements of any energy company, all companies within the industry would be required to transfer any profits made at the end of their fiscal year, as determined by its accounting process, into a special escrow account operated and overseen by each state's licensing agency. Any deposits and withdrawals would be required to be reported to each state's licensing agency daily. These accounts would be overseen by a state auditing committee, and an auditing report would be made public every six months on the current status of the account, including all deposits and withdrawals made. In other words, all transactions of this escrow account would be available to the general public for review, like a giant transparent bank account of the general public, almost like this escrow account was your bank account in some sense. Companies would be able to draw from these funds quarterly, to meet ongoing expenses for the development of their technology. These withdrawals could be allocated towards labor, capital or any normal business operating expenses. After five fiscal years, 35% of the initial first year's unspent deposits, would be distributed to the existing customer base of any given company, in the form of a customer rebate. Energy companies would be forced to spend their profits and reinvest them quickly back into the development of their own technology, which is precisely what we want, in order to speed the process of superior technology development along as quickly as possible.

Step 5. Requiring internal company audits.

Each energy company would be subject to an internal audit twice per year. Regulatory and compliance audits would be performed by auditing companies for a maximum of two years; at the end of the two-year period, another auditing company would be required to perform these transactions for any licensed company. Fraud committed by an internal auditing company would be considered an Economic Crime.

Any suppliers and vendors to this industry could also be subject to random audits by each state's licensing agency, even if they're not directly producing or distributing an energy product. In short, it would be almost impossible for any company to conduct some sort of illegal behavior within the industry, based on the new laws required, in order to keep their license in good status. There would be almost no incentive for fraud, once all companies within the industry became nonprofit, no longer having to worry about the price of outstanding stock shares or acquiring patents to keep their inferior technology on the market, as patent law covering their technologies would no longer be enforceable. Perhaps the only angle for any seasoned criminal within the industry would be to directly embezzle funds; but semiannual audits, along with a transparent escrow account, would most likely prevent that from ever happening.

Step 6. Creating incentives for employees through bonuses.

I will be covering incentives for employees, including a full analysis of employee compensation plans, in detail later on in the text and only provide a brief summation here. There would be quarterly incentive bonuses for any and all employees of any licensed energy-producing companies. The bonuses would be defined by several parameters, including meeting quarterly incentive goals, number of overtime hours worked, safety standards adhered to and the nature of hazardous work per employee.

In addition, there would be a yearly profit-sharing bonus awarded, based on meeting yearly performance goals, for any given fiscal year. I would prefer to see oil workers on drilling rigs become top-tier earners through this compensation plan in making at least 10% more annually than they are now. Working for any petroleum-producing company, because of the risk of loss of life, is far greater than any other employee's job risks within the industry. We should be paying the people who are on the basic production lines—where the rubber meets the road—the greatest amount of money, to make sure we currently meet or exceed our energy needs, through our existing energy technologies. Anything that might cause a decrease in the supply of our existing energy technologies would create a devastating effect on our existing economy and we simply cannot afford that to happen, nor should we plan for it to happen by not incentivizing workers correctly.

Creating an income cap: The income limit for any individual within the energy industry would be limited to $250,000, including salary, overtime and bonuses. This cap would cover all employees and officers including the chief financial officer and chief executive officers of any licensed company. I will expand on this in more detail, as to why I believe this is specifically necessary, in the next chapter.

A bonus of up to $3 million could be awarded to any individual or team, for producing any breakthrough design in energy technology that becomes manifested into a usable piece of "superior" energy technology. The days of shelving superior energy technology by purchasing patents and government sequestration will simply come to an end by enacting the new laws and regulations governing licensing in the energy industry.

Step 7. Forming a state Energy Protection Agency

The state's Energy Protection Agency, or the governing agency designated by each individual state, would be responsible for the enforcement and maintenance of all regulations governing all licensing prerequisites, renewals and audits; the ceasing of existing energy patent laws; and monitoring any type of potential Economic Crime investigations or any other enforcement or monitoring deemed necessary under licensing regulations. We need to ensure that companies within the energy industry run not only in an honest and fair manner but adhere to the designated strict licensing laws and regulations set forth. An enforcement agency would definitely be required to keep a close eye on all energy-based companies, to ensure they remain nonprofit, non-publicly traded and patent free.

Step 8. Sourcing funds for the operation and advancement of new and existing energy companies.

Since we're eliminating initial public stock offerings and private equity placements, as a way of sourcing funds to start new energy companies and maintain our existing energy technology companies, we'll need some other ways to fund these companies so that they can bring or continue to bring their technologies for consumption to the general public in an efficient manner.

The sourcing of funds for new and existing energy companies could be done through any of the following means:

1. The issuance of tax-free, state-issued municipal bonds.

2. The issuance of tax-free federally issued government energy bonds. However, we can only use this source if the federal government enforces licensing laws throughout the entire country and enacts a policy to regulate the energy industry through a licensing system.

3. State or federal energy grants.

4. Allocation of a percentage of yearly state income tax revenues.

5. Allocation of a percentage of ongoing state sales tax revenues. This could include a gasoline tax, tobacco or alcohol tax, fast food tax.

6. Crowdfunding through online donations.

All sources of energy investment or regulation of funds would be required to be held in an escrow account as defined under Step 4.

Step 9. Monitoring, maintaining, supporting and adjusting the industry rules and regulations through a vetting period of at least five years.

The system would need to be closely monitored for a period of at least five years before we consider implementing it in our transportation and housing industries. The overall plan calls for the licensing and regulation of only the energy and healthcare industries at first. Other than licensing healthcare and energy, the United States economy would run business as usual. It is important to realize that we can only change our economy in small increments. We must first take baby steps before we can take giant steps. We cannot run all our industries under this model, at the same time. I believe this type of vastly changed regulation across many industries at the same time would result in disastrous and tumultuous changes for our economy that our general public would not be ready to understand and adapt too quickly. Again, the overall idea is to reduce overhead first and foremost, prior to our country producing and implementing labor-reducing and therefore income-reducing technologies; closely monitoring and maintaining the system; making sure audits are done properly and making sure that people are incentivized properly. In fact, my greatest concern would be that the incentives to the employees in our licensed energy industry would keep the employees properly motivated at all times—we should do everything in our power to keep consumer confidence and morale high in America. We are going to need people on oil-drilling rigs working hard to get oil to our refineries, as much as we'll need new energy technologies developed by properly motivated scientists and engineers. Everyone working together through open-sourced collaboration and sharing technology is the centralized theme that we will need to continue to explain over and over to the public. I believe innately this system will work and produce highly successful, superior survival technology for the American public to enjoy and forever change the lives and daily activities of the average working person, transporting them from a constant state of mental scarcity towards a perpetual state of enjoyed abundance.

What we're trying to do here is drain the swamp. We're trying to use our existing, available sources of funds to develop and continue existing energy technologies, while simultaneously attempting to create superior technology that will no longer require constant perpetual payments of currency.

Let me be honest: It doesn't really matter if we borrow this money. Eventually we will not need to worry about repayment of the debt, because at some point in time the entire country will run on technology that does not require a massive amount of labor for cash to support it. It would make little difference if we actually defaulted on this debt in the long run; over the next 30 years, with the mass advancements in technology, most likely we're going to see all of our financial and credit markets implode anyway, based on the mass development of artificial intelligence. The financial markets are going to implode, so either way, we'll need to make sure we have the right survival technology in place before it happens. Under the current system, government debt is over $25 trillion and household debt over $14 trillion. Who do you think is going to pay back the $39-trillion debt that keeps rising every day? It's not going to be paid back; the government will scrap its currency and issue another one before it does so, making all debts uncollectible, including the current government's debt to all its creditors, before it ever attempts to pay this money back. If you want evidence of this, simply look around the world at countries whose currency systems have already failed, where new currency had to be issued. There have been thousands of fiat currencies throughout world history and all of them have failed. It doesn't matter how smart we've been running our economies relative to other countries; technology is going to destroy the system one way or another. Government debt is not guaranteed; it simply backed by a promise to pay it back by the government of the United States. So the system you're a part of now, is issuing debt it can't pay back and isn't promising you a better life through creating superior technology. We can continue to work with the system built on faulty premises and a currency backed by air, or we can adopt another system that works to the advantage of the general public more efficiently.

Please pause again to remember that this is a broadly outlined plan. The purpose of this book is to raise awareness so that everyone, regardless of their knowledge of economics, can understand how the current laws of our system work against us and what we can do to bring ourselves back to a place of prosperity and abundance. Your questions are important to me, and I understand that many of you may have questions about the system were trying to build; if you keep reading, you will likely find the answers to all of those questions. Please don't be afraid to fact check and explore your inquiries on the internet as well, using this text as a reference guide for your general understanding of the economy.

Now let's define what these energy companies should be creating. All licensed, nonprofit, non-publicly traded and non-patent-holding energy companies should be creating:

1. Energy that can be used in any location on the planet, without use of a power grid for its distribution, to allow 67% of the unpopulated land of the United States to be inhabited by the citizens of the United States, in order to keep real-estate lot costs as low as possible and/or potentially never increase over hundreds of years of time.

2. Energy created at the lowest possible cost per unit to the consumer. Let's set a goal for a free-energy generation device with the cost of $500 or less. Again, if we find extremely efficient solar panels, I'm all for this, but the source of energy must be portable, to allow our citizens to live virtually anywhere and keep lot costs as low as possible. This type of technology should not require a battery backup, as it should produce power whenever desired "on demand," so the requirement for the storage of electricity is simply eliminated when using this newly developed type of technology.

3. Energy that has the potential to be produced at an exponentially lower cost-per-unit over time than what is presently being produced today. This would include the lowest possible per-unit replacement costs and per-unit repair costs, if applicable. Let's set a goal of any energy-producing mechanism that does not requiring any repair or replacement within the first 25 years of its creation.

4. Energy production that has the least amount of negative effects to the environment, including pollution.

5. Energy technology that requires the least amount of human labor to be created. Repetitive human labor is exactly the problem we're trying to eliminate.

6. Energy technology that could be implemented at a very low cost and replicated by all Third World countries.

Only a portable source of energy would meet all six of these very important criteria. What we want here is to be able to live anywhere in our country or as a matter fact anywhere in the world, with free energy for our homes and autos.

Let assume at some point in the next 100 years we'll be able to create an energy based portable shelter. Just by running a program on your phone you would be able to create a holographic projection of your home including; your furniture, appliances and personal items inside it. Can you imagine people being able to travel the world with a portable source of energy and a portable shelter and live in different places around the world, for basically no cost, their entire lives and be able to move from place to place with just smart phone? This would allow people to travel freely and break down the cultural and primitive differences we all have with one another. It would truly be a major deterrent to all wars and hostilities, which represent the byproducts created by the currency system that must constantly promote scarcity to perpetuate itself. We should be imagining goals like this one in our long-term future rather than trying to envision ourselves as millionaires.

A portable energy device could provide the following benefits to the world:

- Permanently lower real-estate lot costs and the overhead living expenses for all people, allowing fewer hours to be worked per week, with a higher standard of living.

- Decease in the likelihood of war. Since all countries would have access to the same energy technology, there would be fewer incentives to attack a country if the competing countries held the same level of survival technology. War for control of oil fields or other scarce resources would not exist.

- Increased health benefits and deceased healthcare costs, due to a sharp fall in financial stress, as savings increase in households and the number of hours worked per year by the aggregate population drops.

- Allow for more savings per household, to avert future financial crises.

- Decrease crime, due to lower survival costs and higher cash reserves attained by the general public, decreasing the likelihood of committing crimes in order to survive.

- Boost the domestic economy, by no longer relying on imports made from cheap labor, as American overhead costs drop. American businesses now become nationally competitive and will be able to produce all the products we need right here in this country. Your own local town, with a population of just a few thousand, may be able to produce all the goods and services you need within its borders, in the future.

- Free energy would create incredibly cheap food production, allowing any local population to utilize massive local greenhouses, or perhaps anyone might even enjoy the benefits of a fully functioning greenhouse on their own property.

- The internet and autonomously driven vehicles could take care of all your shopping needs, and certainly broadband internet provided worldwide, through an extensive satellite system, would take care of all your communication needs. Virtually anything you might need in a small community could either be manufactured and provided to you locally or delivered long distance by a drone or autonomously driven vehicle. Basically, you could reap all the benefits of living in any major metropolitan city, while living in nature, owning your home free and clear and simultaneously reducing your monthly bills to a fraction of what they are now. The present currency-based, for-profit system, coupled with patents, will never allow this to happen.

How can we solve the problem of creating a free-energy device, using our mass consciousness? Once at least 25 states have adopted a licensing system for energy companies doing business within their borders, I would suggest the United States commit 3.2 million people, or approximately 1% of its population, in shifts 24/7, under a new type of Manhattan Project, until the task is completed. Similarly, any state wishing to adopt this policy prior to its acceptance at the national level should commit at least 1% of its population to making this type of energy technology a reality. Every state budget will differ slightly depending on its population, primary industries and local resources. We have more than enough money, artificial intelligence and human ingenuity to solve this problem. If we look at the question of raising money to solve this problem, just from the federal level alone, we do in fact have more than enough money to fund an ongoing project like this for decades; it's just a matter of setting our priorities. Let's look at a hypothetical example here.

If you paid 3.2 million people, or slightly less than 1% of the nation's population, an annual salary of $100,000 per year, in round figures that would turn out to be a $320-billion expenditure per year. Our federal budget deficit in 2017 was approximately $665 billion; this is the amount that went to debt, because our government is forced to spend beyond its means and the aggregate population was forced to create, repurchase and throw away massive amounts of inferior technology that year. The United States in 2014, for example, spent approximately $610 billion, or 34% of the entire world's budget, on military spending. This was more military spending than the other top seven countries combined! If we cut our military budget in half, to fund this project, we would still spend more per year on defense than the top two other players, China and Russia, combined! Three-hundred-and twenty billion dollars would be a drop in the bucket to start a project like this. To continue these expenditures annually until the project was completed, there's plenty of money for a project like this, if it's run properly.

Do you think we could get results with 3.2 million people working on the same project and moving in the same direction, without competition, with no incentives to make the technology inferior and every incentive to make it superior? Perhaps not even that much invention and design work would need to be done, if this type of energy technology has already been invented and was shelved by corporate America or was previously confiscated by our government. I would call this type of project a good old-fashioned barn-raising, in order to create hardware that makes a direct and sustainable change to our way of life. How many actual scientists and engineers do you think we need? We can afford to hire millions of scientists and engineers, each working independently on different types of projects, sharing information, that perhaps might develop several different, portable sources of energy. We would have more than enough money to hire several hundred thousand scientists and engineers initially, creating structures and elaborate labs for them to work in and providing them with the artificial intelligence and the raw materials they need in order to make their designs a reality. We also have the money to fund future scientists and engineers though more intensive scholarship programs. Our tax money is currently being diverted to useless pursuits that will never amount to anything; our labor and knowledge are being misdirected towards a system whose only goal is to produce profit; and our work becomes perpetual, never giving us a means to an end. I cannot stress enough that we need to use our currency, our labor and our creative spirit as means to an end.

The United States will have to continue to borrow money, year after year, until it becomes bankrupt, because it will not allow our overhead and survival expenses to drop, thereby exponentially lowering its own overhead costs. The United States government has no intention to make budget cuts of any significance to any of its major departments, whether they be relevant or irrelevant to the prosperity of America, because budget cuts would cause a rise in unemployment and a bad economy, and would not allow any politician to meet their incentivized goal—which is to be reelected. Let's look at the example of the United States military. If you reduce the military and lay off workers, these ex-military people become our newly unemployed; consequently, the unemployment rate rises, and the politicians can potentially in those affected areas, lose their jobs. In short, the government creates fake jobs, by keeping on government workers and military personnel they probably haven't needed for decades, and keeps funding ridiculous military projects whose only intention is to keep secret the results of these projects from us, and that by design provide no direct benefit to our economy. Meanwhile, the unemployment rate looks great!

This is all paid for with debt the government issues or prints—in other words, fake money. The people of our country are lulled into a false sense of belief that our economy is running smoothly. We will continue to reelect the same people who are forcing us into bankruptcy—a bankruptcy that is sure to come when the interest payments on government debt become so great that the government can no longer run its core departments and make interest payments at the same time. When the government defaults on its debt, it will issue another currency, so that it does not have to pay back any principal, to its bondholders, because under a currency reorganization, our government debt no longer becomes legally collectible. If a treasury bond, for example, states that it's to be paid back in U.S. dollars, but if U.S. dollars are no longer an acceptable form of currency in the United States, the bond becomes worthless. The government might pay back the existing bondholders with new currency, by issuing new government bonds, but the conversion rate between the old currency and the new currency might be just a fraction—for example, less than 1%, of the face value of the old currency. Your money as a U.S. citizen would also fall victim to this new exchange rate, so that you can move forward and have some sort of money to spend, to keep the economy upright, but the account balances of your checking, savings, brokerage or retirement accounts, in this scenario, would be basically a tiny fraction, of what they are now. So again, it's important for us to develop superior technology, look at the positive and preempt this from happening by demanding that we receive superior technology and that our energy, healthcare, transportation and housing industries become licensed over time, so that our overhead remains low and a future currency collapse like the hypothetical one I've described above, would create a far less significant impact to our economy and each citizen's means of survival.

Another way we can develop technology quickly is to take advantage of the mass forms of communication available between individuals around the entire globe, afforded to us by the internet. There are approximately 4 billion people connected to the internet on this planet; by creating free and open-sourced web-based forums and video discussions in groups, we can develop free-energy technology at the quickest pace possible. Everyone on the planet should be able to provide their input towards this massive problem. Do you think 4 billion people on this planet working together in an open-sourced forum, sharing information freely and transparently, could develop this technology? I certainly do! I have absolutely, completely and totally no doubt. All we really need is a small percentage of these people to provide pertinent information, in order to help make free energy an everyday working energy technology on this planet.

Let's take a realistic look at three possibilities regarding superior technology being implemented on this planet right now, whether you're talking about an extremely efficient solar panel, a free-energy device, wireless power or any type of energy technology that might radically change the currency system. I firmly believe the reason why we currently don't have superior energy technology running on this planet is due to one of three reasons:

1. A corporation holds the rights to the patent, which it either developed in its own research and development lab and patented, or bought the patent rights to and then consequently shelved the technology in order to keep selling its inferior technology to the public as long as

possible. At the end of the patent's useful life, or as soon as possible, the corporation holding the patent intends to invent upgraded technology, from the basic design of the patented technology it currently holds, in order to file another patent, to again keep its inferior technology on the market as long as possible, and it willfully intends to legally fight any way it can in court to keep this technology from being distributed to the American public. Any company threatened by emerging technologies would be wise to enact such a defense strategy, in order to keep itself from going out of business.

2. A patent was filed with the United States patent office by an individual, and reviewed by the appropriate government departments, which found the technology to be a "threat to the national security of the United States" and confiscated the patent under the Invention Secrecy Act of 1951. The aim is to hide the patent from the American public for an indefinite period of time.

3. The technology that all Americans are seeking to receive, such as a free-energy device, an extremely efficient solar panel or any device that would radically alter the production and consumption of energy in the United States, has simply not been invented yet!

So, we basically have to follow one of three paths in order to find our solution to our problem—which is a superior source of energy technology. Right now, our odds are very low, virtually zero, of actually witnessing superior technology being developed and distributed to our population based on the existing laws of our country. We know that patents privately allow corporations to control and hold back technology, and we know that the Invention Secrecy Act of 1951 will publicly allow the government, to confiscate this technology when an inventor attempts to follow the law by filing for a patent. Why not eliminate two of the three blockages to our destiny, by following the plan I've outlined in this chapter, thus taking the government and corporate America out of the equation, by making energy producing companies' nonprofit, non-publicly traded and unable to purchase or control technology through patents? Our last possibility, that the technology hasn't been invented yet, we can directly tackle, by putting 1% of our population to work on the problem tomorrow! Following this plan, we are taking a direct path to ensure the superior technology we need is being invented, because it now becomes our goal as a country to make it happen. If we allow a licensing plan to regulate our privately held energy companies, our odds are now a "minimum" of 66% that we will have success, because we need to consider the fact that "if" the technology was already invented, under the laws of the new system, it would be revealed to us in a short period of time by someone being able to openly and transparently recreate the technology from a previously filed patent, without fear of government or corporate intervention. If this is not the case, we're still in a very good position of attaining of 100% success, with everyone in the world focused on solving this one problem, in cooperation—working together to develop the energy technology we need. Basically, what I'm trying to tell you is that by following this plan we eliminate three huge barriers that are holding us back— currency incentives, patents and competition—in order to receive the energy technology we want and truly deserve, rather than staying where we are, keeping old barriers in place and having a few people competing for one spot of glory, who are sure to be bought out or robbed through government confiscation.

We should implement this licensing regulation beginning with our energy and then our healthcare industry, over a period of five to 10 years. Specifically, during this period, the effects and results of regulation on this industry should be studied proficiently. The effects of energy regulation on society, the effects on the overhead costs of the average citizen, the effects of regulation on our current petroleum-based companies and electrical utilities, the general overall health and well-being of the workers in the energy industry—every aspect of new energy technology being implemented into society should be quantified, studied and potentially forecasted. I think we need to understand here that, if a portable source of energy is developed and distributed throughout our country, eventually people will move to more remote areas, where lot costs are extremely low, in order to build homes. Initially, this demographic is most likely going to be filled by retired people, who will be incentivized to cut their overhead, based on their limited retirement incomes. Artists of various sorts might also create their own communities, as well as just about any person seeking to lower overhead and reduce their work schedule. This mass migration out of the cities and into the country would cause massive real-estate defaults or at the very least create a massive permanent drop in the price of real estate. So eventually I believe we will need to face the fact here that if we're going to change our overhead costs, our credit system is going to collapse. How will we deal with this problem? How will property taxes be collected? How will schools be funded?" The short answer to all these questions is that all expenses throughout the country will require less currency because the cost of building, running and maintaining a school, for example, would gradually decrease over time, due to massively decreased labor costs and massively decreased building costs, incredibly cheap lot costs and artificial intelligence driving ongoing maintenance costs down over time.

Perhaps at some point in the future, we will be able to operate from such a position of strength that we would be easily able to just write off all our existing debt and move forward with a new system of currency. This new currency, used for a small portion of our transactions, might be backed by some sort of basket of commodities and real tangible assets and provide even further stability to our future economy.

What we need to envision—from a consciousness, spiritual, physical and mental perspective—is that the for-profit, currency-based economy is only a means to an end and should be cannibalized in order for us to migrate to a technology-based system. We're "shedding our skin," so to speak, from one system to another. We can build this new economy. We have the people, we have a formalized internet to share information, we have the basic technology to expand our ideas and make them more efficient and we have the currency to pay people, provide them with the tools they'll need and to create the structures for them to work in. We have everything we need to make this happen; it's just a matter of coming together as one and agreeing on a formalized plan, for all of us to follow. This is how we're going to make our new economy a reality.

CHAPTER 6

Motivating and Maintaining Licensed Worker Compensation and Morale

How exactly do you motivate people to work themselves out of a job?

Most people would say that if we don't need currency to survive anymore, then we'll just sit on our couches and do nothing. At this point, I hope I've proven to you that a currency-based system coupled with laws restricting information technology is never going to produce superior technology. I hope by the end of this text you will have some insight into the fact that humans can be motivated to create and manifest beautiful things on this planet, without being beaten by a stick or pointed towards a carrot.

Some people might argue that the currency system "builds character" and that without patents companies would never produce any type of technology whatsoever. I would argue that a currency exchange-for-survival system is motivating our workforce only up to the point that provides a person a certain amount of income relative to their safety and security needs, which is probably not much more than the amount it takes to pay the ongoing expenses for an average household in any given month. Humans basically aren't motivated to save money, simply because they are not motivated by currency. Various surveys from 2018 and 2019 report that about 60% of the country does not have $1,000 to cover an emergency expense, the average household debt is over $137,000 and the median household income is only about $59,000/year. Billions of people on this planet survive on less than a few dollars a day and save absolutely no money at all. I think if humans were more motivated to amass currency, we would probably have more evidence to support it in the form of larger savings account balances across our aggregate population. Humans are motivated by technology and the benefits that using technology brings to their lives. Currency is a medium to purchase technology, but technology is what provides us the lasting benefits.

Could we produce better results throughout our economy by distributing technology to our citizens, rather than distributing a byproduct called currency? Would people be more motivated to work directly to receive technology rather than currency?

Survival through currency not only stops our ability to obtain superior technology, but it also deflates our motivation, because we have no nationalized goal to stop repeating endless tasks that machines could easily replicate. Americans end up working endlessly and struggle against their instincts to save currency to purchase their future survival expenses for retirement over a period of 40 to 50 years. Neither the currency nor the price of their future survival technology is guaranteed during this entire period. How can people be steadfast and motivated to save, when there is so much uncertainty in the fundamentals of the system? The currency-based system constantly strips away the abundance in one's life, by introducing complex fundamentals such as competition, scarcity, inflation and confusion, through a labyrinth of laws no one fully understands. Is it any wonder that the vast majority of the public never rises above their current station by saving a massive amount of currency?

All United States debt, including its corporate, government and household debt, is constantly increasing; this is mainly due to the fact that technology has not been applied to our overhead industries to lower the cost of their products, and these overhead costs are innately tied to the price of all goods and services made in the United States. So, from the big picture perspective, with so much uncertainty within the system and ever-increasing debt, the system seems doomed to fail as machines in various forms slowly replace human labor.

The currency system runs on the fundamentals of scarcity, competition, confusion, inequality and greed. It leaves us with widespread assumptions and false beliefs that are based around the fact that the only way we can develop technology to an extremely high level is if ownership is involved; and unless ownership is involved, no one has the incentive to develop anything when actually the concept of ownership itself, through instruments like patents, is the very thing that attempts to slow or halt the advancement of technology altogether. Currency creates quite a number of paradoxes that need to be transcended by the human mind in order for any human to obtain a higher level of awareness and consistent level of happiness.

Let's also understand here that the goal of a technology-based economy, especially following this plan, which only deals with changing four industries initially over decades of time, is not to eliminate all human interaction with the planet and render humans useless as an end-result. Humans with access to machines that can replicate their mundane survival tasks can still fulfill many basic human needs, whether it is the need to belong to a group, participate in creation or just simple contemplation; the need to do some sort of physical and mental action daily toward achieving some sort of goal will always be a part of the human psyche.

Now let's look at how licensing our energy, healthcare, transportation and housing industries would have an effect on our mass population, according to Maslow's hierarchy of needs. Maslow's hierarchy of needs is organized in a pyramid, starting at the bottom with physiological needs, and working to the top with safety needs, love and belonging, esteem, and finally, self-actualization.

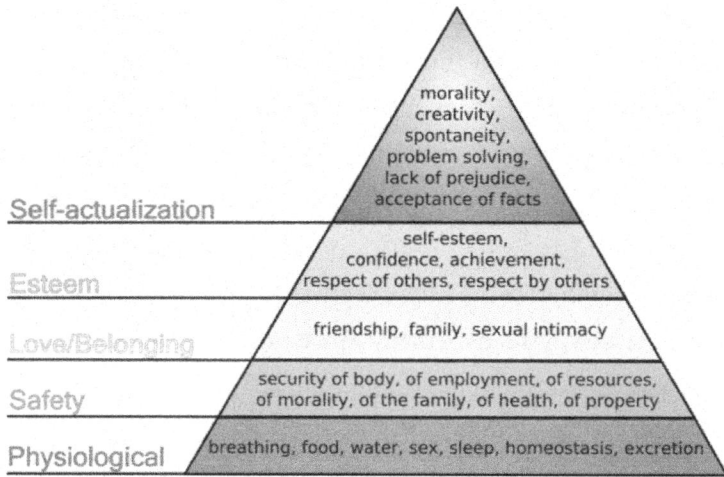

- Physiological needs: These wouldn't change much, as they are intrinsic to organic matter and not currency. We would certainly obtain easier access to water if it could be produced directly in the home, and at least some food if some of it could be grown in the home or in an adjacent greenhouse. Both food and water might be a fraction of the cost they are now as overhead prices drop exponentially.

- Safety needs: Since most people would be working perhaps 10 hours a week or less in this type of economy, security of employment would be a very low priority. Security of health and receiving health treatment would also be a very low concern for the human population of the United States, because there would simply be no incentives to overcharge people in a nonprofit, non-publicly traded and patent-free medical system. Shelter in this type of economy would be incredibly cheap, and almost all the population would own their homes free and clear. There would be plenty of disposable income and time to create more technology. Survival would become easier and simpler on this planet. In tougher economic times, since survival expenses would be a fraction of what they cost today, there would be very little stress, if any, for most of the nation's households.

- Love/Belonging: Since people would not be spending the majority of their time working for their own survival, they would be completely free to enjoy and indulge the needs of bonding through friendship and family openly, for extended periods of time. No longer would long work hours interfere with family and friendship obligations. People would be forced to focus on relationships, rather than work. I cannot emphasize the importance of focusing on relationships as a culture versus the focus of many Americans today, which is basically on their job, their cell phone and shopping. People being forced to focus on relationships would have a massive impact on the culture of the United States, and I believe it would bring people together and bond us emotionally as a culture. Perhaps the biggest thing we're lacking today as a culture is togetherness, a sense of inner connectivity. Last but not least, socialization and care groups for humans could be formed, so that people could interact and love one another without constraints.

- Esteem: In a technology-driven economy, people can no longer differentiate themselves through currency, so they would have to basically rely on their own feelings and actions towards one another to gain mutual respect and confidence in each other. Removing currency basically levels the playing field and allows humans to be judged on their own actions and character. Lies and deception would no longer be in vogue in this new culture.

- Self-actualization: Humans would be free to create, socialize and work together, alone or in a mind-hive if they wish, to basically do just about anything they wanted to, since there would be so much free time available to the general public. Mass movements of meditation would be possible; and mass groups assembled to work on other technologies not pertinent to survival, to help make life easier and more entertaining for everyone, would be the general theme of life. Everyone would have time to understand their higher self, their ability to create and not be hampered by survival fears. People would be free to experience new activities and new careers they'd never tried before, new technologies, new ways of thinking and new emotional states.

Let's continue to look at the concept of what removing currency for survival from our planet, does to the human mindset:

- Most people are already programmed to work. This habit has been formed over the course of their entire lives. This habit programming will not cease to act out in all humans, unless other programming replaces it. So, most people will continue to look for some type of work or interaction to fulfill a sense of self-worth and respect by others, regardless of the level of currency received or not. These needs seem to be innate to the human species, so it would seem that if currency was not a part of the equation, humans would still find some external way to meet them.

- People have a basic need to create, whether it be technology, art, a great meal or anything personally satisfying to any particular human being. This idealism would definitely continue even if currency were eliminated altogether or our dependence on it was vastly decreased. Our population could channel this indelible need to create and work as a means to an end by cooperating together to create superior technology. Even if you are not a scientist or engineer, certainly anyone could support these people, emotionally with their positive thoughts or even physically by an immediate support position in one of these industries. Anyone's continued activities as a successful economic participant would move us toward our plans for success.

- Humans are not interested in repetitive tasks, as they all work toward the same goal their entire lives: retirement. At the heart of the matter, people really don't want to work. The American work life consists of mundane routines, endless drudgery and doing the same acts over and over again expecting a different result. The population of the United States would be able to set a goal to bid a fond farewell to this insanity. It would also stand to reason that by giving people an incentive to retire early by working in an industry that would require the development of superior survival technology, they might through continued planning and work meet that goal even earlier than they originally thought they could, and this incentive might spur great motivation and an even more cooperative nature, throughout any particular industry. Perhaps we can get the American work week down to 10 hours from 40, no longer requiring that we all save a massive amount of money in order to do so. We may not reach the goal of full-blown retirement, but we may reduce our work week to 10 hours, and that is certainly vastly different from the 40-hour work week everyone is committed to now!

Let's examine another roadblock thought process to prosperity, which is that if machines are doing our work for us will we all just become lazy, do nothing and become depressed. Let's look at concrete examples of people working today without mass incentives for a better standard of living, or money in general: The Red Cross and Peace Corps members, volunteers in the United States and around the world, help people every day without regard for money. There are plenty of concrete examples of people who are not money-motivated and not motivated by the fear of loss or endless consumerism. It stands to reason, based on these concrete human examples presented to us every day, that we can potentially build a non-currency-based system where everyone cooperates and enjoys far greater abundance, prosperity and happiness, than we all do today.

The purpose of this book is to help you understand that, in order to create a new economy, we need a high level of confidence and belief that this system will work. If we don't establish psychological and emotional understandings of who we might become without currency, then we will never achieve our goal and see our physical manifestation become a reality. Everything starts and ends with the thought process; without a vision in your mind, there is no way we can make a technology-based economy, a reality. We need to think, act, walk and talk like this has already happened, and hold fast to a vision of what we will become and how we'll interact with each other in this new reality. If we don't change our thought process, you can be 100% assured that the physical reality of a technology-based economy will never become a reality. I will continue to outline and expand, in this text, on a vision of what our new economy will look like and what your potential future might be, so that you can better visualize on a daily basis what thoughts you'll need think and actions you'll need to take to create this reality.

Let's pause for a second and take a look at the fact that the development of the internet, over the last 25 years, has radically changed the views and consciousness of the entire American public. Today, the way we access our bank accounts, look for information, ask artificial intelligence for directions or play our favorite TV or music programs, is completely and totally different from the way in which people completed those tasks just 50 years ago. We're entering the dawn of a new age, and we need to keep the laws governing our country up to date with this explosion of technology, in order to keep its future expansion under of the control of the mass population of America. For profit and shareholder-based companies simply cannot coexist alongside the modern advancements of technology we enjoy today or the advanced technology we will possess in the future. If you were charged one dollar every time you accessed a page on the internet, how much time would you spend on the internet and how much less do you think you would be developed as a person emotionally and psychologically today?

Charging high prices for information restricts access to information, the same way that the ever-increasing cost of overhead technology causes a restrictions on the ease of our survival on this planet. The American public wouldn't be nearly as educated as it is now, nor would it enjoy the abundance of technology that it does today, without having been offered free information to low-cost technologies through a robust credit system. We are realizing that as we progress as a society, we need to streamline the way our economy functions, in order to take advantage of technological advancements as quickly as possible and incorporate them into our mainstream everyday functions. In order to do that, currency will need to become less of a focal point than it used to be. We're changing our consciousness, expanding our horizons and realizing that we don't need to hold on to old limitations that have been keeping us enslaved for thousands of years.

Now that we have an idea about what the motivations and morale would be like for an average citizen in a technology-based economy, versus our existing for-profit, currency-based economy, let's examine ways to specifically motivate industry workers in the energy, healthcare, transportation and housing industries that would specifically be affected by the licensing plan.

Quarterly and Annual Bonuses

The compensation plans of workers in these industries would not change that much from what they are today, and there would be little disturbance, to the overall work-life and routines of these workers. Employees would carry on with their standard 40-hour work week as usual and we would only plan on reducing their hours at some later determined point in the future, once sufficient low-cost survival technology begins being manufactured and mass distributed the public. The bonuses would be defined by several parameters, including meeting quarterly incentive goals, the number of overtime hours worked, safety standards adhered to and the nature of hazardous work. In addition, there would be an annual profit-sharing bonus based on meeting performance goals for any given fiscal year. We should be paying the people who are on the front production lines, where the rubber meets the road, the greatest amount of money, to make sure we currently meet or exceed our energy needs through our existing energy technologies. We'll still need to run our cars on gasoline and make sure we have a decent supply of it as well as oil, available to our country. That means we'll have to keep exploring and extracting oil from the ground, to run our economy as a temporary measure, until other technologies can replace petrochemicals. Anything that might cause a decrease in the supply of our existing energy technologies would create a devastating effect on our existing economy and we simply cannot afford for that to happen, nor should we plan for it to happen. Careful consideration needs to be given to worker-incentivized licensed industries and how to structure their bonus plans. A standard compensation plan for any company could run to least 30 pages, including an explanation of health and other benefits. We'll need to review all the current compensation plans, of all energy-producing companies and look at their basic structures now, in order to minimize changes and avoid chaos. We would attempt to pay the important people, those most vital to ongoing products and services, 10% more overall annually then they are currently receiving, to keep our energy, transportation and housing industries strong.

Our healthcare industry will require higher incentives where lives are concerned, increasing annual incomes for doctors, nurses and other critical medical personal up to 20%, over their current annual incomes now, when a licensing system is implemented into any of these industries. This plan calls for 65% of any worker's existing compensation to remain guaranteed and at least 35% of it to be incentivized through bonuses. We need to make sure the workers in our energy, transportation, healthcare and housing industries that are so vital to us are participating in a highly incentivized compensation plan. An entire book could probably be written on this subject alone. The general idea I'm trying to get across to you is that with any given workforce, in any given company, you can remove guaranteed income and replace it with incentivized income that pays slightly more annually than an existing guaranteed plan. Your input and the input of other experts are also required. This plan is quite comprehensive and requires everyone's feedback including yours. How would you incentivize workers in these industries? Think about it, and start talking to your friends and coworkers about it. That's how ideas become realities.

Creating an Income Cap

The income limit for any individual employed within the energy, transportation and housing industries would be $250,000, including salary, overtime and bonuses; this would include any executives including the chief financial officer and chief executive officer of any licensed company. The medical industry cap, for all employees, would be $650,000. Our goal here is to stop working. So if that is our goal, then there simply is no need to create massive incomes for a privileged few, so that they can save their excess currency for the future consumption of inferior technology, because this economy will produce lower required overhead costs decade after decade. In this scenario, less currency is needed over time. In summation, we will be strategically deflating our economy rather than constantly inflating it with purchases requiring we go into greater debt, as we are now. A $250,000 income is more than sufficient to meet the needs of any survival expenses, for the average American, as well as meet the needs for luxury expenses, of almost all Americans.

Consider the fact that studies have shown that making over $75,000 a year, as I outlined earlier in the text, does not change the overall emotional level and well-being of any individual. A $250,000 per year income is eight times the $30,000 per year income that 50% of the American population makes annually now. I fail to see the hardship concern that might be voiced from the privileged few as to why anyone would need to make over $250,000 a year in a need vs. want industry.

Do you want to know why you can't get ahead? It's because of the mass disparities, in the currency-based system, where CEOs make hundreds of times more annually than any typical employee of the same company. A 2018 article from the Niagara Gazette by Stan Cho states that the average

CEO now makes 164 times the median pay of their employees, yet companies continually ask their workers to do more and make less.[49] This is where inequality, with regards to access to technology, is born. Why would someone need to make more than $250,000 a year, if working for a licensed energy-based company? I will quote the answer that "at will" employers give to their employees when the employees don't like the pay they are receiving or don't like their working conditions: "If you don't like it, you can always get a job somewhere else." Since our plan only regulates four industries, there are plenty of opportunities to earn greater sources of income elsewhere. Those disheartened by this compensation plan would be free to seek incomes in other industries not regulated by it.

Another very important reason to create an income cap for executives is to free up more cash to incentivize the bottom-line workers of any industry: scientists, engineers, doctors, nurses, x-ray technicians, oil-drilling rig workers, auto designers and digital printing designers. The people who actually create the technology that we need the most need to be incentivized the most and paid the most money. Hierarchical structures are not as important in licensed and nonprofit companies. We're working as a means to an end, not to continue to provide inferior technology at the expense of others, in order to propagate a fat paycheck for executives. We want people to speak out, speak their mind, criticize and vent their frustrations over designs and processes that are backed by inefficient, stale and outdated for-profit philosophies. One of the main reasons why businesses across the United States are becoming more inefficient is because people in these companies are afraid to speak out at work for fear of losing their jobs. The loss of any job causes a major drain on the worker's savings and extreme emotional turmoil; these ongoing issues can potentially cause that worker to have to relocate themselves to another part of the country if they can't maintain the same standard of living and a host of other problems. It simply isn't worth it, for the average employee to

---

49   https://www.niagara-gazette.com/news/local_news/ceos-raking-in-big-bucks-compared-to-employees/article_9294c0b9-2168-5bb9-b735-ca497e1ba271.html

speak out or criticize any company today; they would rather keep quiet, put their head down and suffer in silence, than deal with the problem of potentially getting fired.

Employees can potentially be fired for asking for a bonus or raise, calling too much attention to themselves, outperforming a boss or a preferred coworker, starting a business outside of work or standing out in any way, whether positive or negative, because this could potentially send a negative message to their employer and can result in them being fired. Your employer basically has little to no interest in your survival, nor of the consequences you might face if you lose your job; they remain focused on their one goal—maximizing profit—no matter what the cost to the planet or any person on it. I couldn't find any statistics on this information, obviously because at-will employment laws don't require companies to give reasons for firing people or requiring companies to track those statistics; but I can tell you with 100% certainty that people have been fired in the past based on the reasons I've outlined in this paragraph.

Incentives to Invent New Technology

A bonus of up to $3 million could be awarded to an individual or per team, for producing any breakthrough design in technology that becomes manifested into a usable piece of superior technology. An individual inventing any drug that would pass through FDA trials and would show results, in either curing or preventing human diseases or illness, could receive a one-time lump sum payment of $3 million, which would not be counted towards their annual income cap. We can still incentivize the creation of technology without patents, by offering very large bonuses to anyone person or team, working in a licensed industry, to create superior technology. Money for these bonuses could be sourced from the retained earnings of any given company within the industry, through money paid annually to an invention pool by each company within any given licensed industry, state bonds or crowdfunding. A bonus like this would be a drop in the bucket for an existing petrochemical company. Our very long-term goal, perhaps over 50 to 100 years, is to really eliminate currency from our country, so the bonuses themselves are almost a means to an end, from the perspective that it would behoove the receiver of such a large bonus to spend their money almost immediately, on anything that they would like, rather than save the money, because most likely at some point in the future their bonus currency would become worthless, caused in part by their own invention.

Are you beginning to understand the paradox, between currency and superior technology? Once technology is developed to a certain point, the need for currency would no longer be required. Right now, you talk to your phone and your phone is talking back to you, in an intelligent and coherent manner, giving you the data and directions, you need in order to help live your life more efficiently. How long do you think it will be, before currency is no longer needed?" I can assure you, we're not that far away.

In the previous chapter on energy technology, I've already outlined how we might fund projects like building a free-energy device through simple actions, like cutting our bloated military budget, alcohol or fast food taxes, tax-free municipal bonds or crowdfunding. We can easily afford to hire millions of people who work on the frontline of design, intervention, manufacturing and distributing these products, as well as all the support people needed to make this process as efficient as possible. We have the money to build or rent structures for these people to work in and provide them the raw materials and tools they'll need; we have the information; we have the artificial intelligence; and we have extremely educated, creative and bright people who will be no longer be afraid to give their input in order to create superior technology.

We can also provide absolutely free ideas and labor to solve these problems by using message boards, interactive chats or videoconferencing with anyone, in any country across the world, as there are over 4 billion people currently connected to the internet. We have a massive amount of resources we can use to solve this problem—if in fact the technology we seek has not already been invented yet.

Achieving Long-Term Extraordinary Goals by Creating Concrete and Achievable Short-Term Goals

In his 2016 text *Smarter, Faster, Better*, Charles Duhigg does quite an excellent job of explaining how very precise short-term goals can help create a specific pathway to attaining long-term goals. I encourage you to give the book a read. It covers, quite elaborately, how habits are formed in humans and how attaining goals that have been seemingly impossible has been achieved by a team of employees within many companies. I'll paraphrase a few examples from the book, to give you a better idea of the process

Plans to put concrete goals in place, in order for workers to get extremely clear about what they need to do, in order to create a single process or clear a single obstacle to reaching a very extraordinary goal, have been outlined for decades by very familiar large corporations in the United States. A specific system of goalsetting in order to ensure concrete results within companies is not something new to the United States. General Electric started this type of goalsetting back in the 1960s. Workers were given a series of goals to set for themselves. The goal had to be realistic, and the division or manager setting them had to be completely specific about what they were doing. The specific objectives had to be measurable, achievable, realistic and based on a timeline; they had to be provably within reach and described in a way that suggested an achievable plan. If the goal wasn't precisely set and thought attainable by the existing supervisor, it was sent back to the employee, who had to resubmit their goal over and over again, until it was accepted. Studies have shown that the setting of short-term specific and attainable goals leads to the achievement of seemingly unattainable goals over the long term. Duhigg cites studies that have shown that the process of making a specific goal within a specific timeline and proving to a given person that it can be achieved by a written plan, forces a discipline on to the process of creation that good intentions can't ever achieve

Duhigg also uses the example of the country of Japan using short and long-term goals to build its high-speed rail system. After being devastated by two nuclear bombs during World War II, around 1955 Japan decided it needed a faster railway system in order to connect the country, to build its economy around. Travel through the mountains of the country could take as long as 20 hours—one way. This was simply unacceptable to the Japanese government, and they decided to embark on an endeavor to build a high-speed rail system. Engineers were given tasks and goals that at the time were completely unrealistic. They explained to their supervisors that the trains would crash at these high speeds and would be completely unsafe. As versions of the train got faster, management continued to tell the engineers that their results were simply unacceptable. In 1964 the first bullet train was launched in Japan, which attained an average speed of 120 mph.[50]

If you think about connecting the first railway systems in this country, I'm sure that there were people who thought these goals were unattainable at the time, due to the technology and information available; but yet these goals were attained and today we have both highway and rail systems crisscrossing our entire country. Had we not set these goals; we would not have near the level of trade in the United States that we do today.

We will need scientists and engineers to weigh in on these goals, as well as trained human resources people and even perhaps motivational coaches or sports psychiatrists. We have the resources available to us and we should use absolutely every resource we have for the construction of superior technology, because we know it will change the standard of living and make an easier way of life here in the United States. This plan can also change the entire planet, by cloning the system around the world. I can also tell you with 100% certainty that there are many other books and thousands of pages written

---

50   "Smarter, Faster, Better" by Charles Duhigg 2016, Chapter 4 pages 114 to 124.

on the subjects of motivation, compensation, goal-setting and other aspects that have been used in the past to help companies work with their employees to create better products. Motivational programs and specific goal-setting programs have been used by major corporations and even our own military, throughout the last century. Feel free to do more research on the subject if you like. There is also a suggested reading list at the back of the book.

The nature of a technology-driven economy is to work in cooperation together versus a few individuals struggling in competition with one another. We should challenge the assumption that inventors across the world should compete against each other in secret for billions of dollars, and we can increase our odds of producing superior technology in any given industry anytime we introduce the concept of competition into that industry.

Alfie Kohn's 1992 text *No Contest: The Case Against Competition* takes a straightforward approach to debunking the assumption that competition makes us more productive. The text reveals that human beings assume that if people are not in some sort of competition, they cannot be successful and otherwise become malcontent losers, accomplishing absolutely nothing, over the course of their entire lives. Kohn's book goes on to cite 65 scientific studies that found cooperation promotes a higher level of achievement than competition. Cooperation also promoted a higher level of achievement than independent work, in 108 studies reviewed over a period from 1924 to 1980.[51] These types of beliefs have been programmed into people and passed down from generation to generation, through thousands of years of running an inefficient system that has produced disastrous results including slavery, wars, mass inequalities through currency, separate rights to technology and worst of all—destroying the imaginations of the mass population by driving horrible programming into the minds of young children that they cannot achieve their dreams unless they strive to compete against others, in a mass grab for cash, which will always be in scarce supply.

---

51   Alfie Kohn's book *No Contest The Case Against Competition*, 1992, pages 46-48.

So let's ask the question, "Does competition make us more productive?" I wrote this entire book without competing against anyone. Painters, sculptors, artists of all sorts, do not compete against one another. If the cells and biological systems within your body competed against each other, most likely you would live a very short life, if at all. The universe provides balance throughout its scalable structure even at the atomic level, with the intention that all parts are equally important. Personally, I have thrown out the idea that competition holds any benefit whatsoever to my life and removed it from my way of thinking. I'm sure if you start thinking about it, there are literally thousands of examples where people have created things without ever competing against one another.

We will require superior performance from our scientists, engineers and supporting branches in order to build superior technology; a system requiring anything less will not produce the results we require. Cooperation has been shown to produce better results than competition when a small group of people are working on a very complex problem; hence again the need to remove patents and the greed of shareholder interests and simply get to the bottom line—creating superior technology so that everyone can enjoy it.

Certainly, one could argue that any industry, such as energy, healthcare, transportation or the housing industry, that was required to solve very complex problems in order to meet the long-term survival needs of the planet would be served better by being transparent to the public. Potentially tens of millions of people throughout the world could be contributing ideas to creating new superior technology, through message boards, chats and social media, in cooperation with one another, to produce phenomenal results, in just a short period of time.

We have roughly 125 million people in our workforce in the United States, putting in billions of hours per year, with the majority of the population going nowhere but to their next paycheck. Personally, where do you see yourself in the next 30 to 40 years, if we continue on with the same system? If you are able to work over that entire time, would you say that you've lived a good life? I would say any person who worked continuously over 30 to 40 years in endless drudgery, lead no life at all! What I'm trying to get you to realize is that even if you're fully employed the rest of your life, there's really no point in continuing on with the system as it is, because it's not allowing you to live the life that you deserve to live. If you lose your job to artificial technology or just get laid off and can't find work anymore or become homeless, would you rather enact a system now that can potentially alleviate either scenario from happening?

Perhaps working as a means to an end would be the greatest motivational factor for any workforce I could imagine. Let's get everyone working together and focused on creating superior survival technology, rather than being separated through currency and continually being required to fight daily for our survival. Let's forever change the course of our destiny by creating a new system that will allow future generations the ability to achieve any dream they can imagine for themselves.

Forming a State Economic Committee

As some levels of our technology are advancing at an incredibly rapid rate, I think we need to ask ourselves why is it still necessary to have a proxy (an elected official) making our economic decisions for us? We been going along with this idea for over 240 years and accepted it as a fact of our lives as citizens of the United States. How, why and when exactly did the idea of using a proxy to make laws and economic decisions affecting our country start?

When the colonies were first founded, it took weeks in a horse and buggy just to get to the nation's capital, to cast your vote. So, based on the time constraints involved and the level of technology available to the average American, it might've been a good idea to allow a proxy vote for you because you could not be away from your homestead for a long period of time, people were concerned primarily with their own survival—harvesting and gathering enough food to last them through the winter. A short supply of firewood might cost you your life. You had to constantly tend to your survival needs and anticipate potential catastrophic events that might cause a shortage of your long-term food and supplies. A colonial-era citizen someone who did not complete an adequate amount of work and survival planning might end up in a very severe hardship situation, with no real access to healthcare nearby nor any advanced healthcare technology to help them. People of that era had simply very little time and resources to devote to the creation of laws in our country, and the majority of freedoms that people enjoyed were already written into law and accepted culturally through the Constitution, Declaration of Independence and other documents.

Another major reason why the people of the colonial era gave their innate rights and power to receive and enjoy technology over to proxies was simply because barely any type of advanced technology was available to them at that time. A pic, a shovel, a rifle, a pail and perhaps a covered wagon encompassed the extent of all the technology that most people had access to during the 1700s. Citizens got their water from self-dug wells, built a log cabin from the nearby trees, built a fireplace with stones and mortar for heat and had no electricity or running water. Colonial-era citizens could never envision enjoying the type of survival technology we do today, and if the founding fathers of this country could have anticipated the advancement of technology to the level it is today, they would've added extra provisions into the Constitution to make sure that the rights and powers to technology to survive on this planet rested with the citizens themselves rather than with the proxies they elected.

The past citizens of the United States mainly used proxies to deal with the creation of general laws on our behalf and to uphold the laws of the Constitution. People openly, willingly and voluntarily gave up their rights to vote directly and participate in the creation of laws in this country. These proxies were supposed to make fair and just laws that benefited society. During colonial times you could literally walk into the White House and schedule an appointment to meet with the president of the United States in person. Our concept of people directly communicating with our proxies has completely eroded over the last 240 years. We now have over 325 million citizens in this country: How can just a few people make fair and just laws that address the needs of 325 million people? If every senator had to talk to just 20% of their constituents per year, they simply would have no time to do anything else. We have a system of federal government today that is simply out of touch with the needs of the people and massively swayed by corporate lobbyists.

Furthermore we should ask, why do we now need a proxy to vote for us when technology has advanced to the point where proxies are no longer needed? We no longer need to travel by horseback to the nation's capital to write our vote on a piece of paper with an eagle feather dipped in ink and slip it through the slot of a sealed wooden box. We have the ability to read extensive bills that could potentially create laws right on our home computers. Printing presses and the United States postal service provide us with state and national voter ballots and booklets, in order to cast our votes for various propositions and candidates. The entire population is able to access public transportation to arrive at any given polling place in an incredibly short period of time and those in rural areas can easily vote by mail. Since technology has advanced itself further than any of our ancestors could have dreamed since the birth of our country, we no longer require proxies to vote for us on any given subject, and should therefore turn the voting power back over to the citizens of the United States, to whom it rightfully belongs! Please understand that, the voting power, in a democracy, always has and always will rest with the individual citizen. The right to vote on your survival has always been yours. If our ancestors unwittingly decided to make a bad decision and turn over their rightful voting power in regards to controlling technology that would affect the survival of future generations, to a proxy, that's not a mistake whose consequences we should have to keep enduring. Especially when it comes to someone voting for their own survival. Any citizen should have the right to make direct decisions on their own survival, and that includes decisions that affect the development and placement of advancing survival technology for the benefit of the general public.

Economies are best controlled locally, and it is my firm belief that all economies should be controlled directly by the citizens of their own state, with their own votes. This chapter will outline exactly how these goals can be accomplished and how we can turn the power to create laws regulating corporations back over to the general public. People should have direct control of their own survival and politics should be left to politicians. Our economic decisions should not be made by politicians—this is why we're in the mess we're in. I cannot stress this point enough: Politicians or any federal laws they make do not have the "innate" right to decide what technology the aggregate population should have access to, or the innate right to make policies that affect our overall standard of living. You should decide how you're going to survive, and no one else. By allowing proxy control over your survival, you are voluntarily giving up your innate rights to survival technology. In this current political system, the technology rights of all citizens of the United States are being openly and notoriously violated. Current federal laws allow greater access to technology for some citizens versus others and this is a clear violation, of the technology rights innately granted to you as a human being.

The second paragraph of the United States Declaration of Independence starts as follows: *We hold these truths to be self-evident, that all men are created equal, that they are endowed, by their Creator, with certain unalienable Rights, that among these are Life, Liberty and the Pursuit of Happiness.* I hope this book will begin a "technology rights movement" throughout the country—where people understand that their civil rights are being violated by the federal government and the individual states of the United States should use their power to fight against these exploitations.

We've seen how technology in certain industries is not moving forward, and we know the reasons specifically are a lack of information in the form of patents and government confiscations that sequester superior technology or potential superior technology, while at the same time incentivizing greed and allowing a small group of people to control a large group of people through currency. Reacting to this dilemma in the standard traditional

American way is simply not getting us anywhere. What I'm telling to you here specifically is:

1. Don't get angry about the way things are.

2. Don't protest in the streets.

3. Don't call into radio and television talk shows and complain.

4. And finally…don't ever expect your federal government to bring you any type of technology that is going to stop you from working 40 hours a week or stop the majority of our population from living paycheck to paycheck. Government officials are incentivized in every possible way to keep the status quo intact.

The federal government is the driver of the for-profit system. It makes the laws to keep the for-profit currency-based system in place, and specifically these laws are designed to prevent readily available access to superior technology by the general public. The federal government created and continues to enforce the Invention Secrecy Act of 1951, which openly and notoriously stops the evolution of technology in key areas in order to keep our overhead high and requires we use currency for 100% of all our goods and services. Why else would we take profits from the exploitation of people's lives in the form of publicly traded healthcare companies? The simple reason that we don't have government-run healthcare like other countries around the world is because government officials actually own a lot of healthcare stocks! Government officials can legally vote on the creation of new laws that would directly benefit their shareholdings. In other words, government officials can actually take our tax money and put it directly into companies that they own shares in, thus circumventing public money into their private pockets, and all of this is completely and totally legal. An article from State News by Sheila Kaplan in 2015 tells us that the entire Congress combined personally held $68 million of health-related stocks in their own personal portfolios in 2014.[52]

---

52   https://www.statnews.com/2015/12/01/congress-pharmaceutical-investment/

The owners of healthcare companies—the shareholders, who are also our elected officials—are allowed to take our money and put those funds into their own companies, to increase their wealth by voting on policies that directly affects the profitability of the companies they own shares in. Yet people in America still think that they are living in a democracy. The general population still believes that the government is making laws in the best interest of the public, which they have pledged to do. This is a complete lie, yet people ignore it every day or simply cannot understand the complex relationships between stock prices, government spending and the incentives created by allowing representatives of our state and federal governments to cast votes specifically with the intent to increase the value of their shareholdings.

Using government proxies to solve economic issues would not be a wise course of action under our current political system, because proxies are incentivized to vote in their own best interest, for the following reasons:

1. Government proxies make government laws and policies that affect companies and industries that they directly own stock in, causing a direct conflict of interest by using public money in order to further their own private interests. The proxy's vote can also be bribed, with the golden parachute waiting for them, at the end of their term by any corporation that would seek to sway their vote with a high-paying job or shares of stock in their company.

2. The goal of any elected official is to become reelected; so like the for-profit paradox, where any company's only goal is to create profit as a priority above and beyond anything else, the proxy's goal is to become reelected regardless of whether any bill or law voted on during their term benefits the general public. Reelection and attempting to better the position of the public over the course of an official's elected term are not mutually aligned goals.

3. Taxation keeps the government in power. The government would essentially lose all of its power or the majority of its power over its

citizens, if it lost its ability to create passive income from taxation. Passive income is income that is earned without work; an example would be receiving a dividend when you purchase a share of stock. The stock pays you an annual dividend yet you do no form of physical work to receive this source of income. No proxy will ever vote to dismantle the for-profit system, as taxes allow the government budgetary control over a massive amount of passive income, they receive without effort to spend as they wish. In short, if a proxy enacts policies to reduce overhead, which subsequently would cause a massive reduction in the level of tax income collected by the Internal Revenue Service, the federal government would lose its massive stranglehold over the population because they, like corporate America, would be on equal footing with the general public again. Both corporate America and the United States government rely on the population's willingness to work and be taxed, so that they can manipulate the entire population under a labor for cash survival system. Once survival technology reaches an incredibly low cost, all citizens become equal with each other, both rich and poor, and this equality extends to government officials as well, who will no longer be put on a pedestal to ensure that their constituents continue to keep their jobs in order to survive. In summary, if you remove the government's power to make the majority of economic decisions for the citizens of the country, people would become less reliant on the government and any of its actions, which most likely over the long term would be relegated to just dealing with civil issues -like handicapped parking. The government's role would become far less significant to the overall happiness and well-being of the people than it is today. Extremely low survival costs, throughout the world, would cause great difficulties for the United States military to recruit new people. New military candidates would be less likely to risk their lives in military service, as the income needed for survival by the average U.S. citizen would be far less and would outweigh the life-threatening risks of the job.

4. Government officials often don't take the time to read bills fully or review last-minute additions to their content before voting on them. So, the assurance of due diligence, that should go along with the idea of having a full-time elected official who has nothing more to do other than to basically take care of one job and make sure they vote correctly, is an assumption and not a vetted fact.

The more we become aware of the problems that we face and how our current democratic system incentivizes certain behaviors, the better we can understand how to create new laws that produce different results. Voting for a preselected corporate candidate, in a two-horse race, for critical political positions will never solve our problems either. The federal government has become a completely corrupt entity and is incapable of righting itself; in order to do so we will need to make changes to some current government laws and regulations that incentivized corruption in order to mitigate the problem. In the path to license our energy, healthcare, transportation and housing industries, we can be 100% certain that if government officials are shareholders in these companies, they will never vote for the demise of their own investments and retirement savings. Since we know this is a foregone conclusion, we don't need to bother with worrying about what the federal government is going to do or not do, in order to create our new economy. Wow what a relief! No more hoping that someone is going to come along and save us and get elected into office and then lie yet again and do absolutely nothing, like we've seen for the last four consecutive decades. To be honest, the people's interests have probably not been represented by federal government since the New Deal, under the Roosevelt administration, which began in 1933.

The way to break the power of the federal government—as a matter fact the only way left to break the power of the federal government—is to use the collusion power of the 50 states by having these states change their laws, to conflict directly with federal laws. If there is enough collusion power between enough states, the federal government will have no choice but to back down and change federal law as well allowing federal tax funds to be diverted towards developing technology in our four survival industries of critical importance.

In order to begin the process of state collusion, I would suggest that each state form its own economic committee. The laws and restrictions governing the formation and regulation of an economic committee and its members could be voted on by the general public, in one single well-versed state proposition. Any member serving on the economic committee would be so completely restricted by the laws governing their position that they would have absolutely no incentive whatsoever to make a decision that was not in the best interest of the general public. An economic committee member would be appointed to create laws that directly affect the economy of that state. Any state may appoint a department or entity in charge of enforcing the rules, prerequisites, restrictions and ethics of committee members. The economic committee would be governed under the following rules, prerequisites and restrictions:

- Each member of the economic committee may serve a term of no longer than four years and would be limited to two terms within their lifetime, for a total of eight years.

- Each economic committee member would have to swear a public oath to meet the following prerequisites and abide by any personal restrictions required in their particular state, in order to hold a seat on the committee, before they could be cleared by any particular state government to serve on that committee

- An economic committee member may not have served in a political office in any capacity during that particular candidate's lifetime. Those in power will only seek to keep the current system in place, ensuring that their retirement money is safe. We need action at this time and not career politicians who have little knowledge of economics, mathematics, new technologies and how they will impact our economy. Prerequisites for the position would include extensive knowledge of economics, banking, financial investments and currency, as they affect cycles of both consumer spending and credit, as well as manufacturing, production, and other services. A committee member should also have a basic background in software, hardware and computer technology, as well as a some basic understanding and conception of our most advanced cutting-edge technologies such as free energy, ColdFusion and the effects that implementing advanced superior technologies would have on our society, not only in regards to their impact on the currency-based system but safety, long-term durability and concerns for the public in general, if we were to implement new technologies of this type into our economy. Our politicians today are outdated people, who have no idea how technology actually works, how a packet travels across the internet or how to write a basic computer program. Their consciousness consists of thought patterns that are not relevant to today's technologically advanced society. The general philosophy of any economic committee member would be to have an extensive understanding of how to use currency as a means to an end to begin phasing it out of our economy and replacing it with highly advanced and superior automated technologies.

- An economic committee member would be subject to equity restrictions. Any person with any kind of morals and ethics would understand implicitly that it is a conflict of interest for any public official to hold stock, warrants or options, in any type of publicly traded company while they serve in office. A committee member and their spouse would be prohibited from holding stock, warrants or options, in any publicly or privately traded company in their personal possession or in the possession of any immediate family member, for their future safekeeping for later distribution, for the entire term they hold office, in addition to a cooling-off period of no less than 15 years, beginning the day after, their last day of elected term. If the economic committee member is elected for another four-year term, with the two consecutive terms totaling eight years, the 15-year cooling-off period begins, the day after the last day of their second consecutive elected term. If there is a period of time in between reelection, the 15-year cooling-off period applies to the time between terms, not to exceed 15 years, and would begin in its entirety again the day after their second term in office has ended. The holding of stocks, warrants or options, in any publicly traded company, during their time in office or during the cooling-off period would be considered an Economic Crime.

- An Economic Crime would be defined as committing a monetary fraud against over 100 or more citizens of the general public. An Economic Crime against the people would not allow for bail to be set in any amount prior to trial. The penalty for an Economic Crime would be 25 years to life in prison and a minimum fine of $1 million, if the accused person is found guilty.

- A committee member would be required to send their asset statements yearly to the appropriate state department assigned to regulating committee members for review not only during their time in office but during the "cooling-off" period. In order to serve on this committee, you must possess the utmost integrity.

- An economic committee member would be subject to income restrictions. All economic committee members would be subject to a maximum base salary of $200,000 per year during their time in office, which could not increase by any type of state or federal vote for at least a period of 10 years, and then would only be limited to voting on increases to income relative to the cost of living—which should be decreasing at that point due to a drop in overhead costs. An economic committee member would be limited to the salary paid a committee member at the time of taking office and would have a cap to their income of $200,000 per year – in addition to a cooling-off period of no less than 15 years, beginning the day after their last day of elected term. If the economic committee member is elected for a second, four-year term (two consecutive terms totaling eight years), the 15-year cooling-off period begins the day after the last day of their second consecutive elected term. If there is a period of time, in between reelection, the 15-year cooling-off period applies to the time between terms, not to exceed 15 years, and would begin in its entirety again the day after their second term in office has ended. An income of $200,000 per year would be calculated as the taxable income on an IRS 1040 form. If married filing jointly, a couple would be limited to $400,000 per year taxable income on an Internal Revenue Service form 1040. A committee member would be required to submit their consent to allow their yearly tax transcripts to be reviewed by the appropriate state department, assigned to regulating committee members. Exceeding the income limit in any given tax year would result in extreme fines and penalties and could potentially be considered an Economic Crime.

- The income restriction after a term in office closes the loophole for corporations to offer obscenely high-paying jobs as a reward to committee members who could potentially help create and vote in favor of propositions benefiting certain corporations during their time in office. If you allow people access to public funds, in order to manipulate them for their own benefits, through increased stock prices and executive positions waiting for them when they are done holding office, this is a direct form of theft from the American public. Public funds are diverted to private companies, and private companies in turn take the funds and pay them to politicians. This is the essence of our system today. Politicians are paying themselves with public funds, essentially stealing public money and giving it to themselves; this is without a doubt a major conflict of interest, and as long as we have this type of endless carousel going on in our government, we will never release any type of technology that will remove us from an endless stream of debt.

- An economic committee member would be required to pass a criminal background check and never have committed any type of fraud or crime involving theft or a federal felony. An economic committee member would go through a very intensive prescreening background check, to make sure that they had never committed any type of a federal felony or any type of fraud.

- An economic committee member would be required to take an oath to uphold the income and equity restrictions during their time in office and during the cooling-off period after their term or terms serving on the committee. The economic committee member would also be required to take an oath to serve the best interest of the general public and to make policies and laws that would allow the mass manufacture and distribution of new technologies to the general public in the simplest, most efficient and transparent manner.

- An economic committee member could not receive bribes, kickbacks or gifts of value in any amount, both during their time in office and during the 15-year cooling-off period. A committee member receiving a bribe or any type of inappropriate compensation would be prosecuted under the Economic Crime law. Any individual or group of individuals caught bribing or attempting to bribe a committee member would also be subject to prosecution under the Economic Crime law. Basically, what we're doing here is taking away all the incentives for corruption in order to make laws that are fair, just and serve the greater needs of the entire general public.

- An economic committee member would be required to provide their last 10 years of employment history and give their permission to the appropriate state governing department to review their credit report.

Any gross misuse of credit or falsification of employment would result in candidate ineligibility.

- Feel free to add your own rules, prerequisites or restrictions as you see fit. This system is all about a cooperative end-user input. These prerequisites and restrictions represent general guidelines and would be subject to each state's individual interpretation in the formation of its own economic committee.

An economic committee member would perform the following duties:

- Study models that simulate the effects that proposed changes in the current laws governing our energy, healthcare, housing and transportation industries have on the economy.

- Form recommendations to the general public, on the basis of these outcomes being the most prosperous and least damaging to the currency-based economy in the short run.

- Analyze numbers in each state's local GDP, looking at long-term effects on local communities in education, social development, good will and the long-term evolution of each person, in a given geographical area.

- Form and structure written state propositions. The economic committee would only make recommendations to be voted on through state proposition. The economic committee could never make a recommendation that could be voted on by a state general assembly or legislature, nor endorsed by it. This puts the power of the vote back into the people's hands when it comes to running their economy, and that's where it needs to stay.

The state economic committee would run autonomously of the existing state government, and the existing state legislature would not be allowed to cut funds from any of the direct and supporting functions and departments of the economic committee, for a period of at least 25 years from its initial formation.

Economic and math departments from public universities can be used to crunch numbers to show immediate and long-term effects that changing regulations would have on the currency-based economy and on the overall development of superior technology. Certainly, anyone wishing to get a postgraduate degree in economics or business would be willing to crunch numbers and look at the effects that these specific proposals and propositions licensing our overhand industries would have on our economy, both in the short and long run, including any potential emotional and psychological effects that these proposed propositions could have if enacted into law. We have a plethora of highly intelligent people with access to very advanced computer systems, who can build models and study these problems thoroughly before they are proposed to the public. Universities or other higher education facilities are fantastic resources to provide each state's economic committee with the extensive data they will need in order to craft the most beneficial licensing propositions possible.

A majority vote would be required by the committee in order for any proposition to be voted on in a statewide election. The economic committee would only make recommendations to be voted on through state proposition; it's intended to be its own separate entity and act as a guide for the general public, and is not intended to be a part of politics or controlled in any way by any federal, state or local government, nor should it be influenced by the threat of increasing or decreasing funds to its department in order to sway its recommendations to the general public.

The economic committee would consist of 12 members. In order for an endorsement to a proposition to be given by the economic committee, 8 of the 12 members would need to vote yes to allow any proposition to be voted on by the general public.

Based on the income and equity restrictions applied, let's try to understand the potential nature of behavior of each committee member and the type of decision-making and solutions we can expect to receive as a result of these restrictions. Potentially the economic committee could sway the public by giving an endorsement to a proposition that could potentially benefit a large corporation. Let's also consider the fact that receiving any stock from any person or company as part of compensation for attempting to sway the public's vote would not be an option, due to equity restrictions for a period of up to 19 years or even decades longer, depending on the beginning and ending of a committee member's second term. A committee member would be limited to the amount of gross income they could earn from any resource whatsoever, and any company potentially promising a committee member a $4 million per year cushy job after they leave office, in exchange for their vote, is unlikely. I'm not sure why it would be worth the effort to take bribes or do something that could potentially put a committee member in jail for a period of 25 years to life and drain their entire assets trying to make restitution, when a designated department in every state would be auditing each committee member yearly to make sure they have not received any payoffs, kickbacks or bribes from corporations both during their time in office and during the cooling-off period. On the other side of the coin, any of the entities from the bribing corporation or company would also be prosecuted equally under an Economic Crime bill. Our results of sanctions on officials represent real policymaking benefits to the general public, unlike today's structure where without sanctions public officials funnel public money back into their own pockets. I believe a type of system that enacts heavy penalties, restricting committee members from deviating their decision-making towards their own benefit, would successfully introduce propositions into states that would distribute technology in a clear and transparent manner as efficiently as possible. Our goal is about getting technology to people as fast as we can, and getting off the currency merry-go-round while at the same time ensuring that we possess superior technology to sufficiently drop our overhead, prior to reducing incomes.

The federal government today essentially acts as both the shareholder and Board of Directors, controlling its workers or citizens of the United

States. Earlier in this chapter we've seen that federal government, between the House and Senate, owned at one point in time, an estimated $68 million worth of healthcare stocks alone. The shareholders of a company are not going to give up their shares of stock or any of their long-term investments for the benefit of the people; this is like asking an American slave owner prior to the Emancipation Proclamation to simply free their slaves, because all people are created equal. As long as slave owners had the law on their side, they were going to do everything in their power to make sure the laws enforcing slavery were never changed. If the laws regarding the introduction of new technologies into our country had been changed in 1776 as part of our Constitution to state that any person inventing new technology was mandated to produce and distribute it at the lowest cost possible, our country and the mental state of its people would be in a far different position than it is today. Clearly with a population increase in the next 100 years estimated at 50% greater than it is now, and artificial intelligence moving at a pace that may eliminate a large portion of human labor for cash from our economy in the next few decades, we need to take preemptive action now to apply technology to our overhead so that everyone can benefit and does not have to endure a "period of waiting" in a crisis, waiting for the proper survival technology to be available to everyone. The proper survival technology needs to be available to everyone at the lowest possible cost, as soon as possible in order for the general population to avoid the misfortunes of a severe economic depression, which is sure to come if action is not taken to prevent it.

Now that we fully understand the laws and regulations needed to run an economic committee properly, let's look at some state propositions, in order of priority, that the economic committee should be presenting to the public.

1. An Economic Crime Proposition. The first proposition the economic committee should put forth for vote to the general public of their state should be a proposition to pass an Economic Crime bill. As we discussed previously in this chapter, an Economic Crime is a crime of

fraud committed against 100 or more people, for profit or gain. The penalty for an Economic Crime would be 25 years to life in federal prison, with no possibility of parole during the sentence. The fine for committing an Economic Crime would be a minimum of $1 million and could include making full restitution to 100% for all the victims who have had for-profit fraud committed against them. In order to make full restitution, this could mean that the entire assets of anyone found guilty of an Economic Crime could be liquidated in order to make full restitution to the victims. I believe these assets should also include any offshore bank accounts that the perpetrator held. It may be difficult to retrieve such funds from offshore bank accounts. I believe, however, that every attempt should be made over an extended period of years to collect these funds from foreign bank accounts if available, to make full restitution to the victims of an Economic Crime. Any individual or group of individuals found guilty of bribing or attempting to provide any type of incentives to an economic committee member, in order to sway their vote for endorsement of a proposition or influence the creation of any state proposition, would also be guilty of an Economic Crime. I've outlined the basics of this proposition; however, the actual proposition, put forth the vote and endorsed by the economic committee would be far more extensive, in order to close any additional loopholes and exploitations that lobbyists and corporate representatives might take advantage of in order to benefit themselves.

2. A proposition authorizing terms for communication with the State Economic Committee and the general public.

An interactive cell phone application should be created. Alternative ways to contact the economic committee would be website correspondence, telephone or in-person appointments to meet with a committee member directly or a customer service representative who would directly report to a committee member.

No limits would be given to the number of times a single individual could correspond with the economic committee. In other words, no one would be granted more or less time with the economic committee. It would also be illegal for an individual, group or corporation to hire a designated representative to correspond with the economic committee. Anyone who has ever been employed as a corporate lobbyist would be required to register and disclose this information with the department supervising the committee. It would be illegal and considered an Economic Crime to receive any type of compensation from a corporation or group of people, to speak with an economic committee member, or correspond with the department, in any manner. It would also be an Economic Crime in any state to hire a consultant of any type to correspond, advise or attempt to influence the economic committee. The intention is for corporate lobbying to become obsolete under this new system. Good luck in trying to sway the vote against the people in the first place, when a committee member can't be bribed or bought off with golden parachutes, because of the income and equity restrictions that have been imposed on them as a result of holding the office.

3. A proposition to regulate the energy industry under licensing laws.

The third task of the economic committee would be to study the current energy industry, the local economy of the state and the effects of regulation under the new restrictions and licensing imposed on energy companies. The economic committee would study both the long- and short-term effects on their state's economy from the entire industry becoming nonprofit, non-publicly traded and without the option to hold patents. We should use our local universities and colleges who have professors and graduate students, as well as any private economists and input from local counties and communities, in order to create the best economic models possible. Various economic models, both mathematical and theoretical, will simulate different potential scenarios and outcomes based on the enactment of a newly licensed energy industry. We should also incorporate college professors, businessmen and community leaders as a resource, for their advice and wisdom in helping the economic committee draft this proposition. Various economic models would look at the aspects that this type of legal change would have on the following:

A. The emotional effects to humans and the psychological outlook on their lives, their life purpose and the way they interact with their fellow human beings. Humans that have a bad psychological outlook on life generally are prone to not taking part in the workforce or working towards a more prosperous world. You can certainly read books on the subject, but many recessions are simply the result of a bad outlook on life due to a series of tragic financial events, such as past stock market or real estate crashes that caused a perpetual sense of pessimism toward money circulation and prosperity in an economy. I believe the greatest psychological barrier to overcome would be to get the citizens of any particular state to understand how not using currency, or how to reduce their dependency on it, will affect them in the long run and in the short run and how it will change their current identity as a human relegated to a life of current drudgery to a free person in their sovereign power. United States citizens are going to have to embrace a new identity that derives self-worth from helping others and enjoying a higher state of abundance through technology that they simply have never have had before and perhaps cannot even comprehend. Essentially, people will become tourists on the planet and at some point, their entire life goals and creative manifestation will rest more on helping and fostering relationships rather than the constant creation of currency.

B. The immediate effects and long-term effects on the federal currency and how these actions would cause inflation or deflation of the prices, for all goods and services, created locally within the state as well as those imported.

C. The immediate effects on the stock market as it would relate to publicly traded companies that would not be affected through licensing regulation. Stocks trade fundamentally on what is called "the perfect information theory." This theory simply means that any information that is brought forth by any type of report, news, act of war or terrorism, and so on—whether this information is good or bad—is priced immediately into all stocks in the market, and this is the reason for the large amount of volatility in stock markets as new information both good and bad is provided daily to traders and traders' interns, who speculate constantly based on new information. We should anticipate that if an economic committee is formed with a specific purpose to regulate our overhead industries that are the major drivers of the financial markets, the changes to laws and regulations affecting these companies including a buyout of existing shareholders would have a huge negative effect on the idea that owning stocks is actually a good idea at all. I would expect that if one licensing proposition alone were enacted into law in any given state, regulating just one industry, there would be extreme negative effects on the stock market, and it could easily lose 50% of its value in a short period of time. Even though the plan does not call for the removal of shareholders from any industries other than our four outlined overhead industries, setting a new type of precedent to the way technology is created without a mass reliance on currency would certainly cause a panic in the financial markets and we should expect this panic to have a mass negative effect on all types of venture capital funding and the ability for companies in any industry to raise startup money. Enacting licensing regulations may also cause knee-jerk reactions by executives of companies in all industries of America, in order to try to get their stock prices back up, if their stock price perhaps falls artificially low. Regulating just one industry—energy, for example—could result in mass layoffs and extremely high unemployment in an attempt to reduce overhead by executives to show the existing shareholders that their company is committed to long-term profits and propping the price of their stock back up. Another side effect might be the cutting of wages across the board by executives, to accomplish the same goal. Therefore, it is of the utmost importance that we simulate these types of scenarios in order to understand the best way to bring about the order, regulation and timing of our energy, healthcare, transportation and housing industries under licensing.

D. The immediate effects that would be felt by the credit markets. If financial analysts understand that portable energy will change where people are able to live, this action will have a mass effect on credit defaults. If a free-energy device or even an extremely efficient solar panel were to be produced and distributed to the public, over a period of 10 to 15 years' time you would see a mass migration of people out of high-cost areas such as major metropolitan cities to local areas where real estate lot costs and consequently that entire area's cost of living was much cheaper. This could result in mass defaults of real-estate loans because properties in major metropolitan cities would not be desirable anymore, due to their high cost and extremely high level of long-term debt servicing requirements. When we arrive at a point in the future where any American has the ability to purchase superior technology at a fraction of the cost, the old inferior technology essentially becomes worthless. The greatest driver of mortgage lending is equity; in other words, the higher the property value relative to the loan on it, the more secure the lender perceives their collateral to be in the event that they have to foreclose on it. So, the higher real-estate prices are in general, the more apt all creditors are to lend on these properties and loosen their credit qualifications. When the price of homes drops, equity drops and the programs that allow for cash to be taken out of homes becomes much harder to qualify for; this credit tightening further results in reduced economic expansion as fewer people borrow, less spending happens; and we know that one person's spending becomes another person's income, so this has a domino effect on the economy. Real-estate lenders fear defaults on their existing collateral and any new loans they might make, when job losses become more prevalent during economic downturns. In response to this domino effect, all lenders tighten their credit standards in order to make sure that they are originating solid home loans, personal loans and new credit cards that will perform in the future (receive all principal and interest back over the term of the loan). Home equity lines of credit are usually the first credit instruments to be canceled by creditors when real-estate prices drop. A tightening in the credit markets or a lack of available credit to other industries, as well as the general public, could definitely cause a major recession to the current economy.

E. The effect this regulation would have on consumer confidence. When currency is not flowing through an economy as it should, that economy is definitely going to be in a recession. If the credit markets tighten, this generally has a negative effect on the economy, because it becomes difficult to finance any high-ticket purchases, such as automobiles, without extremely solid credit qualifications, which a majority of people don't have. Please remember that the system basically runs on the ability of the average person to easily have access to credit in order to repurchase inferior technology; and if lenders tighten credit standards, you'll see an immediate negative effect on consumer confidence and the ability for all Americans to purchase any type of goods and services. The most dangerous threat to the life force of any economy is lack of consumer confidence. If consumers aren't confident in the likelihood that they can continue to purchase goods and services now or in the future, they will cut back spending on both expensive and inexpensive items and tend to hold their money in savings, to ensure they can meet their future survival needs mainly out of fear of being unable to pay for them in the future. The holdback of these purchases causes an immediate lack of sales revenue for most companies across the board, in any given state or country. When sales revenues drop, employee layoffs are soon to follow. When consumers hear about employee layoffs, their consumer confidence drops even more and a cycle of reduced consumer confidence and spending continues to spiral. Newly laid-off employees will be looking for jobs and collecting unemployment. Companies might be incredibly reluctant to hire people because they feel that over the long run, machines may be replacing human labor and reducing the 40-hour work week and thus reducing all incomes permanently across the United States, potentially resulting in less money to purchase future goods and services. A completely structured and viable economic committee, looking to study and implement a licensing system into the energy and healthcare industries alone, would send a clear signal to the entire nation that new economic laws are going to precipitate gradually reducing incomes by the general public, with a higher standard of living. This type of philosophy might also bolster consumer confidence greatly. Scenarios like those I've just described are the reasons why implementing a licensing system, needs to be studied, and forecasted very carefully before action is taken.

I probably could write an entire book on how a just a few pieces of superior technology mass distributed into our economy alone could destroy the entire economy or put it into a very deep recession in the short run. The purpose of this text is to raise awareness that technology destroys currency, and we need currency right now in order to live comfortable and abundant lives. But without the technology purchased by currency we can't live comfortable and abundant lives. Technology is the only force allowing our planet of seven billion humans to survive in some level of comfort today. If not for the great strides made in agribusiness to provide our population with a massively increased supply of food over the last 50 years, we would have had suffered massive food shortages and the majority of the population might have died. Our advancements in agribusiness allowed our supply of food to keep up with skyrocketing demand as the population of our planet exploded from 2 billion people, to roughly 7 billion, in the last 60 years. It's technology that saved us from starving, and its technology that's going to save us again from service in perpetuity or what we call the 40-hour work week. We have to be very careful about what we do, how we enact these propositions and what their effects will be on the economy. Without careful preparation and anticipation of existing market forces and the population's perceptions, we could wind up in a state where this already enacted regulation is somehow repealed. I fully expect it would take the economic committee at least one or more likely two years of study or longer, before we could bring the first proposition regulating the energy industry to a vote. I can't stress enough that we need to implement a licensing system in a tiered process, only regulating one industry at a time and only after years of preparation.

4. A proposition to regulate the healthcare industry under licensing laws.

The fourth major task of the economic committee would be to study the current healthcare industry, the local economy of the state and the effects that a newly licensed healthcare industry would have in the short and long term on that state's economy. Various economic models would look at the impacts this type of legal change would have on the following:

A. The emotional effects to humans and their psychological outlook on their lives.

B. The immediate effects and long-term effects on the federal currency and how these actions would cause inflation or deflation of prices for all goods and services.

C. The immediate effects on the stock market and investments.

D. The immediate effects related to the credit markets.

5. A proposition to require that portable sources of water be implemented as part of the building process of all future homes and potentially be required to be installed in current dwellings.

Atmospheric water generators have already solved the problem of pulling water from the air, but we lack financing from our credit systems and the regulations to require this product to be mass produced in order to exponentially lower the cost of this technology. We also need to possibly look at developing new sources of portable water technology and a proposition to fund these endeavors. The following concerns should be presented to each state's economic committee:

A. Hooking up a lot to a local water utility company requires massive utility connection costs and limits us as a population to a small number of areas where we can build homes. As we've read in the previous text, we know that requiring any home to be hooked up to any type of centralized utility in any location limits the availability of lots that builders can sell to the general public, and this action causes the scarcity of homes and never-ending price increases.

B. Efforts need to be made in the development of portable water technology, through some type of alchemy, extracting water from the air or by other means. A proposition to develop these types of technologies should be put forth and a source of funding should be discussed in depth, since most likely this funding will need to come from state-issued bonds, grants, crowdfunding or another source, since there is basically no market and very little interest by the private sector to purchase this type of technology today.

C. Local and public water utilities do not need to be regulated at this time in my opinion; however, any local city, county or state should be wary of the fact that any privatized business interests will only seek to exploit the public and the committee should definitely take measures to ensure that private interests do not control the state's water supply.

6. Election law and voter reform

Our economic committee needs to do some basic cleanup to our election laws to make issues, especially propositions easier to understand and more transparent to the general public. Basically, our current system today is driven mainly by special-interest groups that are just buying elections or buying propositions – on the state level, through overwhelming advertising, that has no factual evidence to illustrate how a particular law if passed, in a particular state would affect its economy. These propositions have not been tested or scientifically and mathematically studied to understand how they will be affecting: financial markets, currency itself and eventually how they will affect the number of hours worked per year or the incomes and the spending habits of consumers. All the general public hears are some soundbites about how voting yes on a certain proposition will help the people of their state and is steered in a general direction towards making a misinformed decision, based on a small snippet of information. This is not the way we want to run our economy. We want the general public fully informed and understanding in depth how laws and propositions affect our society, our happiness and well-being and the long-term survivability of future generations. Let's look at a few issues that will require some slight changes:

A. Changing the length of time to vote in an election in a particular state. The allotted time to vote for all annual elections should be at least one week, if not longer. In 1776 it might have been a good idea to have a one-day election when you had 2.5 million people in the United States and nothing better to do but watch the paint dry all year for entertainment, but it's quite a bit harder to get 320 million people on the same page all in one day. It is simply ridiculous to expect people who may be incapacitated on one particular day due to illness or scheduling issues to forgo their right to vote. A single-day voting policy basically caters to wealthier people who would not normally see an interruption to their income by taking time off to vote, as their work schedules and company paid time-off policies are very liberal. Contrast that to impoverished workers who might have two weeks paid time off or less, which is most likely used up taking care of their sick children at home or for other practical appointments, like dental work— scheduling conflicts create difficulties for the average working person to actually make it to the polls to vote within a one-day period, because they are constantly having to attend to creating currency in order to meet their survival needs. I personally have voted by mail and I suggest this option as a more efficient way for people to vote; perhaps technology should be developed to vote online and I expect it will one day; some type of authenticity certificate may be required for each individual to ensure voter fraud does not take place, which could easily be developed. Whether we develop online voting technology or not, we should give ample time for all people of each state to go to the polls, and vote and one full week of time would surely help.

B. Changing the laws for television advertising of propositions and for state and federal office candidates. Television advertising would be limited to one designated cable, satellite or over-the-air channel that would air advertisements only regarding political propositions and candidate endorsements. Any television station broadcasting this information would be required to make their studios available completely free of charge to those interested parties who would like to place advertising in regards to a particular proposition, even if it was just an informational guide for the public. Advertisements would be limited to a maximum of two minutes. After each advertisement regarding a particular proposition or candidate endorsement, equal airtime would need to be given to the opposing viewpoint. This would eliminate government offices and propositions from being purchased through mass advertising expenses. Today's candidates, propositions and all laws made in our country are massively influenced by currency, and I see no reason to involve private advertisers in any of our elections, as they simply leave people with opposing viewpoints out in the cold due to their lack of currency to purchase an opposing viewpoint.

Radio advertising would be limited to one particular station, where again the same airtime rules would apply as to television advertising. Again, we don't want to open the door to our elections being bought.

Funds for television and radio studio time could be paid for by the state, through some of the popular funding methods I mentioned earlier or even a specified tax, to ensure a fair and just election system. Money to fund this endeavor could even be raised through crowdfunding as long as it went into a general fund rather than to a specific point of view. Funds for the election of candidates and propositions should be put into a general fund that should fund advertising for both sides of an issue or all of the candidates running for a particular office, rather than funding just one particular person or point of view. It might be interesting to speculate on the fact that if your candidate or your proposition is so good, then you shouldn't have to worry about the fact that your donation—which might fund both a favorable view and opposing view—would stop your candidate from becoming elected or your proposition from becoming law.

Printed advertising would be required to represent both sides of a proposition issue or all candidates involved for particular office, within an immediate area of newsprint such as requiring that print advertising be located and limited to a particular section or page of a newspaper, magazine or other newsprint.

Important note. Internet advertising could be limited to an online website run by each state that equally represents all candidates for office and both the affirmative and opposing views of each proposition in a similar format to television and radio advertising. Regulation beyond that point would not apply to the internet at this time. It is simply too difficult, if not impossible, to try to regulate the internet in this manner, but it would certainly help the general public, at least in regards to television, radio and print advertising, to at least have both sides of an issue presented to them on equal terms, so that they can make the most informed decision. Perhaps people would return to television, radio and newsprint, if these sources of information could be trusted more. Today, based on the current laws allowing elections to be bought, more people are turning to the internet for their source of truthful information on propositions and candidates in elections. I would expect people to still go to the websites of their choice and ignore issues that they feel are not relevant to them. We cannot attempt to influence free will. If people want to bury their heads in the sand or maintain an immovable position on a certain issue, they are going to do it regardless of how much the other side attempts to reach out to them and reason with them. We should realize in order to move forward, we do have to accept that people come from all walks of life and are going to vote the way they are going to vote, regardless of the information that is presented to them, however intelligent and sensible it may be presented. We should understand implicitly that we cannot fix human perceptions and programming on certain subjects; it would be better to focus on the few subjects that would most likely affect the greatest change in our daily lives and our economy.

Candidates running for governor, federal senator, state senate or assembly members or any state elected position would be governed by these laws. Election reforms could even be extended to local positions like County Sheriff or Treasurer. It would be the responsibility of each person voting on any state proposition to be thoroughly informed about the pros and cons of that legislation affecting their state. Each resident must take personal responsibility to inform themselves about each proposition and take care to vote wisely. The economic committee's purpose would be to provide that information in a logical, summarized and transparent manner, for each proposition.

We already have election booklets that are quite extensive, and I would suggest that they be distributed to the public or available for download no less than 60 days prior to the start of any election. Every citizen should take time to read them thoroughly, to understand what they're voting on; your local bathroom is a great place to start! The bottom line is that unless the average citizen is willing to take personal responsibility for their survival rather than deferring it to others as they are now, they can expect the same results and expect to remain in the same economic situation they are in today.

7. Endorsement required by the economic committee for any proposition to be voted on by any state. It would be the responsibility of the economic committee to review any proposition, that would come forth before the voting public, whether the committee created any particular proposition or not. Any proposition could still be voted on by the general public, exactly as the law specifies today, in any given state. The economic committee would be required to "endorse" or "not endorse" any particular proposition. Language would need to be used in all campaign ads on television, radio or newsprint stating clearly that the economic committee was endorsing, or was "not" endorsing, any particular state legislation or proposition, much the same way the annual percentage rate (APR) has to be specified in any ad

for a home loan under federal the Truth in Lending Act. The general public would have the benefit of the economic committee's expertise in reviewing and evaluating a proposition that might be created by and represented by a special interest group for their own benefit, rather than the needs of the general public. We should reasonably expect special interest groups to fight back, by creating their own propositions in order to counter, almost any of the propositions listed in this chapter because it would reduce their power and income, by requiring an endorsement of the economic committee on all propositions slated for public vote, special interest groups would be deterred from swaying the general public toward voting for a proposition that would not benefit them due to lack of information or influence through overwhelming advertising.

Endorsement for any proposition that was not created by the economic committee would require 8 of 12 "yes" votes, after an extensive review, by all members of the economic committee. The economic committee should be presented a fully drafted proposition and given 6 months' time to fully review it prior to voting "for" or "against" an endorsement. So, the committee would have sufficient time to explain its complexities to the general public. We should try and put as many safeguards in place as possible, and clearly, requiring an endorsement by a state economic committee would help the general public, from being swayed to vote on scams that simply would not benefit their best interests. The public would be free to vote as it chooses whether the endorsement by the economic committee was given or not. People still have to be given the right to choose even if sometimes they're going to make the wrong choice. We have to give people a free choice and free will as to how they want their economy and their government to operate. No matter how tightly you make the rules, there is always an element of darkness and deception that can creep into any situation and lead people astray; it's important to recognize this so our society can move toward in a more transparent and truthful election system.

Let's take a step forward in time, now that the economic committee has been formed, election laws have been properly changed and a few years have gone by to study the issues at hand regarding energy and healthcare. Now it's time to bring these propositions to a public vote. Our TV, radio and print advertising is all set up to do this, in a fair and coherent manner so that the public can understand what they're voting on, but single states still face the problem of being left out in the cold, if other states do not adopt the same licensing laws governing the same industries at the same time. I would call any state that affirmatively passes an open-sourced energy or healthcare proposition in their state a "courage state." These "courage states" could be subject to some massive economic declines if energy companies simply decide to pull out of these states, based on regulations that might have been passed against their "for-profit" agenda. Energy and healthcare companies might decide to move their business operations to other states that have not yet passed such regulation. If states start to adapt new policies regarding energy and healthcare, we should expect a lot of corporate posturing and manipulating of the law in any way for these organizations to save their own skins. After all, we are calling for the death of stocks and the general wealth of these companies, not to mention the long-term incomes of a lot of incredibly overpaid executives, who will fight to the death to keep their incomes high. I think it would be important to understand and to realize that collusion power would be required between the states to pass this legislation either simultaneously or from a majority of states in a connected geographical area, in order to force companies within the energy and healthcare industries to comply. I firmly believe in the collusion power of the states, and it is imperative that neighboring states also adopt similar legislation at the same time. If approximately 25 states were to simultaneously pass licensing laws on both the energy and healthcare industries, these two industries would have no choice but to convert their entire business operations in all 50 states to comply with the new licensing laws enforced by, the initial 25 "courage states." Eventually I would expect all other states to adopt licensing policies as well, and eventually licensing for both these industries might be enforced at the federal level as well as the state level.

Two of the biggest problems of initially getting energy and healthcare propositions to pass in multiple states would be the immediate conflict with federal patent law and that shareholders would be taking massive losses on their investments in these companies. Citizens of any state should expect opposition to these propositions being passed into law, as they are going to directly affect the distribution of power in any given state where licensing laws are enacted. Corporations may sue "courage states" and try to appeal these propositions in court, as federal patent law regarding all energy and healthcare patents would no longer be enforceable in a "courage state." We've already seen same-sex marriage enacted at the federal level through collusion pressure from the states, and this process is also happening with current regulations regarding marijuana. Eleven states have legalized marijuana for recreational use, not for any type of medical purposes but for recreational use only; and 33 states have legalized the use of medical marijuana. All of these states are directly in defiance of federal law and prior state laws that have sent people to prison for decades just for having marijuana in their possession. This act is so defiant to federal law that it is basically the equivalent to committing an open act of war against the federal government, and the federal government is "not" invading these states to force each state to comply with federal law. Most likely the reason for this lack of federal invasion is that there is absolutely no way the federal government can overturn an existing state law like legalizing marijuana, back to its original illegal position, since the citizens of that particular state recognize the benefits of making marijuana legal versus keeping it illegal. Simply put, once you change the consciousness or mindset of the people of a given area, it is almost impossible to reverse this type of mental programming, on an aggregate level. The federal government is very aware that once people get a taste for freedom and are able to make their own laws on a local level, regarding any subject, the prior federal laws can no longer be enforced upon that particular group of people. When this type of consciousness shift takes place, it will likely be impossible for the people of a given state to go back to their old way of thinking. I can tell you with great certainty that the federal government is very aware of the fact that a change in consciousness can change our material reality. The federal government does not want people to change their habits and start new ways of thinking and they specifically do not want people formulating laws that would distribute technology equally to citizens throughout any given state, as they are quite well aware that it would destroy the existing currency system as well as the existing hierarchy of power in the United States. Please remember that the United States has always been a "separate rights through currency" country, and will continue to be so until we move out of the currency-based system itself and into a technology-based society where the same level of technology is freely distributed at a very low cost to all citizens equally.

Let's not forget American history, and how throughout its course, state laws have conflicted with federal laws and one state's laws have conflicted with another state's laws. The American public has not always agreed with one another throughout the course of American history. At one point they were states in America that were designated as "free" states and other states that were designated as "slave" states. There was quite a contrast between one state's law, which allowed for the constant bondage and slavery of other humans in order to serve the self-interests of slave owners, while other states made laws that strictly forbid it. Civil rights became another large issue in the 1960s that divided the idealism of Americans. I believe the technology rights movement will become the next form of civil rights activism in this country, once people understand how they are being exploited and manipulated to a life of never-ending service through currency and patents.

Corporations may sue "courage states" and try to appeal these passed state propositions, in federal court. In order to win a court case, these corporations would have to show why they are specifically "aggrieved" by the new enforcement of licensing laws in their industry. So let's ask the question: "How are these companies and corporations going to show a grievance being committed against them or some sort of emotional pain and suffering as a result of these new rule changes to their industry?"

I think it would be difficult to show any vetted studies that making more than $75,000 a year would cause any human direct emotional pain and suffering. Executives would not be able to make a case for a grievance from this perspective, based on the host of studies showing the amount of annual income a human being needs in order to be happy or live a useful and purposeful life. Most likely based on the level of compensation and bonus plan that they are expected to receive under the new regulation, they would be making at least $75,000 a year, so a loss of income would be difficult to prove as a grievance. Furthermore, if the goal of the industry was to reduce the price of all goods and services by reducing overhead costs in the long run, that $75,000 a year may trend down to a $35,000 a year figure over the next decade or so, making the case for permanent emotional pain and suffering from loss of future income even more difficult to argue in court. Let's look at it from the viewpoint of the 1%, who have the money to fund extensive legal action against new types of laws. If a billionaire is left with a small income of perhaps even $250,000 a year or less, and still has billions of dollars in in savings in the bank, how do they prove emotional pain and suffering from loss of future income as a result of licensing regulation? It would be extremely problematic, if not impossible, for them to prove an emotional loss using some sort of expert testimony in court.

I think the focal point of any existing energy or healthcare company's argument against licensing would be that new licensing laws might affect a massive amount of jobs in their industry, causing unemployment and loss of future incomes for their employees. The real truth to that point from the opposite perspective is that none of these companies are guaranteeing these jobs to their employees anyway! These are private-sector jobs and can be replaced by automation or outsourced to an overseas labor force at any time. So I'm not sure where the argument of saving jobs would specifically be able to gain any type of leverage here.

Another argument might be that allowing a small group of companies to keep their intellectual property rights to technology in force, actually benefits the public. How these companies will be able to show that by keeping their patents, they can evolve technology over time, faster than at its present pace, versus developing technology through a cooperative and transparent manner would also be extremely difficult to argue against. I have no idea how, based on the for-profit paradox and other major limitations to the system, already outlined in this text, that these arguments could be conceded in a courtroom. I'm not sure how any of these companies could make a reasonable argument that by continuing to keep existing federal patent laws in place, which directly retard the evolution of technology in this country and allow companies to purchase and shelve new technologies that could reduce our 40-hour work week, advances our society and benefits the general public. Corporate America will simply not be able to prove in any type of civil case that they can evolve their technology faster or to a higher level through secrecy and competition then they could through open sourcing, and thus not be able to overturn state law because they simply cannot prove that overturning the law would be of benefit to the general public.

Let's move on to another concern that we might need to address in order for a licensing proposition to become law: Are people smart enough to vote for themselves? That is a question only you can answer. It is my personal belief that through proper guidance by an honest and fair economic committee that is heavily regulated to a point where there are almost no incentives for that committee to deceive the general public on any economic issue, that any person should be able to make an informed and correct choice beneficial to themselves. If the general public keeps deferring its power to a small group of people to make their economic decisions for them under the current system, where private as well as public entities are heavily incentivized to make laws that serve their own interests, our economy will certainly continue on its present course. The general public under the current system should not reasonably expect to receive any type of superior technology to begin freeing themselves from an endless state of drudgery in order to survive, unless it takes serious personal responsibility to ensure these new laws become a reality.

Let's explore the assumption that members of the House and Senate do an incredibly diligent job of understanding the pros and cons of any bill that comes before them, before voting on it—because this is the type of diligence the general public expects from a full-time employee being paid an exorbitant salary. Is this statement really true? When we examine and scrutinize this assumption, we find it is, like a lot of other assumptions we have explored in this text, to be false. A 2018 article from Rob Elving on NPR.org tells us that Congress repeatedly votes on bills without reading and understanding them fully, and often times other legislation is added into a bill at the last minute, that politicians are not fully aware of prior to casting their vote.[53]

If these bills are thousands of pages long in some cases, we should reasonably expect that no one can read them and understand them fully before voting on them. So why should we expect different results if a full-time paid government proxy voted on a bill, they did not read versus any United States citizen who voted on a bill they did not read? This is one of the specific reasons that each state needs to have its own economic committee to craft and review propositions before they become available for vote. An economic committee member is required to have a specific background in economics, technology and other pertinent areas relative to drafting the laws affecting the economy and would be required to use extensive due diligence before drafting propositions to be voted on by the general public. Furthermore, an economic committee member is not incentivized to vote for short-term fixes, in order to be reelected or sway their vote, through corporate bribes of stock or income after they leave office. The proxy you elect is not required to meet such prerequisites. Since proxies represent the votes of potentially millions of people, and so much money can be spent as a result of the passing of one

53   https://www.npr.org/2018/03/26/596921441/is-this-any-way-to-drive-an-omnibus-10-questions-about-what-just-happened

bill, they become pressured into quick decisions, without fully processing that bill and all of its contents. The current system fails us by not doing its due diligence. The primary motive here is greed. The primary goal of any proxy is to become reelected, so we should expect that if additional debt is issued or our long-term future is sacrificed, in order to produce short-term fixes, all government proxies are incentivized to vote for bills that are the most likely to guarantee their reelection and are not in the interests of the general public. I believe anyone with the right information can make an intelligent decision, and anyone who is directly affected by a potential law should have the innate right to vote for or against it, especially when a piece of potential legislation directly affects the survival of that person. The general public has been deferring its power for over 240 years to proxies, and based on the technology we have available to us today, there is simply no reason I can find whatsoever for the population of the United States not to vote, on its own behalf on any matters that concern their economic survival.

I believe blockchain technology should definitely be used in elections as a way of validating votes, and we can certainly use this technology if we are implementing propositions that directly affect the survival and overall well-being of any given state. Blockchain technology uses a ledger system to verify and cross-check transactions. Each ledger is spread across many computers, so if a computer hacker tries to break into one of the ledgers and change its data in order to benefit themselves, the other ledgers on the network will in collusion together show a different result, which will refute the data of the hacked or tampered ledger and prove it to be false. This is an excellent use of technology to meet our short-term needs for transparency to insure at a very high level that altering voter counts, ballots or potentially rigging elections would become nearly impossible. Blockchain technology can provide the country with the proper checks and balances we finally need to make online voting possible. It would encourage people to take control of their own economy through the passing of state propositions. Blockchain technology can help make the results of elections more transparent to the public, in order to implement a licensing system into our energy, healthcare, transportation and housing industries.

Summary

Throughout this chapter we've explored the fact that the federal government, which is actually represented by private shareholders, is never going to vote against the interest of their own stock portfolio or pension plan. The initial enactment of licensing restrictions on just two industries, energy and healthcare, will need to come from the states themselves in a heavy form of collusion to eventually force the federal government's hand to adopt these licensing laws on all our overhead industries at the federal level. It's time we use the collusion power of the states to actually help us change our world. The first step in this process would involve forming an economic committee. The first proposition for the economic committee to get on each state's election ballot would be an Economic Crime proposition. Just enacting an Economic Crime law in each state would send a clear message to Wall Street and the federal government that financial criminals will be held accountable for fraudulent crimes against the public, and that turning a blind eye like the federal government chooses to do every time there is a mass fraud committed against the public resulting in an economic collapse, would no longer be the status quo. Ultimately this type of system puts the power back into the hands of the people again. I hope that by reading this chapter, you've come to a better understanding of how to regain your power over your own survival.

CHAPTER 8

Reforming our Healthcare Industry

The idea of nonprofit healthcare has traditionally seemed fearful to most Americans; they fear they will sacrifice quality or even increase their risk of death as a result of lowering the cost of their existing healthcare premiums. The accepted business practices and cultural beliefs held in this country tend to steer people in a direction of believing that an overall decrease in price will have a direct effect on the quality of care and prescription drugs they receive. In the plan I'm outlining in this chapter—which is an exact replicate of the energy industry licensing model already outlined in this text—I would like to expose some hidden costs that can greatly reduce the overall healthcare costs for all Americans yearly, without sacrificing any bottom-line service or quality to the customer.

I personally believe that for-profit healthcare is an immoral abomination, and this industry should have never been allowed to operate on a for-profit basis. I think a rhetorical question all Americans should begin to ask themselves is why do we need to make a profit from someone's misfortune, accident or disease? And how is paying ever-increasing costs for healthcare going to increase our standard of living over time? A 2017 article from *The Atlantic* by T. R. Reid tells us that in 2016 America spent $3.4 trillion on healthcare; this figure represented about 1 out of every 6 dollars that Americans spent that year, and was higher than anything else we spent money on the entire year—even higher than the amount we spent on housing and our military.[54]

We've already reviewed the fact that Senators and House members of the United States Government are in fact major shareholders of both pharmaceutical and healthcare stocks, and cutting healthcare expenditures or making major wholesale changes to the system would cause severe job losses most likely resulting in proxies not being reelected to another term; hence the reason we have not been able to advance to a nonprofit healthcare system or even remove health insurance companies from the system. Attempting to understand how this elaborate system works and what the true costs for the actual services and drugs are, is almost impossible for the average American to decipher. Under the current system, Americans prepay their insurance first, so they don't really understand and feel the true financial effects of the cost for drugs or services when they incur them. Healthcare premiums and coverages vary from employer to employer, as does the volume discount based on the number of people covered under a particular plan, and these costs are deductible from income taxes. Furthermore, the consumer does not understand specifically what they're paying for drugs and services, because the insurance company may be fighting on their own behalf to lower the prices paid for these good and services, in order to increase their profits or remain within their budget goals. Federal and state healthcare programs, such as Medicare part D or Covered California, have their own eligibilities, costs and restrictions. Consumers who actually need customized medical solutions to their healthcare problems end up navigating a financial minefield in order to receive the drugs and treatment they need.

I sincerely believe that by regulating the healthcare industry through a licensing system that I will outline in this chapter, we can create a new

54 https://www.theatlantic.com/health/archive/2017/06/how-we-spend-3400000000000/530333/

financial system to fund healthcare while massively decreasing costs and keeping doctors, nurses and all bottom-line employees that directly affect the quality of healthcare service, motivated and time efficient. This type of open sourcing and transparent regulation will translate into a far more satisfying experience for all of our citizens, who will be able for the first time to use healthcare the way it was meant to be used rather than buying an insurance policy and then never using the service, simply because there are so many uncertainties and hidden costs involved, resulting in debt collection, massive reductions to their credit scores or even bankruptcy. Many Americans pay for health insurance that they never use, basically because they are terrified of the hidden costs associated with hospital and other medical visits, yet they still spend an exorbitant price monthly for these unused services just to avoid paying tax penalties or keeping themselves out of a hypothetical "what if?" situation, that could destroy them financially if they ever befall a major accident or disease.

To understand the problem in the broadest sense let's look at the percentage of where each dollar paid actually goes, as part of a typical monthly health insurance premium.

I extrapolated these numbers from the AHIP in an article from 2018 that presented the expenditures from 2014 to 2015 in cents per dollar of health insurance premium paid, as a percentage basis. The percentage of expenditures will vary slightly year-to-year

23.3%	*Prescription drugs*
22.2%	*Physician services*
20.2%	*Office and clinic visits*
16.1 %	*Hospital stays*
15.9%	*Operating costs*
2.3%	*Net margin* [55]

---

55   https://www.ahip.org/health-care-dollar/

The bottom line is that it is very difficult to actually break down specifically where the percentage of every premium dollar paid really goes, especially when we are looking at long-term costs of CAT-scan machines or newly created devices offering advanced medical technologies and so forth. Pharmaceutical companies, as you can see, represent the greatest percentage expenditure of healthcare premiums.

At the end of the list above, we see operating costs and net margin or profit broken down as a percentage of healthcare premiums. About 82% of every dollar paid for health insurance premiums actually went to claims in 2014, so we could at least "potentially" eliminate or potentially reduce the cost of monthly premiums nearly by 18% by eliminating private insurance companies, which are simply middlemen that collect money and then turn it over to medical facilities. Applying a licensing policy to the healthcare industry would not directly decrease, healthcare premiums by a figure of 18%, as there may still be a need for customer service at hospital billing departments to collect the payments and other financial accounting employees required under licensing regulation, but certainly the broad figures, at least on the surface, would seem to be less than those borne by the existing profit-driven system.

The current system complicates matters further through a federal-government-enacted medical loss ratio that sets a minimum for the amount of money insurance companies have to spend on actual medical services and drugs, for every dollar they receive. This legislation potentially stops insurance companies from charging higher prices to its customers and pocketing the difference. So under the rules of the current system, we are "capping" the income on medical insurance companies anyway even though they are profit based and publicly traded; in essence we are asking them to not abide by their best practices that will incentivize their profit, for the sake of the general public's welfare. These types of revenue caps are typical of short-term solutions enacted by the government, and will result in medical insurance companies in the long run trying to exploit loopholes in the law for any reason they can, in order to move more dollars toward their revenues even if they have to hire more people to provide a higher-quality customer service experience for the customer. All of these increasing costs in the long run will be borne by the consumer.

There are some government regulations in place to try to put a cap on insurance company prices that could potentially gouge the public, but I fail to see why we still need these middlemen at all to collect our premiums. Everyone would happily pay into these programs because they need them collecting payments on behalf of medical facilities; advertising and sales teams simply aren't necessary, as the public desperately needs these services. Medical insurance companies also require a vast number of customer service representatives in order to explain to customers what is covered and what is not covered under the plans they offer, and the industry is hiring people specifically for this purpose. So, by running a for-profit industry, which needs to hire people in order to explain the limitations of its for-profit product, the industry directly increases the cost of healthcare premiums. This is another perfect example for-profit paradox. The incomes that are paid directly to these customer service people could be going directly to the customer's healthcare benefits. This type of customer service is necessary because people are vastly concerned about what their "potentially uncovered" costs are going to be before they seek treatment. Many times, customers are given an explanation so complicated as to what their costs are going to be for a particular procedure that they may not seek treatment at all. Do you see the paradox here? If we eliminated privately held profit-driven insurance companies, Americans would certainly pay less in monthly premiums and receive an actual increase in their quality of service due to the fact that extra money would now be available to spend on actual medical services and prescription drugs, and making costs more transparent would mean more Americans would likely seek medical treatment. Federal taxes and any state taxes paid by insurance companies would also be freed up directly for prescription drug and physician services costs, under a nonprofit licensing system that does require the use of insurance companies.

State-run healthcare programs, like Medi-Cal or Covered California, have programs with income restrictions that charge monthly premiums, based on the level of income of each applicant. Health insurance premiums are now based on progressive costs similar to income taxes, in that the monthly premium is increased based on the amount of annual income earned by the applicant. In order to ensure that consumers aren't taking advantage of state healthcare by falsifying income in order to receive reduced premiums, consumers under these programs have to send income verification, letters of explanation and a host of other documentation to legitimize their claims. This means that the state has to employ another army of people to verify the correct eligibility of each applicant, such as underwriters, caseworkers and customer service representatives. These additional state jobs—and thus the additional costs borne by the states offering these types of programs—would no longer be necessary under licensing regulation, which would could free up additional monies to pay actual medical costs through eliminating all these unnecessary jobs. These additional funds could be directly applied to prescription drugs or physician services that the public desperately needs. The entire medical industry is simply paying a massive amount of people to do jobs that are not necessary, in order to ensure that Americans continually pay increased healthcare costs.

A 2017 article by Michael Wyland for Nonprofit Quarterly stated that the number of working Americans from ages 18 to 64 on high-deductible health plans was about 40%.in 2016.[56] Speaking from personal experience, my annual deductible as a single person enrolled in a high deductible health-care plan in 2016 was $3,000; the minimum deductible defined by the IRS in 2018 was $1,350 per year for an individual and $2,700 per year for a family. In general, the cost that you're paying for healthcare directly coincides with

---

56   https://nonprofitquarterly.org/2017/06/09/cdc-americans-high-deductible-health-plans-skyrocket-since-aca/

the company that you work for; the more your company wants to save on healthcare costs, the more likely you are to have a high-deductible healthcare plan. We do not have equal healthcare for all Americans. Almost all companies in America have "at will" employment, and workers are forced accept whatever particular benefits a company offers in order to obtain income to meet their immediate survival needs through currency and must accept as a consequence of this system whatever health benefits they are randomly able to obtain. The majority of our country basically lives paycheck to paycheck and cannot save enough money under the present currency-based system for an unexpected $1,000 repair, so those Americans would be forced to use debt as an option to cover their portion of any deductible payment. If credit was not available to this consumer, this deductible would most likely be forwarded to a collections company, thus ruining that individual's credit score.

It is also noteworthy, from my personal experience as a real-estate lender, that medical collections show up on credit reports all the time and the customers applying for the loans in many cases have no idea that these unpaid medical bills ever went to a collections company and are reporting as derogatory on their credit report and lowing their credit score. They simply assumed that the costs and bills that resulted from their treatment were covered by their insurance company, when they were not, because they simply had no idea what their insurance company actually covered or did not cover on a per-expense basis. Even medical collection accounts as small as $25 or $50 can make a huge difference on a credit score. This represents another reason that the general public is deterred from using the medical benefits that are available to them. What we offer in America today are for-profit healthcare plans that most Americans cannot afford, so when Americans actually must seek treatment at a hospital for emergency purposes or other legitimate reasons, it results in further debt incurred by them, or potential collection accounts on their credit report, leaving them ill prepared for any upcoming future financial crisis. Is it a wonder most people can't save money in this country? I personally do not trust medical facilities any more than I trust a local mechanic to tell me what's wrong with my car—both entities are profit driven. It would be better for people to seek multiple medical opinions concerning almost any medical issue they might have, however minor, before they actually follow through with any procedures.

Unfortunately, if you're one of the almost 40% of Americans under a high-deductible medical plan, you're essentially paying for the majority of your basic services out of pocket and the insurance is simply there to cover a catastrophic event. I firmly believe the fallout and aftermath from all the bills that need to be paid and accounted for by any person having major medical treatments in America today causes each patient severe stress, which further compounds their healing process and could extend the time for them to recover and even possibly deter the healing process, in the case of a chronic disease. In short, people get flipped out over their medical bills, and this is the worst type of emotional position to be in when any person is attempting to heal their body. A 2011 news article from Science Daily sites Dr. Robert Lefkowitz from Duke University as stating that chronic stress can be directly shown to cause human DNA damage.[57]

If a cancer patient undergoes radiation or amputation in order to temporarily remove their cancer, this can leave them in an extremely stressed state not only due to their physical state but due to their potential loss of income from not working and being suddenly deluged with a massive amount of medical bills that they neither understand why they are receiving nor comprehend, that it could potentially take them years to pay off. I fail to see how the excessive stress caused by this financial crisis would aid them in their healing process. In essence, this potential financial crisis could potentially cause further medical issues from extensive stress and failure or slowness to heal and create yet a greater financial crisis! Is it really necessary to have for-profit healthcare, based on the grief it causes citizens?

---

57   https://www.sciencedaily.com/releases/2011/08/110821141135.htm

A 2016 article by Amy Martyn for Consumer Affairs stated that health insurance companies were making record profits in 2016, and that UnitedHealth's CEO made $66 million dollars in 2014 although his pay was reduced to a mere 20 million dollars in 2015.[58] How many people can you hire for $20 million? Well, you could hire 20 people and pay them $1 million a year, or you could hire 220 people and pay them $100,000 a year. I'm simply amazed by the fact that the board of directors of any American medical company could actually believe that one person could do the work of potentially 220 people being paid a six-figure income, regardless of their vision, crisis-solving abilities or business plan. No person could ever justify such an income for their services; the utility value of the service they provided to their company could in no way ever justify this type of compensation.

Let me state here unequivocally that you can never ever have equality under the present economic system. This is just one of the many examples of that inequality and the damage it causes. Currency is always going to block the way to creating the most technologically advanced society we, as humans, are capable of; that's why we need to reduce our need for currency as much as possible in order to produce the most resilient and robust economy possible. Let's begin by regulating our healthcare industry and making it nonprofit, non-publicly traded and patent free.

In the broadest sense, as statistics will vary from year to year, 22% of each dollar you pay goes to prescription drugs. Could we vastly reduce this cost if we eliminated patents from medical industry? Would this stop the invention and creation of new drugs that we may need to heal our people, in the future? These are very good questions to ask, and we should be asking them rather than not asking them to find solutions. But as we saw in my explanation on patent law, what's really happening here is that the entire industry is incentivized to collude and control medical technology, and this technology can be legally hidden, shelved or monopolized, as long as patent

---

58   https://www.consumeraffairs.com/news/health-insurance-industry-rakes-in-billions-while-blaming-obamacare-for-losses-110116.html

law exists. Most people do not have the money to pay for these drugs, and if they can't purchase them, they aren't much good to them. A 2017 report by the Association for Accessible Medicines stated that generic drugs made up 89% of prescriptions dispensed but only totaled 26% of the total drug costs in the United States. Their 2017 report also concludes that abandonment rates for patented prescription drugs were 266% higher than for generic drugs. People in many cases never actually pick up potentially lifesaving drugs from their local pharmacy because the cost is simply too high to purchase these patent-protected drugs. [59]

Based on the numbers already outlined so far in this chapter, 74% of the 22% of each dollar spent on healthcare in America today goes directly to patented prescription drugs. Obviously patent law is the direct reason for this incredibly high per-unit cost. What happens to the consumer if they need a certain drug and no generic substitute is available? They're going to pay an incredibly price for it, and if their health insurance doesn't cover that expense, they're going to lose their long-term savings by paying for it. Not to mention the fact that surgical procedures come at a cost beyond measure and can easily bankrupt the majority of Americans if they don't have the proper healthcare coverage in place.

Let's never forget the one rule of capitalism, which is to make the greatest amount of profit possible So all companies, especially those like pharmaceutical companies, that possess the ultimate leverage—your life itself—are constantly finding ways to pilfer any long-term savings away from Americans. The currency-based system is incentivized to ensure that every American basically has nothing in their long-term savings, because if every American has nothing in their long-term savings, then that money has been diverted to purchasing goods and services for other companies and corporations in order for them to reach their goal of maximizing their profit. Corporate America's goal directly conflicts with the consumer's goal, whose purpose in life is to enjoy peace and prosperity. For-profit agendas result

59   https://accessiblemeds.org/2018-generic-drug-access-and-savings-report

in the consumer dealing with constant stressful and fearful survival issues trying to save as much money as they can, in order to potentially combat them. Clearly, this is a system where the goals of one entity are diametrically opposed to the goals of the other entity. The old-school way of handling things was to say that we should resist temptation not spend money and save it, to make sure we have enough money to survive in our old age. Is it really necessary to keep suffering day after day, in order to ensure that we have amassed money to meet our survival needs later in life? Why waste the time trying to amass cash over the course of your entire life, in order to meet uncertain future survival prices, when we can make the cost of our survival as low as possible, by applying technology to our overhead industries with the goal over the long term of making these costs inconsequential, or potentially even free! Most millennials will never have enough money to retire, based on the massive amount of automation that is going to replace jobs in the next 40 to 50 years anyway.

In defense of the pharmaceutical industry, after filing their patent, which lasts for 20 years, 10 to 12 years is usually spent in FDA trials trying to get clinical approval before the drug can actually be sold to the general public. So this leaves a window in most cases of eight years or less for the pharmaceutical company to recoup its costs. Let's also remember that anyone employed under a research-and-development department for one of these companies does not receive any patent royalties or income whatsoever if they invent any drug that is approved for clinical trials. They get nothing. The corporation owns the patent, and who exactly is the corporation? Again, it's a small group of people made up of stockholders and executives who have access to purchase cheap insider stock through warrants and options, or even given shares as part of their compensation package in exchange for their startup money. The majority of our population basically does not have the kind of long-term savings required to invest in stock, or to take this kind of risk because they only have access to a limited supply of money. Are you starting to understand capitalism? It's a rigged system.

In 2019, the United States Department of Health and Human Services estimated we spent nearly $360 billion on prescription drugs, in contrast to 1960, when we spent just under $3 billion, on pharmaceuticals. Wow! That's a lot of incredibly unhappy people and a whole lot of pain! The bottom line here is we haven't even conquered major diseases like cancer or diabetes, and we can expect to be shelling out an unconscionable amount of money over the next century before we might see actual cures dispensed to the general public for these diseases.

A 2016 article in *Money* by Brad Tuttle states that the price of a life-saving drug called Daraprim was increased by 5,000% shortly after the manufacturer that held the patent was acquired by another company, and that Epi Pen prices have increased by 450% since 2007.[60] As you can see from these examples, the pharmaceutical industry exploits people with a need for potentially life-saving drugs in order to maximize its profit. Patents allow the pharmaceutical industry to control this technology, and the industry will continue on its path as long as the laws governing it remain in force. Once you remove the patents, shareholders and for-profit aspects from an industry, you effectively remove all the incentives to exploit the public with higher prices.

Let's look at some ways the pharmaceutical industry is currently exploiting the laws governing our currency-based economy, so that they might extend a 20-year patent they currently hold up to another 5 years. Some common methods of skirting around the law are:

1. Simply take two different compounds whose patents have already expired, and combine them, and voila! You have another new compound, ready to be patented.

2. It is completely legal to give money to doctors to promote the sale of any particular prescription drug. However, it is illegal to give money to a doctor to prescribe a drug. Pharmaceutical companies easily skirt around this very loose law to influence doctors to prescribe medicines

---

60   https://money.com/high-prescription-drug-prices-facts/

that their patients might not need through exploitation of their greed over their Hippocratic Oath. A doctor can't be paid to prescribe you a drug directly, but they can be on the payroll of a pharmaceutical company to promote the same drug to other doctors, so that these doctors can prescribe that same drug to their patients. In my mind this is in fact giving a kickback for prescribing drugs to patients. No practicing physician with patients should be allowed on the payroll of a private pharmaceutical company in any manner whatsoever. That person should either be employed as a designated spokesperson of the company or as a practicing physician but not as both. To be employed as both would no doubt be a conflict of interest. This industry is screaming for regulation!

I believe physicians working with pharmaceutical companies in order to develop drugs the public needs in an efficient and cooperative manner, would be of great benefit to the public; but again, while our medical industry flounders under the rules of the currency-based system, people can be incentivized to be led astray from the solutions that might meet the public's best interests. I see no need to change this practice and make it against the law, because if we remove patents from the pharmaceutical industry as part of a licensing proposition, most likely there won't be any extra money to put doctors on the payroll anymore. If this becomes an issue of concern for the public, the economic committee can certainly spend extensive time reviewing it and add it to an existing licensing proposition, or create another proposition make this practice illegal at a future point.

3. Either time-release an already existing drug, to make its effects last longer; or change the method of uptake into the body, such as a liquid versus a pill, which might be absorbed faster by the body. Either method is allowed to be patented. Basically, the FDA is just doling out money to pharmaceutical companies and making you pay for it. Pharmaceutical companies are using compounds that are available

in generic prescriptions and changing them from a pill to a liquid, in order to create an entirely new patent. The FDA's perception of this is no different than an ancient King's perception of allowing "salt" to be patented 500 years ago. We're talking about personal opinions here, and not matters of fact or merit—and the public keeps paying for it. How long do you want to keep going along with this insanity?

4. Take the active chemical molecule of an already existing drug that uses several different active chemical molecules in its formula, by using only one particular portion of an already existing drug in a purified form. This magic or rearrangement creates a newly patented pharmaceutical. This deception is usually carried out prior to a patented pharmaceutical expiring.

5. Pharmaceutical companies also regularly engage in the practice of purchasing the entire inventory of a newly expired patented drug, or just directly pay off generic-producing drug companies in order to keep selling newly expired patented drugs at an exorbitant price. The industry can also use fake people to file petitions to extend a patent an additional six months. When you're making billions per year, you certainly have the funds available to run operations of this sort. As far as the FDA is concerned, corporations, under this aspect of the law, are given the same rights as individuals

The many processes I just outlined are referred to as Evergreening. Evergreening is a term used to describe the many ways that pharmaceutical patent owners exploit loopholes in patent law to create greater profits for themselves over a longer period of time than their standard expiring patents normally would afford them. Anytime you involve patents in an industry, you are going to involve lawyers who will manipulate the law any way they can in order to keep profits rolling in. They will roll up their sleeves for years, to try to find loopholes in the law. If they can't find loopholes in the law, they will simply lobby to create laws that serve their self-interests against those of the general public. If you try to sue these people or take them the court, their pockets are so deep they can hold you out of a court trial for decades because they know the majority of people in this country who purchase these drugs basically have no savings to fund any type of a court trial.

The process of evergreening illustrates exactly why you cannot have patents in a need industry. It creates the incentive to endlessly manipulate the law. The United States Government has no intention whatsoever of changing these laws at all, because they are influenced so heavily through lobbying. A2017 article by Megan R. Wilson for The Hill cited that in 2016, fifty companies spent nearly three-quarters of a trillion dollars on lobbying Congress and the Federal Government. Some of the top five spenders included the National Association of Realtors, Blue Cross Blue Shield, the American Hospital Association and the Pharmaceutical Research & Manufacturers of America.[61] Again, as an American citizen you are forced to pay these companies to lobby against your best interests with your own money, by purchasing their products and services. You need to understand unequivocally that every month you pay your healthcare premium some of that money is directly used to influence the government to make laws to continue to ensure that you continue to pay those healthcare premiums and their cost keeps increasing over time. Every time you pay for-profit healthcare companies, you are literally giving money to corporations that can legally buy game-changing patents and put them on the shelf, and you're paying for their lobbyists to create laws that work directly against your best interests, thus holding you in a paradox forever. Until law is changed, you're literally paying monthly to fund your own demise. This is the specific reason we need to remove the incentives of the stockholder and the profit-maker. We're simply caught in a financial paradox in this country, creating an endless loop that we can't get out of or ever allow us to plan and create a different system.

---

61   http://thehill.com/business-a-lobbying/business-a-lobbying/318177-lobbyings-top-50-whos-spending-big

The federal government is not going to change any of the patent laws governing either healthcare or energy. Other countries negotiate their drug prices under nationalized healthcare; but the United States does not, under Medicaid part D. Since 2003 the federal government has not even brought to vote a bill that would allow the government to negotiate prescription drug prices. Our government would rather let people suffer and die than cause pharmaceutical companies to make less profit. The federal system has failed the people of the United States, luckily are there is a civil system that still exists, whereby we can create the law with our own hands and take back our power in a nonviolent manner.

Let's propose some mythical legislation to make a certain section of our population a lot of money. Since it's such a hard job raising children, I would like to propose the creation of the Future Young Americans Fund. This legislation, if passed, would state that at the time of the birth of the any child in America, its parents can apply for government assistance, for as much money as they need for ongoing child-rearing expenses until the child is 18 years of age, at which time the government adds up all the disbursements and charges a 5% interest rate on a new loan, that must be paid back by the 18-year-old adult for the rest of their life. At the time of every monthly payment, the government will extract a 20% processing fee and give the remaining 80% to the parents in the form of a monthly lifetime annuity until the loan is paid in full. Children should be grateful that their parents have raised them, and of course they should pay back the money to their parents for decades, because they might cease to exist without the care of the parents. Why should parents in the United States continue to raise their children for free and not expect full reimbursement, over the course of their child's entire life?

Certainly, we could justify such a program in our society based on the massive amount of government scams that are going on today! Does this sound insane to you? In my opinion this scenario is no different than the idea of for-profit pharmaceutical companies using patent law against the general public and the medical insurance companies collecting payments for healthcare. Merit and hard work have nothing to do with creating laws to force people to pay you for things that they need.

Let's play a game. If you win the game, I'll give you my entire life savings and I'll become your slave for life, doing anything you want me to do. The game is called tic-tac-toe, but there's a catch: I get the first three moves in every game, and after that you get to play. Do you think you're going to win that game under these rules? How far away do you think this game is from the realty that is being played out every day on the American public, by pharmaceutical companies, energy companies and so many others? You can never win a rigged game, and waiting for someone that has all the advantages - to be a nice person and allow you to win is never going to happen. In order to form a solution to your problem, first you need to understand how you're being taken advantage of, so that you can move forward towards a more prosperous and abundant life. So why not change the rules of the game, so that the outcome is more advantageous and equal between you and the companies that create your needed survival technologies?

There still some costs that need to be addressed regarding every premium dollar:

22.2%	*Physician Services.*
20.2%	*Office and Clinic visits*
16.1 %	*Hospital Stays*

Let's address how these costs can be further reduced, in the broadest sense, through a nonprofit, non-publicly traded, patent-free regulated licensed system that would be required for all healthcare companies, doing business in any particular state throughout the rest of this chapter.

Let's look at the basic steps of regulating and removing the currency-based system from our healthcare industry, while at the same time removing incentives from short-term profiteers, who currently block or slow down the evolution of vital life-saving technology, while simultaneously creating incentives for the workers (mainly doctors and nurses) who directly impact the level of healthcare services. This nine-step process is quite simple:

Step 1. Requiring a license for all healthcare-based companies.

Step 2. Removing the shareholder.

Step 3. Removing all patents from the industry.

Step 4. Requiring all healthcare companies to become nonprofit, in order to maintain a current healthcare license.

Step 5. Requiring internal company audits.

Step 6. Creating incentives for all employees, through bonuses.

Step 7. Creating a state Healthcare Protection Agency.

Step 8. Sourcing funds for operation and advancement of new and existing healthcare companies.

Step 9. Monitoring, maintaining, supporting and adjusting the industry through a vetting period of at least five years.

Since you're already familiar with the process from our chapter on energy, I will try to be as brief as I can and emphasize the critical points as they directly relate to the healthcare industry and the direct changes in its regulation.

Step 1. Requiring a license for all healthcare-based companies.

Any company that produces or offers any type of healthcare service, pharmaceutical drug, prescription, medical testing equipment, medical equipment or tools would require a specific license to operate, produce and sell these products or services to the general public or another licensed vendor. This would include holding companies, limited-liability companies, partnerships and sole proprietorship's as well as any corporate entity, even if the sole purpose of the company was to act as a holding company and redistribute any healthcare-related product or service at no cost. Licensing would be required for any company that produces any type of medical instruments, medical tools or medical equipment for the purposes of surgery or inpatient or outpatient care, including hospitals, HMOs and care clinics as well as an entity that buys, sells, holds or redistributes any healthcare product or service used by any consumer, regardless of the size of its market. The state Health Protection Agency or any department designated by a particular state to regulate this industry would require all employees and companies to hold a current license, in order to provide any healthcare product or service. A state-formed Health Protection Agency would supervise and approve licensing requirements as well as be responsible for the renewal of licenses and supervise any required ongoing license renewal education The following individuals would also require state-approved licensing as individuals: surgeons, practicing physicians, nurses, orderlies or any person that would come in direct contact with any patient seeking medical treatment, diagnoses or request for medical services.

Heavy fines and loss of a license would result if misconduct might occur, and potentially that individual could be charged with an Economic Crime. Penalties could also include the suspension of a license or the revocation of a license to transact business or work in the healthcare industry of any particular state. In the event of revocation of a license, the guilty company and any individuals charged would no longer be able to transact business in the healthcare industry. As individual states adopt this practice, a national licensing system should be formed, in order to ensure that individuals found guilty of past licensing violations in one state can't simply move to another state to resume their practice.

Step 2. Removing the shareholder.

The issuance of stock, options or warrants would be prohibited by companies within the industry as a requirement of their licensing. It would also be illegal to create or trade any type of investment that speculated on the supply or distribution of any healthcare product or service to the general public. These would include exotic investments like derivatives. Our goal would be to eliminate all the incentives to take advantage of the general public.

The existing outstanding stock of any companies now producing and distributing any healthcare product would be purchased by the state in which the company did business or by the federal government, at a price equal to 5% of the average of the last three years daily market closing price.

Step 3. Removing all patents from the industry.

In order to hold a healthcare license, any corporation or company entity as described in Step 1 would be required to release all of its patents to the general public, and would not be able to hold, buy, sell or redistribute any type of patent regarding healthcare or pharmaceutical technology. The term "health-care Technology" would be defined under an incredibly broad spectrum to include all existing and past healthcare technology known on the planet as well as any healthcare technology that could be used by a consumer as a form of healthcare technology in the future, and should be broadly defined enough to close any future loopholes of exploitation. All patents, both past and present, would be released to the general public and distributed to all licensed companies within the industry through a centralized database, for development. This policy would allow complete transparency and any particular licensed individual or company to produce healthcare-related technology without the concern for filing a patent. The main function of removing patents is to allow technology to be created and distributed as quickly as possible, keeping planned obsolescence and maintenance concerns to a minimum.

If a given state enacted this type of licensing regulation, anyone in the world could go to that state, start a company, produce healthcare tech-nology under licensing laws and restrictions of that state and never have to worry about anyone suing them for patent infringement. The law would be all-encompassing regarding healthcare patents. They would no longer be enforceable within the borders of the state. The public should see and hear everything when it comes to the development of their technology, and be able to ask questions and get answers from on-site customer support people whenever anyone in the general public requests it as well as having mandatory chat and e-mail response teams in place. A policy of a no-patent industry would allow complete transparency and anyone to produce healthcare technology without the concern for filing a patent and allow technology to be created and distributed as quickly as possible, keeping planned obsolescence and maintenance concerns to a minimum. All trademarks and copyrights currently held by existing licensed healthcare companies would have a two-year expiration.

All new technology could be accessed through a central database by all the licensed companies within the healthcare industry. The central idea is for the companies to cooperate and create the longest-lasting, most efficient healthcare products and services possible. Cooperation is basically proven to beat out competition, in many scientific studies virtually every time. Allowing companies to share knowledge and build on that knowledge together is the quickest way to creating superior technology. A mind-hive type of environment, in complete cooperation, is certainly a better way to develop technology for the general public, in addition to using supercomputers and artificial intelligence.

Another major federal entity that provides massive power and incentives to keep drugs off the market that can potentially save human lives is the Food and Drug Administration (FDA). The FDA is simply too powerful and is too under managed for the massive role it plays in approving or denying the consumption of prescription drugs by the general public. It has the potential to single-handedly keep a life-changing drug off the market in order for inferior products to continue dominating their current market share. There are simply too many incentives to bribe FDA officials in order to thwart potential drugs that represent mass leaps in technology and can provide massive benefits or lifesaving efforts to the public. I'm not directly accusing the FDA of anything, I'm merely pointing out that placing the public's fate in the hands of one small federal agency incentivizes bribery, and the FDA deserves a certain degree of culpability because of the position our currency-based system has put it in. When we concentrate the power of assimilating all our technology into a few small federal entities without a system of checks and balances, like having a president without a House and Senate to balance the spectrum of power, corruption will abound. People are being massively price-gouged to purchase FDA-approved and federally patented prescription drugs; this is a fact that can't be debated. When it comes to life-saving drugs or other medical devices that can potentially save lives, power over these survival technologies is too concentrated in the hands of the FDA without any other checks and balances to offset its powers.

States should highly consider creating their own version of the FDA that could potentially listen to appeals from doctors or other nonprofit pharmaceutical companies that are still being denied their ability to sell their drugs to the general public by the FDA. The entities asking for appeal would have no reason to do so other than for the benefit of the general public, because all companies and corporations, under licensing regulations, would be nonprofit, non-publicly traded and patent free. There are simply no payoffs, profits and incentives for these companies to obtain other than trying to look out for the general welfare of the public. Funding for a state-run FDA could be accomplished by pooling the resources of all the newly licensed states together to effectively create a state run and state financed version of the FDA. In the case where the federal FDA denied a drug and this multi-state funded entity could approve the drug in one state or several other states for consumption by their general public, in this case state law would again conflict with federal law.

How will pharmaceutical companies make a profit or break even on their investment into new drugs, so that they keep attempting to make new drugs to heal people? To assume that drug companies will go out of business and find no other way to fund the creation of new drugs to be consumed by the general public without the use of patents is a fallacy without merit. There are many ways the public can ensure that the creation of new drugs not only continues forward today at the level it does now but actually increases from its current pace. Let's look at several ways the slack can be taken up when patents are eliminated from the pharmaceutical industry. First of all, pharmaceutical companies that are nonprofit will require less revenue for normal business operations because the profit element has been removed from the price of any new drug. Perhaps the general public may have to fund these companies from new taxes or debt that is issued by a conglomeration of newly licensed states. This option would be massively cheaper than continuing to fund private equity pharmaceutical companies through the massive price-gouging, we experience today. Newly licensed pharmaceutical companies would now all be nonprofit, so most likely they would be directing fewer concentrated efforts on more substantial long-term solutions to our healthcare problems and diseases since their for-profit motives have been completely removed. The newly licensed industry would be completely transparent again, as patents are no longer a part of the equation, so all pharmaceutical companies can cooperate, sharing technology between one another rather than hiding it under rules of the current system, where companies compete and fight against each other for market share. Cooperation will facilitate huge strides in creating drugs cheaper and faster. We could use outsourcing and off-shoring at least to some small degree in order to further cut production costs. We could use other countries' technologies and resources in online forums and videoconferencing in order to assist us in the design and creation of new drugs and simply have the FDA and the new state-run version of the FDA approve them for final consumption here in the United States.

Step 4. Requiring all healthcare companies become nonprofit, in order to maintain their healthcare license.

As part of its licensing requirements, any healthcare company would be required to transfer any profits made at the end of its fiscal year as determined by its accounting process into a special escrow account, operated and overseen by that state's Health Protection Agency. Any deposits and withdrawals would be required to be reported to the state Health Protection Agency daily. These accounts would be overseen by a state auditing committee and an auditing report would be made public every six months on the current status of the account including all deposits and withdrawals made. All transactions of this escrow account would be available to the general public for review, like a giant transparent bank account of the general public. Companies would be able to draw from these funds quarterly, to meet ongoing expenses for the development of their technology or ongoing medical services. These withdrawals could be allocated towards labor, capital or any normal operating expenses. After five fiscal years, 35% of the initial first year's unspent deposits would be distributed to the existing customer base of any given company still in possession of saved funds, in the form of a customer rebate. Healthcare companies would be forced to spend their profits and reinvest them quickly back into the development of their own technology in order to speed the process of superior healthcare technology development along, as quickly as possible.

Each state would set up a designated escrow account to receive healthcare premiums from its citizens. All healthcare services and pharmaceuticals would be invoiced and paid through this account. It would be subject to audit two times per year by independent companies. Each auditing company would be limited to a maximum term of no more than two consecutive years.

Healthcare insurance companies would be required to close their doors permanently, as they would not be able to obtain licensing. Unfortunately for those employed by healthcare insurance companies, they would no longer have jobs. Insurance company middlemen, or middle persons if you like, are simply not required for this type of system to function, and the cost of keeping these jobs as we can see now is incredibly expensive for the general public and causes a major financial burden on the citizens of United States. Employees of these insurance companies would receive a six-month severance package in the form of six months of their present monthly salary paid in a lump sum at the time of their employment termination and up to 12 months of their existing benefits, free of charge. I would also suggest that each state would cover 50% of the cost of any schooling through any public university or technical college for any person in the industry who would like to retrain for a job in a new industry, and that any supplemental educational expense would be applied only towards schools within the state where that particular healthcare insurance company employee lost their job. Perhaps we can also offer low-interest or zero-interest student loans to these employees to cover the remainder of their educational expenses, to retrain themselves. These student loans could be offered to employees in this industry up to two years prior to removing the insurance companies themselves. These employees might be forced to work a 40-hour work week and attend school on the side, but at least they might have some type of job waiting for them when their job is finally eliminated. This is why it's so important to think things through and make changes slowly and deliberately over time so that the transition from a currency-based economy to a technology-based economy can be the least destructive to the overall well-being of everyone of society as possible.

Apparently, I'm becoming a big spokesperson for Kaiser Permanente, which is already nonprofit and non-publicly traded. A 2014 article from Jeffrey Pfeffer in *Fortune* magazine wrote that Kaiser had about 9 million members and does not use an insurance intermediary to collect money from their customers. When pricing healthcare costs for himself and his wife and comparing Blue Shield to Kaiser, he found Kaiser's overall yearly costs a staggeringly 39.7% less then Blue Shield. The main reductions to costs were cited as simplification of process and a reduction in administrative overhead; the article noted that U.S. doctors spend an average of one hour per day dealing with insurance paperwork when they could be seeing patients.[62]

That's potentially a 40% drop just by becoming nonprofit and not having shareholders to answer to; perhaps that's not a precise estimate, but potentially thee actions could substantially reduce monthly healthcare premiums for the American public, and we haven't even got rid of the patents specifically for prescription drugs, which still makes up a sizable portion of monthly healthcare premiums. Remember that companies like Kaiser still have to pay full price for patented prescription drugs, patented medical equipment and medical supplies, and large fees to potential price-gouging third parties, such as emergency medical flights by helicopter, which can easily run $75,000 or more for just one accident.

If we eliminate the insurance companies from the equation, how much could we potentially save? Look no further than Medicare. We may be able to potentially take up to 13% of the existing budget and move those funds directly to medical expenses and prescription drug costs, just by adopting a similar plan. A 2017 article by Daniel Marans for the Huff Post states that Medicare only uses about 6.4% of its existing budget on administrative and overhead costs, whereas the standard model requires 18% of every dollar paid to administrative costs and 3% to profits.[63] At 21% versus 6.4%, the numbers speak for themselves. Here's your single-payer plan everybody! Just pay an amount to your local state government every month and your medical expenses would be paid through the account I've outlined in Step 4.

A 2017 article in CNBC by Ester Bloom noted that Americans that year paid $3.4 trillion for medical care, and yearly per-person healthcare costs were expected to increase approximately 50% from $10,000 in 2016 to

---

62   http://fortune.com/2014/10/20/health-insurance-future/

63   https://www.huffingtonpost.com/entry/insurance-companies-medicare-for-all_us_58c1b1fae-4b054a0ea690dc8

almost $15,000 per person by 2023. Adjusted for inflation, healthcare costs are nine times higher now than they were in 1960.[64]

In 2019 America spent approximately $3.8 trillion on healthcare costs, or about $11,575 per person, so it seems we may actually be on pace to meet a $15,000 per-person figure at some point. Approximately 50% of all American workers make $30,000 a year or less. So, if we expect healthcare costs to rise per person, in the next 5 years or less, to almost $15,000 or half of what the gross income is of 50% of the working population, just how is this all going to work itself out? We simply cannot keep perpetuating a system like this, and we have to take a serious look at eliminating some of the existing laws governing our healthcare system before we get into very serious trouble and potentially a very serious currency collapse from the massive amount of debt that is being incurred by Americans today. Clearly America's debt levels have been rising decade after decade, and that's one of the reasons our nation's credit card debt is over $1 trillion today, or about $8,500 per household. The system can't keep running this way. The currency-based system relies on debt service to remain functioning, because it pairs obscenely high and ever-increasing overhead costs with stagnant and potentially decreasing incomes, as simultaneously we lose human-labor-created incomes to technology.

We have a great dichotomy to overcome if the overhead monster is not fed. Corporate earnings would drop; consequently, we would have layoffs, massively declining stock markets and tight credit markets. Contrast that with the fact that the majority of poor people in the United States will continue to have no savings, no retirement plan and to most likely rely on public assistance to survive, which would come in the form of welfare and food stamps. Simultaneously artificial intelligence is destroying the labor for cash, for survival process, alongside a massively expanding population and ever rising real-estate costs. Either one side suffers or the other side does. Either the majority of the people in the United States continue to live in debt

---

64   https://www.cnbc.com/2017/06/23/heres-how-much-the-average-american-spends-on-health-care.html

slavery, in perpetuity of service to a small group of people, which will eventually end in a currency collapse due to amassing an insurmountable level of debt that can no longer be serviced by the general public; or there will be massive adjustments to our survival technology and the potential extinction of our existing financial markets, if we license our overhead industries.

Personally, I would expect health insurance premiums to drop drastically, perhaps by 50% or more within the first year if licensing regulation is enacted, so the average American would have more income to spend on other goods, which might fuel economic growth. What jobs would we specifically be losing by instituting this type of licensing legislation regulation, regarding the healthcare industry, in any given state? Statistics tells us that there were about 463,600 people employed in the home offices of healthcare companies in 2016. Most likely the near one-half million people employed in the home offices of healthcare companies would permanently lose their jobs under this type of licensing. In addition, there could potentially be up to another 300,000 to 500,000 people including health insurance agents or vendors of the insurance companies and other miscellaneous people associated with the healthcare industry that might also lose their jobs as a result of eliminating health insurance companies. So, we could be looking at up to an additional 1 million people being unemployed initially by eliminating just the health insurance companies themselves. Do you see why Obama Care never got to the point to actually regulating the cost of healthcare and just forced people to pay health insurance premiums by federal law, in order to merely provide guaranteed care and eliminate pre-existing conditions? This is about all the government could get accomplished based on the fact that the Senators and Congressmen are in fact the shareholders of these companies and would never allow that kind of loss to their stock portfolio. In the meantime, the general population continues to see their money to spend decrease after taxes and after their monthly bills are paid over the long term as healthcare costs will continue to rise under a for-profit system, in order to meet shareholder demands. If potentially our prescription drug bill as a nation reaches a $1 trillion annual expenditure, premiums may soar to a level that can no longer be serviced by the general public. If you're not using prescription drugs yourself, your premiums, deductibles or other out-of-pocket expenses are going to be adjusted in order to cover this massive cost to pay for the cost of others anyway, so everyone will pay regardless of the level of services that they actually use. What happens to the other businesses that rely on Americans still having extra money left over in their paycheck after they pay their overhead expenses? These businesses, like many of your local restaurants, will simply cease to exist at some point, if our overhead expenses are allowed to continually increase unchecked.

What this system involves is sacrifice. Sooner or later healthcare insurance company employees are going to lose their jobs because their jobs simply aren't necessary, with the level of technology we have today coupled with the fact that these jobs create such an overall financial burden on the general public that they directly affect the overall financial security of all Americans. Based on these facts, it is simply pointless to continue with the current system.

Step 5. Requiring internal company audits.

Each state would set up a designated escrow account to receive healthcare premiums from its citizens, and this account would be subject to audit two times per year by independent companies. Each auditing company would be limited to a maximum term of no more than two consecutive total years.

Each licensed healthcare company would be subject to an internal audit two times per year. Regulatory and compliance audits would be performed by auditing companies for a maximum of two years. Fraud committed by an internal auditing company would be considered an Economic Crime.

Any suppliers and vendors to this industry could also be subject to random audits by the state Health Protection Agency, even if they were not directly producing or distributing a healthcare product, service or pharmaceutical drug.

Step 6. Creating incentives for all employees through bonuses.

There would be a yearly incentive profit-sharing bonus for any and all employees of a licensed healthcare-producing company as well as a quarterly performance-based bonus. The theme here would be to use profits directly toward present and future employee salaries and bonuses rather than towards creating the continued wealth of passive shareholders. The performance and annual profit-sharing bonuses would be defined by several parameters, including meeting quarterly and yearly incentive goals, number of overtime hours annually worked, safety standards adhered to and nature of hazardous work. I would prefer the compensation plans for all doctors and nurses to make up the greatest part of our healthcare expenditures, because they put in the most hours and have the most direct effect on patient recovery. These types of incentive bonuses would allow doctors and nurses to earn the income they really deserve for all the hard work that they do. There would be an annual income compensation cap of $650,000 per employee, including base salary and bonus. The general population seems to have an angry reaction any time salaries are potentially capped, especially in the healthcare industry where they believe that their standard of service may be lowered as a result of not properly incentivizing employees or any particular individual. However, I think we need to look again at the big picture of where we're going and why any person would need an obscene amount of money when the "specific" purpose of our new technology-based economy is to drop overhead costs, thus eliminating the need to save currency, for their current and future survival expenses.

We should be paying the people who are on the basic production lines of the pharmaceutical industries as well—where the rubber meets the road—the greatest amount of money, to make sure we have a well-defined, streamlined and abundant level of healthcare services available to consumers. An individual inventing any drug that would pass through FDA trials and would show results in either curing or preventing human diseases or illness, would receive one-time lump-sum payment of $1.5 million, or $3 million per team, which would not be counted towards the annual income cap. So, there would be plenty of incentive for individuals to keep providing great healthcare services and essential pharmaceuticals to the general public. Funding for these types of bonuses would initially be sourced through, the pharmaceutical company's existing retained earnings that might be available prior to licensing to add to an invention pool. A bond fund could be established in each state at the time licensing is passed where up to $2 billion, for example could be allocated towards the existing and future operation of pharmaceutical production companies.

I would expect all doctors and nurses in the industry to be making at least 20% more than they are now, which is double the amount of expected increase I proposed for energy companies, through their annual profit-sharing and quarterly bonuses, which would be performance-based. Hospital personnel would not experience any staff reductions; perhaps there would be some adjustments to the higher-paid employees of hospitals such as the administrators or specialized surgeons, since the cap of $650,000 gross income per year for any employee would be in effect. This may cause a decrease in tax revenue to state governments or organizations like the IRS; however, I would expect that this decrease in tax revenue could be offset with a decrease in pay to state government employees, relative to the decrease in costs to healthcare, and eventually passed on to all federal employees if the states colluded together to adopt this licensing plan on a national level.

Step 7. Monitoring, maintaining, supporting and adjusting the industry through a vetting period of at least five years.

The system would need to be closely monitored for a period of at least five years. All companies, outside of the energy and healthcare industries would be governed by the same laws that they are today and run business as usual. It is important to realize that we can only change things in small increments. We must take small steps before we can take giant steps. We cannot run all of our industries under this model at the same time; it would result in disastrous and tumultuous changes for our economy. It may be a decade of time before a licensing policy is adapted to either the housing or transportation industries, I believe these two industries definitely need to be regulated under a licensing plan at some point, because they represent a large portion of overhead expenditures monthly for all Americans. Again, it's very dangerous to provide every good and service in your society on a for-profit, privatized basis. For-profit incentives, especially when dealing with survival issues like medical care or housing, can cause severe volatility in economies and perhaps even their complete collapse. Prior to the Civil War we had privatized fire departments and police forces in America, and there's a specific reason that these organizations now run in a nonprofit manner; a private fire company, for example, could potentially extort any price from you to put out a fire burning currently your home.

The general idea here is to reduce overhead first and foremost, prior to our country producing labor-reduction technology on a mass scale. We need to monitor and maintain the system over basically a minimum 5- to 10-year period of time, making sure audits are done properly, and making sure that people are incentivized properly. In fact, my greatest concern would be for the incentivization and compensation plans of the employees of the energy and healthcare industries. We need our doctors and nurses properly motivated and seeing the proper number of patients per day, working hard and feeling good about what they do. Emotional attitudes are a very important contributor to producing excellent results.

Step 8. Forming a state Healthcare Protection Agency.

The enforcement and maintenance of all regulations governing all licensing—prerequisites, renewals and audits, ceasing of existing patent laws, monitoring of existing technologies or any type of illegal healthcare practices, potential economic crime investigations and any other enforcement or monitoring deemed necessary—would be the responsibility of the state Healthcare Protection Agency or the governing agency designated by each individual state for this regulation. We need to ensure that companies within the healthcare industry run not only in an honest and fair manner but adhere to these strictly enforced licensing laws and regulations. Any enforcing agency, whether at the state or federal level, would definitely be required to keep a close eye on all healthcare companies to ensure they remain nonprofit, non-publicly traded and patent free and continue to operate, over time, in an ethical and fair manner.

Step 9. Sourcing funds for operation and advancement of new and existing healthcare companies.

The source of funding for this licensing system in regulation could come from the following sources:

1. The issuance of tax-free state-issued municipal bonds.

2. The issuance of tax-free federally issued government healthcare bonds, if collusion by the states causes this licensing policy to be enacted at the federal level.

3. State or federal healthcare or pharmaceutical grants.

4. A portion of yearly state income tax revenues.

5. All or a portion of state sales tax revenues. This could include a gasoline tax, tobacco or alcohol tax, or tax on fast food.

6. Crowdfunding.

All sources of healthcare investment or regulation funds would be required to be held in an escrow account, as defined in Step 4.

Most likely exorbitant healthcare premiums would be replaced initially by larger taxes, in order to fund the healthcare industry and service any principal-and-interest bond payments. It's important to note that if any state that passes a law requiring an increased tax to cover healthcare costs, this tax should come with a mandatory expiration of five years. There should be a mandatory required vote through state proposition to continue the tax, at any amount going forward, after a five-year vetting has passed. Any taxes would be ironclad in their designation for healthcare and pharmaceutical expenditures only. These taxes could not be used for the state's general fund or any other purpose, even during times of war. Rebates to customers from all nonprofits would begin after a five-year period, and would be required annually going forward; so as time passes if it's determined that larger taxes are being enacted on the public only for them to be rebated at a later date, it would be a good idea to lower taxes accordingly so as to minimize the number of rebates given the general public. These per-state, per-person rebates would be calculated as: the total of all rebates from all nonprofits, including all healthcare and pharmaceutical facilities, divided by the number of citizens per state, and that specific dollar amount could be applied as a state tax credit toward state taxes owed or in addition to a state tax refund for any specific calendar year. Our goal here, again, is to lower the bottom-line production costs and services for healthcare over time so that eventually, within 50 or 100 years, the cost of this service would virtually be inconsequential or essentially free. It is important for any members of an economic committee or members of the state enforcement agency to keep focused on this cost reduction role as its number one priority.

After crunching the numbers, I would expect to see at least a 75% decrease in the cost of money spent on pharmaceuticals per year today, rather than seeing the 50% increase that is forecasted to occur over the next 10 years. Though I have not extrapolated the numbers as it would be impossible to do so based on a system that has not been active yet, I would expect that in 10 to 15 years the United States would be spending $100 to $250 million per year on pharmaceuticals rather than $1 trillion per year.

It should also be noted that a major complaint from physicians seems to be the lack of a centralized legacy system to store and view medical data records. Many physicians claim that when a patient visits them from another hospital—if they're on vacation, for example— information from their medical records has to be faxed over to them from their primary care physician or other facility. Oftentimes the physician on duty receives faxes of 30 pages or more when they simply need one paragraph's worth of data and have to sort through this extensive fax data, which takes time and directly increases our healthcare costs. It may take many hours to receive medical data from another facility, as medical records offices may only be open 8 hours of a 24-hour day. There are many different brands of software that track medical records data, and having to use so many different types of software can be very cumbersome for the attending physician. A CAT scan for a brain may actually be ordered as a CAT scan for a foot, to the particular department that performs such scans, because the data-entry fields and graphical user interfaces involved with different types of software are most times so small or unclear for the user to read and interpret, that they are filled out wrong by the attending physician regardless of their skill or intention. Having access to a patient's medical data records via an electronic tablet at bedside, with an easy-to-use and universally accepted standard of software, would be extremely beneficial to all patients. The speed at which treatment and/ or pharmaceuticals could be prescribed could also directly help to save lives, so it is paramount that we develop such a system in each state and a universal standard for the software being used, so that interstate access to medical records is both transparent and efficient. A 2016 article by NEJM Journal Watch noted a medical study that revealed for every hour a doctor spends with a patient they spend two hours working on electronic health records.[65] The failure of the current healthcare system to force the industry to adopt a universal standard for its medical record software is causing a massive increase in the cost of our healthcare premiums. Two hours spent on health records, for every one hour spent with the patient, is a disgustingly inefficient business practice that we need to end. Under the currency-based system, companies are incentivized to provide inferior software that requires constant upgrades while at the same time many different companies within the industry offer similar software for this one specific purpose. Once again, we can see where the incentives of this for-profit driven industry help to keep increasing our insurmountable healthcare costs.

I would also propose under this licensing plan that one software company be used to create a medical database for any given state, and that the software should be accessible to all physicians and hospitals from other states within the country. For example a physician who is examining a patient that is on vacation from another state would need access to that patient's medical records, and there should be mandates between the states to offer uniform standards and minimum requirements for both the software and hardware from the computer vendor providing the software and uploading any patient medical records into it, as well as monitoring and maintaining it. I could write a book on this subject alone. It would be an understatement to say that there will be major conflicts between various hospitals as well as software companies currently providing these services. There are huge profits to be made from offering electronic medical records, so many other companies would be eliminated if we only use one company as a primary provider of software. Electronic medical data records companies would put up huge resistance to such a proposal. This is exactly my we need a licensing system in our healthcare industry, because if we try to tackle one issue at

---

65   https://www.jwatch.org/fw111995/2016/09/06/half-physician-time-spent-ehrs-and-paperwork

a time, there would be so much resistance to each individual issue that we would never accomplish any real change. When the new systems are up and running, the old private legacy systems should run alongside them for no less than a period of two years, just to make sure there isn't a problem with accessing or losing any past patient data.

Conclusion

I hope that from reading this chapter you can see the mass exploitation involved in the pricing of pharmaceutical drugs and medical services in the healthcare industry. The goal of any for-profit industry is to maximize revenue, which means to push the maximum amount of volume, or number of units they can sell, constantly to a higher level—and more importantly, if possible, to always push the price of their product higher to create maximum revenue, which creates maximum profit. Perpetuating a for-profit, patent-enforced healthcare industry will always result in pushing our healthcare costs higher year after year. These results are absolutely guaranteed, because it's natural for companies to follow these for-profit incentives. You can expect your healthcare premiums to never stop increasing over the course of your lifetime, until they become absolutely unaffordable for you or the government issues additional debt to cover such costs, or until the government can no longer service its ever-increasing debt and creates a new currency to replace the old one. This system is on a collision course, and getting for-profit incentives out of the system as quickly as possible should be our main goal.

Do we have some problems to work out here? Absolutely. We need to get feedback from doctors, financial administrators of hospitals and of course directly from the citizens in each state, on their response to implementing a licensing system. It's so important to get feedback first, because this system affects the future viability of healthcare companies as well as their bottom-line service to patients. It is my sincerest hope that this book provides you with some solid insight into solving this problem! There are going to be quite a number of logistics that need to be worked out, regarding the initial stock buyouts and access to operating funds needed for any of the newly formed nonprofits, in addition to making sure that existing established companies continue to receive the funding they need and offer great service—potentially a higher level of service than they offer now. Let's not forget that we'll need plenty of incentives for doctors, nurses and all care providers and a lump sum payment for anyone or any team that produces a pharmaceutical drug of benefit to the public that passes FDA trials and becomes approved for use by the general public. I feel very positive about the overall impact that this type of regulation would have on the entire population of any given state passing this system into law.

Over the last hundred years we've stripped the diversity of our ecosphere, and it is having a massive effect on our wildlife, lands, oceans and the health of our human population. If we can bring down our overhead:

1. Americans will have more disposable income and more money to spend on higher-quality organic, non-GMO vegetables and more time to prepare foods at home and hopefully avoid unhealthy fast foods.

2. Americans will experience fewer stress-related diseases and organ failures due to a reduction in their overall stress levels, by being able to survive by working fewer hours per week, and potentially increase the possibility for more available savings to draw from in uncertain economic times.

3. Fewer traffic accidents will result as rush-hour traffic diminishes greatly due to staggered start shift times and shorter working days.

In summary, any time you have a workforce that does all of your labor, healthcare expenses will drastically increase over time. It's much cheaper to have robots doing automated labor than it is to have humans performing labor in any given economy. If a machine is broken during a work accident or car crash, it can easily be replaced or repaired, unlike a human being; and the cost of that repair is also a fraction of what it is to repair a human being. There is simply an astronomical cost associated with repairing a human body, and that cost correlates into increased working hours per year by all Americans. The more human labor a country employs, the more car crashes, work-related accidents, mental-health issues and overall disease is created across the working population. The less human labor we need to involve in our economy, the lower our healthcare costs will be, and correspondingly we will need to work fewer hours per year in order to pay those costs off on an annual basis. This is exactly the type of domino effect that we need in order to increase our standard of living and enjoy life more!

Let's assume for a moment that we can get these two industries— energy and healthcare—under a licensing system, making all these companies non-publicly traded and nonprofit and removing the industry patents. Most people might be asking at this point how can these laws be changed when there is going to be so much opposition, resistance and lack of initiative to change them, specifically from the majority of the human population that is under a mass delusion that only more currency, created through more hours worked, can solve their problems? I firmly believe that through the strong unbiased guidance provided by each state's economic committee, in order to create state propositions that directly benefits the public and are voted on directly by its citizens, coupled with state collusion on a national level, will be more than enough support to get the job done. If we put the vote back into the hands of the people to directly affect their economy with the proper guidance and regulation, the plan set forth in this text should work quite well.

The reason for the specific plans I've outlined so far in this text, regulating our energy and healthcare systems under licensing systems, is to illustrate to you that these plans allow us to move forward in a specific and direct manner, addressing the assimilation of technology into our economy, reducing our overhead first rather than income for survival first as we are currently attempting to do today, which is sure to result in disaster. Rather than waiting for a certain dream technology to randomly pop into our sites created by a random inventor—which we know, based on the currency paradoxes we've reviewed, is never going to happen—this plan galvanizes our entire country and its population toward creating and receiving the following benefits:

A. Lower energy costs for the entire country with a mass emphasis on bonusing the existing employees directly responsible for the extraction of raw material. The United States population would be far less subject to price gouging as ex-profit-driven executives would now be forced to concentrate their entire efforts solely on the production of their product rather than quarterly earnings reports. Our existing energy industry would run in a far smoother and more consistent manner, and we would see greater employee retention, happier workers and decreasing costs, as both short- and long-term profit schemes would cease to exist.

B. A mass emphasis on developing a portable and completely self-contained source of sustainable energy, such as a free-energy device or extremely efficient solar panel, in order to drop real-estate lot costs over the long term, thus reducing the size of home loans and the overall debt issued yearly to Americans, while simultaneously increasing disposable incomes (money left over to spend monthly after paying existing overhead debts). Overall, the idea here is to decrease the amount of our reliance on credit, by producing superior technology requiring far less replacement and repair for our energy and healthcare technologies.

C. Promote the openness and willingness between all citizens not only in the United States but around the world to share their technology, as there would be little incentive left to keep such information secret. The emphasis would be to eliminate our reliance on currency by developing superior technology, so that in the long run venture capitalists would realize that currency was a sinking ship and not worry so much about getting huge paydays for themselves. Overseas corporations might be more open and

willing over time to just open-source their patented information and technology to the general public, and this would greatly
increase the speed and efficiency with which we could incorporate
new superior technologies into our own country.

D. A massive decrease in the amount of healthcare premiums
currently being paid to private insurance companies in order to
service privately held, for-profit pharmaceutical and healthcare
facilities, offset by a far smaller increase in state sales or income
taxes in order to provide universal healthcare coverage for all
citizens. We really shouldn't be worried about going into debt,
whether at the state or federal level, in order to license these two
industries, because the end result of what we're trying to do here
is eliminate the need for future currency expenses, since basically
at some point our financial markets will collapse anyway from
automated labor. There simply won't be enough currency circu-
lating in the system, at some point in time, because no one will
have enough cash to keep buying anything at the level they are
now; and as a result, stock prices, home prices and credit instruments like mortgages will no longer increase in value over time
and become useless investments. What we're trying to accomplish
by adopting this plan, is to tide ourselves over, with the currency
we need, to build a new technology-based economy until we no
longer need the currency itself. Licensing these two industries,
removing the patents and shareholders and making these companies nonprofit is a means to an end. Reducing the 40-hour work
week opens the door for a much better life for all of us. A massive
drop in monthly healthcare premiums would immediately result
in a large surge in the disposable incomes for all Americans. So,
as these disposable incomes rise, money would be freed up to
purchase all kinds of local products and services. American companies might see an increase in the demand for their products and

services and began hiring people locally, thus creating massive opportunities for domestic job growth. There would certainly be more money for the purchase of organic foods, gym memberships, and so on. Just eliminating the number of people sitting in a chair 40 hours a week alone, would have a great effect on the overall health and well-being of our entire population. I firmly believe that the greatest threat to the health of all Americans is debt slavery. Debt slavery is a mandatory requirement for three out of four Americans, and we should do everything possible to change the rules governing this system in order to make the system work for us, rather than against us. In addition, by implementing this plan our exports would become massively cheaper than they are now and we would hold a world competitive advantage because our exports would no longer require high healthcare costs and other high overhead costs built into every product and service we create. If our president really wanted to eliminate our trade deficit, these are the types of policies he should be championing, to institute at the federal level. Finally, it would be far easier for employers to hire new employees because the costs associated towards the ongoing healthcare benefits of any newly hired employee would be drastically reduced; therefore, it would not be unreasonable to assume that a massive amount of job growth could be created in our country. The outsourcing of American labor, which I still expect to be popular, will be far less incentivized, as the cost of a single American employee would become far less relative to the cost of an outsourced worker, worldwide.

It's important to note here that we should apply this licensing system to the energy and healthcare industries only for a period of at least 5 to 10 years before we even consider adopting licensing regulation to our transportation and housing industries, and to take care and exercise caution to ensure we do not disrupt the flow of currency to our general population , as this might cause them harm or potentially create a major economic recession or depression.

I believe firmly this system can and will work. It's simply a matter of 328 million people getting together, going along with this plan and accepting it as a common business practice, in order to better their lives. If you want to make this plan a reality, I suggest you begin by discussing it with your friends as an alternative to discussing two-party politics, which offers no solutions for anyone. just repeats the same acts and produces the same results. You might find this type of conversation to be a lot more positive and rewarding than the last conversation you had with a friend about the economy!

CHAPTER 9

Reforming Our Transportation Industry

My own personal opinion is that the transportation industry should not fall under licensing guidelines until at least a 5- to 10-year period has elapsed since instituting licensing regulations for our energy and healthcare industries. The major reason or concern over licensing this industry would be to require all the manufacturers of automobiles to mandatorily use a free-energy device to power their vehicles, if in fact such a device was available to the general public for purchase, rather than continuing to force the use of inferior technology to power these vehicles on to the public through the use of collusion practices that that would continue to force the American public to keep purchasing old forms of gas and electric vehicles. As I've already outlined in past chapters, changing too many industries at once would potentially cause too many disruptions to the current system and could destroy our financial and credit markets, causing an economic recession or depression for an extended period of time. This is the reason why I have stressed first and foremost that a "free-energy" device—whether that be some sort of portable generator, ColdFusion device, an extremely efficient solar panel, wireless power or some extremely efficient alternative way to power our vehicles—needs to be invented and available for mass distribution first, before we mandate it be used in our transportation industry. I think you will find some interesting facts about the transportation industry as you read this chapter; and based on the evidence presented, you'll see how it is essential for this industry to undergo licensing regulation.

The first internal combustion engine was invented in 1859 by Nikolaus Otto, 161 years ago. At that time of his invention, the only means of communication technology was the telegraph; there were no telephones, smart phones or computers. This technology was invented with two design tools—a pencil and a piece of paper—and constructed by a primitive lathe (metal milling machine) to carve the metal to specified design dimensions. Today we're still using the internal combustion engine, whether it is gasoline or diesel powered, the latter invented by Rudolf Diesel in the 1890s, as the main form of propulsion to move our vehicles across the United States.

Is our technology really advancing in the transportation industry? A 2009 article from New Atlas tells us that the original Model T Ford averaged 25 miles per gallon, and that U.S. fuel efficiency has only increased by 3 miles per gallon between a span of over 80 years from 1923 to 2006.[66] For many of those years—specifically in the 1970s—the miles per gallon used by most vehicles decreased to around 11 or 12 miles per gallon. A 2016 article by De-Ann Durbin for phys.org notes that the U.S. Environmental Protection Agency stated that the average fuel economy of 2015 model-year vehicles increased one half mile per gallon that year, to a record high of 24.8 miles per gallon.[67] Contrast that with Henry Ford's clunker, which averaged 25 miles per gallon—so the average fuel economy for all the vehicles on the roads 100 years later, versus the first one that rolled off an assembly-line, has basically not changed at all! There's no difference, folks! Miles per gallon could actually

---

66   http://newatlas.com/us-vehicle-fuel-efficiency-improves-3mpg-80-years/12410/

67   https://phys.org/news/2016-11-average-fuel-economy-high-mpg.html

decrease again, like it did in the 1970s, depending on the pressure put on by automobile companies towards federal and state governments to loosen environmental standards. Sure, there are electric cars that get higher MPG, but the public is not going to embrace them as long as they are being steered toward gasoline-propelled vehicles, and electric vehicles represent just a tiny fraction, of the total vehicles on the road worldwide.

In roughly the last 60 years we have increased the power of computer processing chips, in terms of the performance of floating operations per second, by one trillion times. This is an actual and not exaggerated figure. So if you look at the parallel between computers and automobiles over the last 100 years, we've mass-produced inefficient gasoline-burning vehicles, year after year with virtually no change in MPG, while in a span of about the last 60 years we've increased the performance of computer processors, by one trillion times! One of these industries is producing transparent technology to the public and trying to make is faster, more efficient and easier to use by the general public, while the other industry colludes with its competitors to make sure we never lower our transportation costs. There is a mass collusion between the oil industry, which sells gasoline, and the makers of automobiles to keep selling the same system of propulsion in all automobiles around the world, decade after decade. Clearly, based on the evidence, there is absolutely no intention whatsoever for automobile manufacturers to change what they are doing. The motive here is profit, and you simply cannot make increasing profits over time with a higher-MPG automobile if you are interested in selling gasoline to people. We went to the moon almost 50 years ago and we can build thinking robots that can learn how to walk, yet apparently, we've never been able to transcend to another type of technology to power our vehicles in the last 160 years since Nikolaus Otto's original invention.

People are looking to mandatory minimum MPG sanctions which won't even serve as a Band-Aid, in terms of solving the main problem of the entire industry, which should be to power all vehicles using some sort of free-energy device. Under the currency-driven, for-profit, shareholder-run system, this type of technology has no hope of replacing any existing propulsion systems. Minimum MPG talk is just a false flag to divert your attention away from the real issues. People are under the assumption that we will keep progressing our technology and one day 200 years from now we'll never need currency. I wish someone could explain to me how this is exactly going to happen without changing the laws governing our idealisms of ownership outlined in the book.

Electric cars have been around since the 1920s. I love the desire and inspiration that Elon Musk puts into developing new technologies and also admire his work with Tesla in trying to create a new mode of transportation for our society, yet Tesla is only one company! Elon Musk basically gave away most of his patents regarding the propulsion system of his electric vehicles, because he felt that was the only way he could get the existing auto industry to incorporate this technology into all the vehicles mass-produced by the entire transportation industry. Do you see the need for licensing now in this industry? Our old friend, the for-profit technology paradox, has come to greet us again. Internal combustion engines have cooling systems that break down, oil changes that are needed, fuel systems with problems, air filters that need changing and layer upon layer of repair problems that allow the sale of aftermarket parts and huge profits for the automobile industry. Elon Musk has basically given his technology away for anyone to copy, in the hopes that the industry will adopt this system of propulsion on a mass scale; and yet the industry has basically no interest in doing so because the old technology is simply too profitable to replace. This is exactly why we need a licensing system to force a free-energy device to be installed in every vehicle in order to eliminate the internal combustion engine and even electric engines powered by coal-fired power plants, as the primary source of propulsion for our transportation industry. As you can see, trying to get the transportation industry to use another source of propulsion, even if it's patent free and more energy efficient, than the existing technology, isn't profitable, so it simply isn't being embraced and we're not seeing its physical manifestation in any type of mass production whatsoever. Clearly, we can see the goal is for-profit and not on the advancement of technology, a cleaner ecosphere or a higher standard of living for all Americans. If we can produce a portable source of energy to propel these vehicles, this device could easily be dropped under the hood of any vehicle and potentially we might not have to re-purchase another vehicle for a period of 25 years or longer; but we'll need a licensing system imposed on the energy industry in order to make sure a "free-energy" device is actually created and available for use by the general public, and licensing regulations to cover the transportation industry in order to make sure they comply with its installation into all of their mass-produced vehicles. Without these regulations, we'll never see a free-energy or low-cost energy-powered vehicle.

Let's look at another assumption: Electric car sales are taking off and becoming a major portion of all automobile sales in America; at the same time, despite Elon Musk basically giving away his patents, electric vehicles only represent about 2% percent of all vehicles on the road today. The simple reason this is not happening is that the entire automobile industry does not want you to purchase these vehicles. In the long run, companies again make more money through the planned obsolescence and repair costs built into gasoline-powered vehicles. Personally, I feel that the body styles of electric vehicles not specifically made by Tesla are being made to look undesirable, and the specific reason I believe this is happening is to steer the American public away from purchasing these vehicles. Electric propulsion systems could certainly be dropped into any brand of popular gasoline-powered vehicles today, but except for a Tesla, electric vehicles are not being made to meet the same demands for style, demanded by those in the market for a new automobile today. Discerning car buyers will still opt for the gas-powered vehicle because the body style and the overall way they feel about the vehicle - better meets their psychological and emotional needs.

ExxonMobil earned over 20 billion in net income in 2018. How many patents do you think you can buy out and take off the market with $20 billion? If I were running any oil company today, without question and hesitation I would buy all the competing technology that I could and keep it secret forever. Stop hating oil companies! Oil companies aren't the problem. We'll need to change the regulations that affects these industries if we want to produce different results. Again, we have to look at patent law as the major obstacle to inventing, creating, mass-producing and distributing technology into our society. If you do not understand that patents are playing a major role in the speed in which technology is assimilated into our society, keeping us bound in a labor-for-cash loop, at this point, then there is little that I can do to save you from your plight! I realize that you're trying to do all you can to understand why the system is not working and why the system is not helping you, and that's probably the reason why you decided to pick up this book, in the hopes of finding a way out. I can assure you that we, as a species and certainly here in the United States today as a population, are quickly beginning to figure out the trap that we're in and how to spring ourselves from it!! I only have sympathy for those who will continue to struggle with currency-based concepts over their lifetime in the hopes of experiencing dramatic results to their lifestyle yet constantly experiencing disappointment. The fact that I've experienced major disappointments and financial struggles throughout the course of my life is the direct reason that led me to write this book. If we all simply raise our awareness and understand the problems we're facing, we can implement solutions quite quickly and begin to reduce our overhead.

Another massive reason the transportation industry needs to be regulated is related to the outrageous prices charged for vehicles in America today. The current industry has no type of price regulation, not to mention the fact that despite having no regulations on the price of its product, the American public had to bail out this for-profit industry in 2008. Another point of contention is, why is the American public being forced to purchase vehicles that depreciate like a 747s without fuel? According to Car Fax.com, on average a new car will lose 60% of its total value over the first five years of its life.[68] Over decades of time we're putting in more hours of labor per day

---

68   https://www.carfax.com/blog/car-depreciation

to purchase transportation technology and it continues to become worthless over a short period of time. The reason that planned obsolescence is built into every newly produced vehicle is to require the purchase of another new vehicle at regular intervals. We're never going to make a car last a hundred years, or decrease the rate of depreciation per year, with a for-profit transportation industry regulated under the laws we have now. So we're again were back on the carousel, making money to purchase inferior technology that will never become superior, based on the fact that everyone right now must make money to pay overhead and as long as overhead (energy, healthcare, transportation and housing) goes unregulated, for-profit loopholes, lobbying and every possible effort will be made to continue the insanity of going nowhere.

We might all assume that our advancements in technology over the last 50 years would have helped us to decrease the number of human hours worked per year in order to purchase a vehicle, but this is actually untrue, and depending on the vehicle type in question, we're worse off than we were decades ago in terms of the number of hours we need to work per year in order to purchase a new mode of transportation. An article by Kurt Ernst from Hemmings in 2014 noted that in 1965, the average worker was only required to put in about 911 hours in order to purchase a Ford Mustang, versus 1162 hours in 2013.[69] In 2013, the average person had to work 1162 hours in order to purchase the same type of gasoline-powered vehicle that someone in 1965 could do by working only 911 hours. Did the 2013 vehicle perhaps have more technology and luxuries available than the 1965 vehicle? It certainly did, but also remember that things like Bluetooth technology, GPS or MP3 players weren't invented by the automobile industry. I can certainly get around just fine using a "free" map app on my cell phone that I can attach to my dashboard, with a cheap holder, for $25 or less rather than paying an exorbitant price for a built-in navigation system. Isn't technology supposed to be working for us? Aren't we supposed to be working fewer hours per year, in order to purchase vehicles with more technologically advanced

---

69   https://www.hemmings.com/blog/2014/03/07/have-cars-really-grown-more-expensive-since-1965/

propulsion systems than people did a generation ago? Apparently, according to the source above, we're going backwards, and I believe at this point the reasons why are obvious.

It seems very obvious that technology that's allowed to be freely developed like computer chips can massively increase its performance in terms of its utility value over decades of time, whereas technology that is clearly sequestered and purposely held in check by certain industries goes nowhere. The evidence to support this supposition is overwhelming. The transportation industry needs a mass overhaul and infusion of unregulated, unconfiscated and unmanipulated technology, in order to rid ourselves of a perpetual and seemingly infinite 40-hour work-week loop.

Our tier-based plan calls for open sourcing and taking the for-profit incentives out of both the energy and healthcare industries after a minimum period of five years, which may extend to a decade depending on the reactions to this licensing and the consequences to our economic fundamentals and the general public. Once our energy and healthcare industries are well-established and running smoothly under our licensing plan, we should follow the same type of licensing regulation with our transportation industry. It would be important to enlist the help of our college and university systems nationwide to run scenarios to make sure that we understand the full effects of permanently changing the basic fundamentals of this industry—especially when we are going to permanently remove a large amount of currency circulation throughout our economy due to permanent job loss, through technological innovation. On the other side of the coin my concern here is that if a free-energy device is invented, it needs to be adopted by the transportation industry in order propel all our vehicles. If there would be resistance in the form of collusion by the transportation industry to continue running gasoline-powered or electric vehicles that require hookup to a power grid to charge, the transportation industry as a whole would be very reluctant to take on a source of propulsion that would massively decrease its annual revenues and potentially permanently eliminate jobs in its industry—an industry that continually relies on an inferior form of technology that constantly needs repair or replacement in order to create an endless stream of cash flow.

Our familiar plan follows a nine-step flow:

Step 1. Requiring a license for all transportation-based companies.

Step 2. Removing the shareholder.

Step 3. Removing all patents from the industry.

Step 4. Requiring all transportation companies to become nonprofit, in order to maintain their energy license.

Step 5. Requiring internal company audits.

Step 6. Creating incentives for employees through bonuses. Transportation workers could expect to see their annual incomes increase by 10% through a structured bonus system.

Step 7. Creating a state-run Transportation Protection Agency.

Step 8. Sourcing funds for operation and advancement of new and existing transportation companies.

Step 9. Monitoring, maintaining, supporting and adjusting the industry through a vetting period of at least five years.

Let's begin:

Step 1. Requiring a license for all transportation-based companies.

A transportation company would be defined as any company that creates any type of vehicle on its premises, including the following: snowmobiles, motorcycles, all-terrain four-wheel vehicles, motorized yachts and motorized boats, automobiles and trucks—used for both personal and commercial duties by the general public. A transportation company would also be defined as any company that directly or indirectly provides a product or service for the industry; this would include any original or aftermarket parts or any service used to alter any parts, for a vehicle manufacturing company or corporation, for the sole purpose of producing any vehicle that requires a propulsion system to the general public. Any companies or corporations that produce "aftermarket" or OEM (Original Equipment Manufacturer) parts to be used to replace the existing parts or sell these parts to the general public—for example, a salvage yard that was in the business of retiring, shredding or melting vehicles—could still do so without a license. However, if the salvage yard sold any type of aftermarket parts or scrap metal to a licensed company, they would require a license and be required to operate under nonprofit directives or under the umbrella of a separate company.

Two of the main companies providing replacement parts to the transportation industry, besides the oil companies, which obviously make money from oil changes and petroleum-based parts, would be the companies that currently produce tires and brakes. The U.S. tire industry had total sales of about $38 billion in 2016. Tires need to be replaced an average of every 3 to 5 years depending on the mileage and driving style of the owner. We can expect this regular replacement expense to continue forward indefinitely under the current system. If there are 300,000-mile tires or axles whose bearings could turn 1 million miles before replacement that can be produced today, then we should be mass distributing them immediately. Antigravity technology would eliminate the tire industry altogether, so its development is most likely impossible under the for-profit incentives governing the current industry. Todays' intellectual property laws and incentives leave the development of these types technologies to private companies making private purchases of private patents, to shelve the technology with no transparency required to the general public. Just like housing with its tax-deductible mortgage interest and property taxes, varying from person to person based on their yearly income, the American public has absolutely no idea what the true cost of owning an automobile is today based on the different depreciation rates for vehicles and varied repair costs.

Let's draw some conclusions based on what we know so far about a transportation industry that is for-profit, publicly traded and patented, and the effects the laws governing this industry have on the American public:

1. The average American is now going to spend more than $36,000 for a new vehicle, and that's about $6,000 more than the average annual income of 50% of the American public! The prices of vehicles rise directly proportional to the amount of inflation in any given economy. Now that times are good again and people are making more money, the rising prices of vehicles attempt to zero out any net benefit the general public might attain from better economic times, in order to increase their savings. The currency-based for-profit system does everything in its power to keep Americans right where they are now with the small benefit of perhaps enjoying a slightly better substitute vehicle with some minor upgraded electronic technology, whose propulsion system is exactly the same as it was 50 or even 100 years ago. The relative number of hours a year they need to work for this purchase hasn't really changed all that much since 1965; as a matter of fact, the relative number of hours to purchase a typical vehicle is actually more now than 50 years ago, and about 98% of the vehicles on the road today across the world are still powered by gas or diesel.

2. About 50% of the American public can also expect the investment of their annual salary into an automobile to depreciate by about 60% within the first five years of owning the average vehicle.

3. According to AAA.com, Americans can expect to have extensive and numerous vehicle maintenance costs while owning a vehicle, and at least one in three of them will not be able to cover the repair bill without going into some type of additional debt.[70] Let's also be very honest in saying that once a vehicle reaches 150,000 miles or more on its odometer, the repair cost per year becomes exponentially higher

---

70   https://www.aaa.com/autorepair/articles/planning-for-auto-maintenance-and-repair-costs

with major repairs needed for things like water pumps, timing belts, valve replacements and potentially transmission repair, which can cost between $300 and $1,000 per instance or more depending on the type of vehicle being serviced. These types of breakdowns leave consumers scrambling for cheap do-it-yourself fixes on the internet in a state of panic, trying to keep their vehicle on the road as their income and expenses are constantly being tested under this type of system.

In summation, this is a debt-driven industry based on inferior technology that constantly needs to be repaired or replaced! Why should we continue to support an industry that leaves us powerless to evolve beyond an endless cycle of income and spending? I wish I could give you an answer to that question, but I can't. Perhaps it's the way our multifaceted society has developed over the last hundred years in a wide variety of ways. All I know is that it's time to get rid of the idea that constantly repurchasing the same inferior technology is good for us. It's time to stop working just to work or just to support industries that aren't making our lives better. The products produced by this industry have a short-term useful life and are thrown into a hole or the ocean, causing damage to our ecosystem and damage to our bodies by ingesting toxins that further increase our healthcare premiums. Do you see the vicious cycle here? These industries have all very quietly orchestrated collusion between themselves to keep Americans from using the superior technology that they really deserve, transportation technology that could potentially last 25 or 50 years without replacement. Dwelling technology that could potentially last 100 years without repair or replacement. Healthcare premiums that should be a fraction of what they cost now with less people going to doctors, because they are less stressed out and work less. Isn't it time the American public stop being forced to pay exorbitant prices for housing, automobiles and pharmaceuticals just to keep on surviving to work yet another day? We're not striving for any of the goals I've just outlined. We're not even making any effort, because we have no goal to do so and we are not unified as a country to make any goals. We are divided as a country due to the laws of for-profits and patents that transform us into individuals who are striving constantly to the meet the demands of exorbitant, ever-increasing overhead and have little time or energy left to ever look at the big picture, in order to help ourselves transcend beyond our daily rituals.

Let's set a goal of $5,000 as the average price for any vehicle in America, and 300,000 miles for the first scheduled maintenance to be required on any part of any newly produced vehicle, including the windshield wipers. If we could produce this type of technology, it would solve basically all of our problems; the price of a new vehicle would be a fraction of what it is now and potentially trending lower over the long run. Perhaps a vehicle's useful life might easily extend a to a period of 25 years and most likely during the first 10 years there would be no maintenance required whatsoever, and we might expect the depreciation of a vehicle of this type during the first 10 years of ownership to be minimal. Most likely due to its nominal price, the majority of the general public would not need financing to purchase these vehicles, thus eliminating additional interest payments, which further lowers the cost of each vehicle. Enacting a licensing system sets all these goals in motion and will help us to create the technology to make it a reality.

Step 2. Removing the shareholder.

Stocks trade on the perfect information theory, which basically says that any information, good or bad, that is known by the public is already priced into any stock today. Licensing our energy and healthcare industries, with the known potential for the entire transportation industry to come under the regulations of a licensing system would have an immediate negative effect on all of the stocks traded in the transportation industry. Potentially the shareholders being removed entirely from these companies that are going to be made nonprofit would have a large negative effect on the stock markets, and over the course of 5 to 10 years, of the licensing of the energy and healthcare industries the value of transportation stocks may only be a fraction of what it was before those two industries became fully licensed, because of the threat of losing those shares to a licensing system. So instituting a buyout for a price equal to 5% of the average of the last three years daily market closing price, for the stocks of all transportation companies, might possibly be executed at a higher price than the current market price of their stock and might offer the shareholders some sort of profitable gains at that point in time.

I'm also quite aware of the fact that pensions in this country are invested heavily in the stock market, and if we start taking the profit out of our energy and healthcare industries, we would see pensions not being able to meet their monthly guarantees or goals to their recipients. This could have a negative effect on the incomes of retired people in particular, especially due to the fact that the baby boomer generation is only expected to grow over the next two decades. What I'm trying to illustrate to you with this specific plan is to follow the lesser of two evils. One way or another, cash for labor is going to be eliminated from our society, either through robots that simulate both skilled and unskilled labor tasks and through cheap outsourced labor, as the world population expands another 50% over the next 35 years; or by reducing overhead through enacting a licensing system throughout the 50 states of America.

While we continue to operate a for-profit currency-based economy, we can expect the cost to repair or expand roads is going to increase, and we're going to have to issue more government bonds just to repair and replace our crumbling infrastructure. The cost of maintaining an environmentally sound ecosystem is going to also massively increase and put a heavy burden on all businesses in the United States, and most likely increased taxes will be placed on our businesses to cover these costs. Large corporations will look to swallow up any mom-and-pop industries in instances where they can use volume sales to destroy them, thus replacing viable small businesses with minimum-wage local labor or outsourced overseas labor. One way or another, the currency-based economy of the United States is going to fail—it is on a collision course and this cannot be avoided. We are in a cycle of continually increasing our debt. I don't think I need to present those statistics anymore for you to understand that the government has no funds saved to cover any future disasters, spends everything that it takes in every year and is horribly in debt. The American public will continue to increase its debt as well until it becomes crushed under the weight of monthly payments that it will no longer be able to afford due to longer periods of unemployment and wages falling relative to increasing overhead prices.   What I'm trying to illustrate to you is that we will have a soft landing, if we can cut our overhead costs prior to our incomes being substantially reduced. In the long run, perhaps in the next hundred years the currency system itself will be largely eliminated. The pace at which this happens will most likely be quicker than many people would prefer and that they might be mentally able to handle. It's always important for us to understand that our future is bright and positive and moving towards a better standard of living, a future that is no longer based on debt and maintaining endless hours of work just to receive our next paycheck. Once our overhead technology begins working for us, we will only need to make a small amount of money and hopefully will able to do the things we love to do for a living. Make no mistake about it: We're moving to a better place than we are now, it's just a matter of how we get there. I'm still quite amazed by the fact that Americans want to work more and still believe they can solve all their problems through increased income, when in fact the currency-based economy is incentivized to keep the general public forever in repurchase mode. Things are definitely going to get better than they are now, because we're coming to an understanding of what we need to do to live life on a more permanent and abundant basis rather than clinging to old models that no longer work.

Step 3. Removing all patents from the industry.

Simply put, removing patents from the industry is necessary to create vehicles that will last 25 to 50 years and eliminate ever-increasing vehicle prices and massive repair costs.

Step 4. Requiring all transportation companies to become nonprofit, in order to maintain their energy license.

We would follow the same licensing process, similar to the energy and healthcare industries.

Step 5. Requiring internal company audits.

We would follow the same licensing process, similar to the energy and healthcare industries.

Step 6. Creating incentives for employees through bonuses.

Workers would receive quarterly bonuses based on performance incentives and an annual profit-sharing bonus based on the cumulative effect of their performance in their previous four quarters. Bonusing and incentivizing should be an essential part of human resources policies. It's also essential that we remove the old quarterly-profit-driven style of management, which constantly micromanages and pushes workers into increasing performance by threatening their survival through the termination of their employment. There are other ways to motivate people to perform at their highest level, and other labor-management systems that have already shown incredible progress in productivity in current and past American corporations.

Charles Duhigg's *Smarter, Faster, Better* discusses in Chapter 5 how the New United Motor Manufacturing plant in Fremont California was completely transformed be a new style of management. Workers were made to feel a part of a family and their input was highly regarded, as to how to best execute their jobs. Over the next 30 years, the plant never had a one lay-off, which was mainly fostered by the fact that the majority of executives of the company were willing to take major pay cuts during economic down times.[71] Executives taking pay cuts is quite rare for any industry, but if people are properly incentivized and understand their specific role within a company and how it affects others, sacrifices are more likely to be made. It's very important to keep workers in all these industries motivated and focused on goals. I encourage you to read Duhigg's book, which gives many examples of innovations and breakthroughs that have been made during very dark times by large corporations in America. These organizations have completely turned around their workforces and their fortunes by setting specific goals, reinforced with specific planning, coupled with a specific mindset, to achieve audacious results.

The United States has created some amazing technology over the last hundred years. Trust in the fact that there are ways and means to motivate people to reach specific goals, and there are a number of books already out there that can show us what actions we need to take in order to meet them. I would urge you take a look at the books listed in the preferred reading list at the back of this text as well as seek out other books on your own, relative to satisfying your own curiosities and questions that I'm sure have popped up into your mind throughout the reading of this text. The purpose of this text is to raise your awareness so that you will seek other information, in order to form a new mindset to assist you in changing our economy.

Step 7. Creating a state Transportation Protection Agency

This federal or state agency would grant all initial transportation licenses and enforce all rules and regulations, to ensure all licenses are properly maintained.

---

71   Charles Duhigg's *Smarter, Faster, Better* discusses in Chapter 5, pp 139-155.

Step 8. Sourcing funds for the operation and advancement of new and existing transportation companies.

There are numerous taxes, debt instruments or even forms of crowdfunding, which we've already discussed in detail, that could be enacted in order to fund this industry's existing companies and help to provide seed money to foster the creation of new companies and to maintain funding for newly licensed companies.

Step 9. Monitoring, maintaining, supporting and adjusting the industry through a vetting period of at least five years.

I would suggest monitoring the transportation industry closely, for a period of 5 to 8 years, before applying any type of licensing to the housing industry. Changing the energy, healthcare and transportation industries in the United States would have a mass impact on the price of housing, as I have already outlined in this text, by massively decreasing lot costs—if just a portable source of energy was actually made available for purchase to the American public. Most likely 10 to 15 years or more would have already passed since the initial licensing of the energy and healthcare industries began, and we would have already seen massive fundamental changes to our economy as a result of licensing these three industries.

We're moving toward a new world here, a new world where we're using our money to build superior technology to eliminate the number of times, we use money as a source of exchange. In short, we're reducing our dependency on currency by creating superior technology. Take a moment now to envision what our society and country will look like 15 years into the process of regulating these three industries. How will people feel, and what will be the general mood of our country? How will people dress? What types of social gatherings might be going on? What will the music industry look like? How easy will it be to start and run a local business in America? How much money do you think the average person will need to make, in order to enjoy a happy and prosperous life? What will the health of Americans be like? What do you think our attitude towards foreign countries will look like? Your vision of your future is extremely important in bringing about this process into a reality.

I've had a hard time during the writing of this book to keep up, over the course of the last few years, with all the newly developing technologies that are quickly becoming realities at least on a small scale in America today. In the big picture there are transportation companies that have plans to eliminate car ownership altogether in the future. Autonomously driven vehicles will most likely be part of a monthly subscription service at some point in the future. We won't buy or lease cars anymore. I can tell you this is going to be a foregone conclusion on some level, as big cities have massive parking problems and the use of autonomously driven vehicles shared by many people would vastly eliminate time-consuming and expensive parking problems. I can understand people not wanting to randomly share the car they use daily with the general public, so perhaps these companies might limit their subscriptions to 10 other people who the consumer has some power in choosing. Ownership use could be time-stamped and ownership habits tracked through some sort of database. So, if my autonomously driven vehicle comes to pick me up, at 5 o'clock after my workday and there's ice cream spilled in the backseat, a database ledger would tell me who the previous user was who is potentially responsible for the mess. Users who practice bad ownership habits, similar to unsafe drivers who pay higher insurance premiums, might end up getting grouped into pools, where they pay higher subscription fees per month for the same vehicle service. In the case of driving long distances, perhaps there would be autonomously driven, subscription-paid vehicles available for long-distance trips only. Tube technology is another type of high-speed mass transit technology that we could also make great use of to meet our long-distance travel needs. A change in ownership practices will vastly reduce the number of cars required to be produced each year, compounded with automation replacing human jobs in factories and over the long run, these new practices translate into a massive reduction in labor needed to produce and maintain automobiles.

We're entering into a world where technology is compounding its expansion at an incredible pace and redefining our illusions of ownership. When your car is sitting in your garage, or outside your house, it's not being used right now but you are still paying for it monthly, and it's still depreciating at a very rapid rate even though you're not using it. This translates into a mass inefficiency of your income and requires your perpetual labor to keep up with this mass inefficiency. Autonomously driven vehicles, which can be created in almost fully automated plants, requiring just a few people to run, will be driven to autonomously operated carwashes. Certainly, antigravity technology would eliminate the use for tire production or building roads altogether, thus eliminating another massive expense for our citizens; and as we go through time, we'll see more and more that the more superior our technology becomes, the less we rely on currency.

In a 2017 article for Electrek by Fred Lambert, Elon Musk stated that almost all brands of cars on the road would be self-driving within 10 years, and it would take about 20 years to replace all cars on the road with autonomously driven vehicles.[72] I think it's important to take into account the fact that an increase in the use of automation in the building of these vehicles could radically reduce that timeframe. Everyone is heavily incentivized to replace vehicles that are 10 years old or older simply because single repairs can run up to thousands of dollars and the yearly expense in order to keep these vehicles on the road is greater than the opportunity cost of buying a newer car. So only a smaller fraction of the general public ever drives automobiles for 10 to 20 years or longer. If we want to replace the approximately 2 billion cars on the road today with more efficient vehicles to potentially save our ecosphere, most likely we're going to have to run plants 24/7, and the only way we can do this is to make our manufacturing plants fully automated and

---

72 https://electrek.co/2017/02/13/tesla-elon-musk-all-new-cars-self-driving/

devoid of human labor. A licensing system dovetails the entire transportation industry's practices and goals perfectly, in every aspect, to meet our future demands while steering the general public out of a constant income-and-spend cycle.

I personally would love to see cars run on ColdFusion or some sort of portable free-energy generator. A fully developed ColdFusion device might power a vehicle for a period of perhaps up to five years without replacement of its power unit, or possibly even longer. In other words, your vehicle could potentially be equipped with its own power supply which would not require any source of energy throughout its useful life—no fill-ups or plug-ins for a period of five years or longer, and as we develop this technology perhaps we could extend the vehicle's power supply to as long as 50 years or more! We could use devices of this type in all of our electronic equipment including our computers and household devices. Even our vacuum cleaners would not require an external source of electricity or fossil fuel in order to run them. These are examples of the type of world we can build if we change the laws running our energy, healthcare and transportation industries. I firmly believe that we're heading toward a better future and this plan is going to help facilitate the speed and efficiency at which we arrive at our destination: a technology-driven economy whose main focus is on distributing technology at the lowest possible cost. Rather than continuing to deal with the same old problems of scarcity, fear and confusion that the currency-based system perpetuates daily and over the long term helps to incentivize our inevitable technology-based economy from ever being constructed. The idealisms and emotions that you're newly creating, as you read this book, are the most important factors in turning your current thought energy into a manifested reality for all of us to share. Only together, through a determined level of understanding and willingness to change, can we create a world of abundance and peace that we've never experienced before!

CHAPTER 10

Creating a Licensed Housing Industry

Since housing represents the biggest cost to Americans and is the direct cause of lifetime debt slavery, we should begin to address this problem as soon as reasonably possible. Americans have been guided under false programming that real estate must always go up, and this is simply a fallacy creating an insurmountable debt for our future citizens; one generation works today for the frivolity of another. People take cash from homes through loans, sell them or they are inherited and sold by their beneficiaries. The young generation buying these inflated homes is forced into paying a higher price for the same level of technology and that price is constantly increasing decade after decade, forcing the new owner to work more hours than the previous owner, in order to own the exact same structure free and clear. The false idealism that real estate will continue to rise in value forever and ever creates debt for future generations that at some point will no longer be affordable based on dwindling incomes due to outsourcing and automation. Exorbitantly high real-estate prices in crowded areas like Tokyo are already facilitating the need for 100-year mortgages, and it is almost impossible to live in a city like San

Francisco without multiple renters in one structure to cover the mortgage payments. In larger metropolitan cities we're seeing the need for people from almost all walks of life regardless of income to be forced into sharing housing, due to its ever-increasing scarcity and rising cost.

Americans need to stop treating homes like a collectible item, such as a rare antique or a limited-edition stamp or coin, and take a different approach to building real estate. We need to shift our idealism of American culture towards creating housing that becomes cheaper over time, similar to our current expectations of purchasing durable goods, like television sets or other electronics. In the electronics realm we expect more technology with declining long-term costs for the product over time, because in this case technology is freely being applied to enhance the product in order to drive the cost down. Any older version of such a technology would be considered obsolete and almost worthless over time compared to the amenities available in the current version. The idealism and expectations that we commonly apply to almost everything we purchase is not applied to the creation of livable structures for humans, in this country. A technologically advancing society's goal should be to create a better standard of living than the previous generation experienced through advanced technology. From the perspective of evolution, the fact that something we need so desperately—shelter—constantly rises in value and the American public participates in this idealism enthusiastically, makes no sense.

The only way to truly solve the real-estate problem in this country is by applying technology to the physical problem itself so we can begin to lower our lot development and on-site building costs and increase the supply of homes throughout the United States. If we keep the current system in place that uses old- style utility connection technologies, through a centralized provider to any prospective residential or commercial lot, we can only expect the price of real estate to continue to rise in the long run. If we keep creating housing this way, we can expect the financing will have to chase the ever-increasing price of this inferior technology. It is inferior because it's simply not able to be supplied at a level to meet the demands for usable living space of our ever-expanding population. Superior technology applied to this industry would create a superior product at a fraction of the cost, so until we remove the for-profit system, along with the incentives to keep the technology inferior in order to create ongoing profits for the industry, we can expect higher housing prices, more occupants per unit and longer-term mortgages in order to meet the enormous debt that will be created by a lack of available living space.

The current system will never meet the needs of our expanding population, which is expected to reach 9.7 billion in roughly another 30 years and over 11 billion by the year 2100. We simply cannot keep the current system in place with that type of population on our planet. If we do so, we should expect to experience severe economic problems. Why keep on with the current system, when instead we can just apply technology to create and clone low-cost superior housing, to increase the standard of living, for all Americans? Computers can help us create the designs and facilitate manufacturing of the technology, and robots can do the work of assembly. The question has to arise at some point in the intellectual progression of our species on this planet: Why keep the old system in place at all? What are the real benefits to keeping it in place? Why keep working forever in service in perpetuity, to pay off inferior technology over a 30- to 50-year period, when we can simply create technology that potentially doesn't require any type of debt service at all?

Let's do a quick review from the previous housing chapter. In order to solve a housing shortage that is plaguing the United States, we basically need to solve two problems:

1. A lot-cost problem, which is driven directly by utility connection problems.

2. Expensive on-site building costs.

Our lot-cost problem consists of a two very easily resolvable sub-problems that can be resolved by granting each lot access to completely portable and self-contained utilities—electricity, water and sewer—while at the same time being able to grade and pave the lot for easy access from any available road, so that we can connect the population of the United States, now roughly 328 million, to the 1.9 billion acres of available land in the lower 48 states. That's about 5 acres for every man woman and child in this country; we don't have a land scarcity problem here like Japan does, we simply have utility cost connection problems to overcome. Right now, about two thirds of the population is squeezing themselves into only 3%, of the usable land in the United States. We need to move people out into the country, into sustainable local communities, powered by solar, ColdFusion or free-energy generators, provide water to the lot through Atmospheric Water Generators and dispose of waste through digitally printed sewer tanks. We also need to provide these local citizens with access to medical centers, grocery stores, trade stores and so on, that in turn operate on portable utilities, are digitally printed and extremely low in cost to build. These digitally produced commercial structures should provide access to the same local goods and services that people expect and receive today in large metropolitan cities. We already know that we can receive delivery service pretty much anywhere in the United States, in just a few days. The internet, satellite TV, and so on can easily connect us to the communications we'll need to stay in touch with the rest of the world. Local residential as well as commercial greenhouses could supply a majority of the fresh food for people and local livestock to consume throughout the year.

Let's review some of the basics we need to address in order to solve our utility connection problems:

We'll need to develop a strong portable source of energy that does not require any hookup to any type of centralized utility.

Next, we'll need a portable source of water created through capturing rainwater depending on the location of the structure, or the ability to find and dig wells at an incredibly inexpensive cost; or perhaps the ability to extrapolate water directly from the air through Atmospheric Water Generators, which are now available for residential and commercial use; or develop another unknown technology that might create water through alchemy or other means, in order to provide drinking water for the humans, plants and animals.

Next, digitally printed sewer tanks. Our ability to produce them thankfully already exists.

We'll need a fully automated system to grade our lot and connect our proposed building site to a local road without distance limitations. If we currently possess technology to create lots in the form of bulldozers, graders, backhoes and the like, and we currently possess autonomously driven automobiles, wouldn't it make sense to produce autonomously driven bulldozers graders, backhoes, bucket loaders, heavy-duty trucks and fully automate the lot-preparation process? Could these vehicles be operated remotely, in a corporate office, from a computer screen?

Finally, will need a machine to digitally print our road, driveway, parking area and walkways, that is fully automated and could be operated or managed remotely through the internet or satellite communication, at a very inexpensive cost.

Currently using today's available utility technology, the above lot development costs pre-build, are estimated anywhere from $35,000 to $80,000, varying greatly depending on location. Since 50% of the American population makes $30,000 a year or less, the goal for our final completed structure should be $25,000 or less. So, breaking that down, we should set a goal for our lot cost preparation, including all on-site utilities, to be no more than $8,000, preferably even $5,000, so we have $20,000 left over for our structure costs, in order to meet our $25,000 on-site purchase cost for a brand-new home. Under the present system of technology, there is absolutely no way that the 50% of our population that makes $30,000 a year or less is ever going to change their current status as a renter to become a free and clear homeowner unless we apply technology to the problem and apply it with the intent over time to produce it at the lowest cost possible. A licensing system applied to this industry, making it essentially nonprofit, non-publicly traded and patent free, is the only way I see this becoming a reality.

Currently there are millions upon millions of acres of land available in the United States, with absolutely beautiful weather and climate that can be used for real-estate development. Phoenix, Arizona is the fifth largest city in the United States and the fastest growing city in the United States; people are clearly flocking to the desert Southwest because there is cheap land there to build on. The southern United States still has vast amounts of land in desirable areas available for building, including coastal areas. In California, the entire coastline has very little urban development between the San Francisco Bay area and Los Angeles; the entire coastline, with breathtaking views is available for usable living space. In short, there is land everywhere to develop sustainable and local communities that could meet the climate and other critical demands of virtually any potential homebuyer. A migration out of the cities would certainly leave the existing metropolitan populations in a far better financial situation, as the demand for real estate there would drop, causing more affordable housing prices with a readily developed substitute available, as an ever-present option for city dwellers within any given state. We must also consider the fact that once sustainable local communities become culturally accepted, trendy or popular in our society, as an exciting and fun place to live, that the basic structures and foundations of our economy will forever be changed. In short, once people find out it's a great deal to live in these types of communities, where people no longer struggle from paycheck to paycheck in order to survive, many people will opt to migrate out of the cities, most likely to a point where city life becomes far cheaper and much more desirable for the remaining residents. I fully expect that based on already established cultural and human thought processes, that it will take decades of time for the populations of major metropolitan cities to migrate fully to more remote residential areas; in the meantime, having a low-cost substitute readily available to all city dwellers will certainly provide a boost to their immediate standard of living.

For the on-site building cost problem, the focus here is going to be on shifting your idealism and imagination towards the idea of portable self-contained living. A Russian company known as Apis Cor has already digitally printed the first living structure. We can also use this digital printing technology to digitally print a driveway access to the main road, the home's foundation, the parking areas, walking areas and sewer tanks. Our intention should be to create a completely self-contained structure that does not require any type of connection to any type of centralized energy or water utility; rather all utilities are produced on-site. Earthships already meet all these criteria: electricity through installed solar and wind power, a portable supply of water through rainwater capture and water recycling, and a portable sewer system that recycles gray water and sewage waste without smell. All utilities in this case are created and produced on-site. These structures are partially buried in order to create natural insulation from the earth, and use a series of ventilation systems and open glass areas to help facilitate natural heating and cooling from the sun and wind, without connecting to any type of a centralized energy, water or sewage disposal.

Problems with Bringing the Digitally Printed, Superior Structures to Market

1. Cost. The cost to build one of these structures on a private lot would most likely run anywhere between $350,000 and $600,000. This price is simply too high for the average person to own and does not meet our goal of $25,000. Since the purchase price for these structures is so high, the product cannot be mass scaled to reduce production costs because the product in its current state of development is simply unaffordable for the general public. Certainly,

I believe all housing manufacturers would like to see their prices come down. Lower prices would make their product available for sale to a much larger market and could exponentially increase the revenues, but until we apply serious technology and automation to the creation and distribution of housing, it's unlikely we will see prices trending lower anytime soon.

2. Financing. This is the largest obstacle to making affordable housing a reality. We can't reduce production costs over time without mass production, which drives more innovation and overall lower unit costs over time. We can't produce these structures on a mass scale without readily available financing for these units to the general public. There is no real way to finance structures of this type. Major banks won't finance these structures because they are considered unacceptable collateral and do not fit most major government loan guidelines. In the event of foreclosure, a certain degree of uncertainty is relevant for the entity making the loan, if the noteholder might actually be able to sell the structure for its appraised value within just a few months of time in order for the provider of the loan to receive back their initial principle investment.

Financing is the major problem in trying to bring the cost down on structures like these and build them anywhere. We have a huge gap between the size of current mortgage loans today and the credit card limits for the average American, we need to find ways to make the purchase price low enough for a cred it card. It's virtually impossible to facilitate any type of production on a mass scale in this industry, in order to reduce costs to the point where they might become affordable to the general public, because these types structures, which are vastly different from track homes, can't be financed under the current lending laws today. Therefore, not a lot of homes can be sold, and this leaves the availability of the technology to just a very small market of wealthy people. Thus, the industry under its current regulations can never achieve the economies of scale it needs, in order to bring this technology to every single American citizen who would like to buy a home. In summary, the greater volume you can mass-produce of any product, the more production efficiencies you can attain, creating that product for sale with lower bottom-line unit costs and then pass those lower cost costs on to the consumer.

Unless we regulate this industry, making it nonprofit, non-publicly traded and patent-free, it's probably unlikely we will ever evolve at all beyond the post-World War II track-home style of neighborhoods that are being created now. It might certainly be possible to finance a structure like this today, after making countless phone calls, arguing with various parties, filing endless paperwork and perhaps working tirelessly for six months to a year to make it happen, but this type of agony should not be a part of the process of buying a structure to live in. Uncertainty, chaos, dead-end phone calls and endless paperwork create a huge deterrent to home ownership in our country. Based on my personal experience, I can tell you that purchasing a home—whether it be your first purchase, a move up or a downsize buy—is one of the most stressful transactions you will ever experience in your life. Obtaining financing for any home is an incredibly difficult task. Even though we have federal fair lending laws today that do not discriminate based on race, ethnicity or sex, the entire population is deterred from financing homes because the process is both incredibly complicated and expensive. Our intention should be to create a housing industry that is transparent, welcomes new homebuyers and makes homeownership as easy as possible. Currently, the system is filled with so much paperwork that the average person might simply give up after just a few hours of futile effort, trying to finance a structure that does not meet the standard lending guidelines for a bank or savings and loan. Our chances are unlikely or even impossible to mass scale this type of technology, to the general public, without severely regulating this industry from the rules and guidelines it operates under today. The federal government's answer to the problem of home ownership has always been to make home ownership affordable, by making the financing easier to qualify for, rather than applying technology to the creation of the structure, in order to lower its cost. In summary, it's easier to apply technology to the creation of the structure, thereby lowering its cost and making it more affordable to the general public, than it is to continue to come up with fancy financing programs and credits to purchase the existing, ever-increasing, inferior housing technology we have access to today. When you continue to use the currency system, everyone, including the government, will look to currency as a solution to the problem, as the first line of defense rather than simply allowing people to have access to the most advanced, cutting-edge technology on the planet. Are you starting to see how your technology rights are constantly being violated?

3. Utility Limitations. It's uncertain based on the vastly different climates we find in North America, from extreme cold in the north to extreme desert heat in the south, as to whether these homes can operate under the available sources of portable energy, such as solar or wind power, which can be purchased today. It's my personal belief, that these sources of energy may not be enough depending on location of the structure, and a third source of power for this home might be needed for use as a tertiary backup system. This is why I have stated that our target energy goal should be to create a portable energy device according to the extended specifications outlined in the chapter on energy. ColdFusion or a free-energy device is what we really need to develop, in order to provide all the power needed to meet all the demands put on it by the homeowner, no matter where the location.

4. Desirability. At one point in time during the Great Recession of 2008, you could probably buy a house in the city of Detroit for under $25,000 on a credit card. Of course, the reason for that was because of mass foreclosures because there was no sustainable employment anywhere near the structure. The neighborhoods surrounding these low-priced homes were probably quite blighted and filled with a large number of vacancies. So, we can basically say that recently the currency-based system has produced homes under our $25,000 goal. However, most likely the resident would not have been able to secure nearby employment to sustain their living expenses. Probably these homes were purchased for cash by wealthier people and then rented back to the poor as jobs became available in the local area again. Typically, during

bad economic times, wealthier people increase their wealth by taking advantage of cheap real estate and stock prices, which are sold at a high price to the general public once the majority of low-income people have reached the point of financial stability again.

Desirability is an unknown factor for humans when they are considering purchasing a home. As to what is desirable and what is not, is based on all types of mental stimuli: television and marketing practices, cultural trends, access to entertainment such as a town square, restaurants, bars, nightlife, the ability to purchase highly differentiated specialty items, and the depth and of extent products available at local retail stores for shopping, and so on. Local communities and rural areas generally lack these amenities, but I can tell you with 100% certainty that if we are able to create structures that are completely self-contained, exempt from utility hookup and that can be built anywhere, we will see communities springing up all over that will represent various cultural attitudes and will become very desirable living areas for many of our citizens. The ability to create low-cost commercial structures that also run portable utilities and can be digitally printed or created at a very low cost will allow us to create new communities virtually overnight across the country. Communities may differentiate themselves based on the type of people inhabiting them: Artists, musicians, retired people or even perhaps scientists and engineers, may start banding together to form their own communities. Living among like-minded people is usually the goal of anyone attempting to move any type of distance so that that people might evolve themselves intellectually in a more efficient manner. Local and sustainable communities that offer extremely low costs of living would most likely be safe havens to people of all walks of life. People will always want to live in cities for one reason or another, but by providing a low-cost alternative to city dwellers, this substitute should keep the cost of city living perpetually decreasing rather than increasing and hopefully provide a better source of housing, such as single-family dwellings, for city inhabitants to live in, rather than overpriced, small-sized apartments.

Creating a More Streamlined Housing Industry

After we fully vetted the licensing process in her energy and healthcare industries for a period of at least 5 to 10 years, and then spent an additional 5 years regulating our transportation industry under the control of licensing, we can now move forward and begin to apply licensing to our last industry of importance: housing. Let's remember that at the present time the industry has absolutely no incentive to build homes unless there is an immediate demand for them at a price that will meet the builder's needs The builder has absolutely no incentive to produce homes during times of recession or for that matter at any point in time where they deem the market will not meet their for-profit goals. There's always going to be a housing shortage in the United States, unless we change the way the industry is regulated. If a homebuilder actually holds back the number of units that they build and offer for sale, in any local given area, this creates an automatic housing shortage in that area; and since we have an ever-expanding population growth, the price always rises over the long term. Large homebuilders have the ability to directly manipulate the market price for their homes by holding back the supply of housing, by not building homes or producing them at a decreased rate, thereby increasing the demand for housing and increasing the per-unit price. Simply put, the builder makes more money by producing fewer homes because they can sell them at a higher price than they would if they produced more homes, at a lower price.

The for-profit paradox and all the incentives of a currency-based economy apply directly to our home-building industry. The builder is always incentivized to hold back production, to keep the price of homes as high as possible. Builders know this and can collude together to keep prices high, since homes are very expensive to produce based on the level of technology we currently apply to their creation. Builders usually don't start physically building homes until a contract has been signed by a purchaser ahead of time. During economic downtimes or times of recession and decreased demand, the builder can simply lay off workers and reduce home production to a fraction of its capability to ensure the price for their product remains as high as possible. Taking things, a step further: What factor is forcing the builder to produce a structure with additional technology at a cheaper price, when people are lined up to buy it as it is? In fairness, there are studies that show that housing production in the desert Southwest, for example, has over time approached production costs in areas like Las Vegas, for example; but the bottom line is, there is no incentive to apply technology to the product and offer a decreasing price in order to meet the scale we're discussing in this text. In order to reach the goal of a newly created structure costing $25,000 or less, we can't use privatized building. No privatized builder would ever attempt to create such a structure because they would simply go out of business.

Technology has not been seriously applied to the problem of providing affordable housing and shelter to the population of the United States, and technology never will be seriously applied to this problem under a for-profit, currency-based system. There are simply too many incentives to keep the system "status quo" by the current suppliers of homes.

A 2016 article for the Urban Institute by Laurie Goodman and Rolf Pendall states that housing demand has been far greater than housing supply since the great recession began in approximately 2009. In 2015, for example, more than a million new households required housing while only 620,000 units were created that year, creating a shortage of over 430,000 units.[73] So basically since 2009, the industry has gone back to normal after the crazy 100-year bubble that happened between 2004 and 2008. Builders control everything and the consumer is left with simply no power in the transaction. My question to you, dear reader, is why should you expect this to change over time? Unless we regulate this industry, nothing will ever change. We need these structures in order to live; they are a necessity for our survival. Why should they be controlled by shareholders and for-profit incentives? As I've stated earlier in the text, the financing must always follow the price when purchasing a home. We should expect longer-term mortgages over time and

---

73   https://www.urban.org/urban-wire/housing-supply-falls-short-demand-430000-units

more occupants per unit based on an industry that is constantly incentivized to limit production. Couple that with reduced incomes that we know are sure to come, due to eventual automation and outsourcing, leaving consumers to play the role of exploited drones and slaves living on tiny incomes trying to keep up with massive overhead costs. In an attempt to change this insanity and end a never-ending spiral of debt creation, let's review the licensing plan that I've outlined for the previous three industries:

Step 1. Requiring a license for all companies that create residential or commercial structures.

Step 2. Removing the shareholder.

Step 3. Removing all patents from the industry.

Step 4. Requiring all residential and commercial housing corporations and companies to become nonprofit, in order to maintain their licensing status.

Step 5. Requiring internal company audits.

Step 6. Creating incentives for employees through bonuses. Housing industry workers could expect to see their annual incomes increase by 10% through a structured bonus system.

Step 7. Forming a state Home Ownership Protection Agency.

Step 8. Sourcing funds for the operation and advancement of new and existing residential and commercial housing companies.

Step 9. Monitoring, maintaining, supporting and adjusting the industry through a vetting period of at least five years.

Step 1. Requiring a license for all companies that create residential or commercial structures.

This would include any sole proprietorship, limited liability company, subchapter S corporation or any entity that produces any type of shelter, whether it be residential or commercial, for human living or the storage of goods and services. This would include one- to four-unit single-family residences, condominiums, hotels, hotel condominiums, warehouses, commercial spaces, high-rise living structures, parking structures and any other type of specialized building used to accommodate humans for shelter or the shelter of any produced goods and services in the United States. Collecting income by providing any type of good or service in this industry without a license would result in prosecution under the statutes of an Economic Crime. Again, we should keep serious watch over this industry before we implement any type of licensing system upon it. At this point, we would've already licensed the energy, healthcare and transportation industries, so we should have extensive knowledge of how licensing would affect this industry and should be well-versed in the actions we need to specifically take to ensure a smooth transition through it. Licensing would also be required for any and all companies that provide any raw materials and/or goods used to erect these structures or design them, including architectural firms.

Step 2. Removing the shareholder.

The issuance of stock, options or warrants would be prohibited by companies within the Industry as a requirement of their licensing. It would also be illegal to create or trade any type of investment that speculated on the supply or demand of housing to the general public, even a private side bet between individuals; this would include any futures and options contracts or derivatives. The goal here is to eliminate all the incentives, to take advantage of the general public.

The existing outstanding stock of any licensed housing entities currently producing and distributing raw materials for housing or creating, erecting or building any residential or commercial structure would be purchased by the state or a conglomerate of states in collusion together, passing a licensing proposition for housing industries simultaneously in states where these licensed entities physically practiced business would be purchased at a price equal to 5% of the average of the last three years daily market closing price.

The remaining steps have been reviewed and explained extensively in the prior chapters on energy, healthcare and transportation:

Step 3. Removing all patents from the industry. Again, all copyrights and trademarks would lose their enforceability 24 months after the initial date of licensing, for any licensed entity.

Step 4. Requiring all residential and commercial housing corporations and companies become nonprofit, in order to maintain their licensing status.

Step 5. Requiring internal company audits.

Step 6. Creating incentives for employees through bonuses.

Step 7. Forming a state Homeownership Protection Agency.

Step 8. Sourcing funds for the operation and advancement, of new and existing residential and commercial housing companies.

Step 9. Monitoring, maintaining, supporting and adjusting the industry through a vetting period of at least five years.

If we license the housing industry, make it nonprofit, non-publicly traded and patent-free, and reach our goal providing a $25,000 purchase price to the general public, we've created a superior housing substitute. Once we create a superior substitute the existing inferior collateral, backing all the home loans in the United States would be expected to fall below the price of a newly created superior home. So, by reaching our goal, all existing wooden built homes and commercial structures would be worth far less money, mainly due to the fact that they require expensive maintenance costs over time, whereas the existing superior structures would not. In the previous chapter on real estate, we've looked at the fact that about 1% of the purchase price of any home in the United States should be set aside in a savings account to cover the expected maintenance expenses for things like dry rot, roofing repair and plumbing repair. The new technology would most likely not have any maintenance expenses over the first 25 to 50 years, of its useful life.

Based on a $25,000 purchase price, there is simply no need to finance a structure, under a secured loan. This would eliminate essentially all the jobs associated with the home and home financing industries as we know them today: appraisers, title and escrow personnel, loan processors, loan officers, loan underwriter's and all the managers, executives, human resources and supporting personnel surrounding these jobs. In addition, due to the extremely low purchase price, there would be little need to insure a transaction like this with title insurance, so title companies would most likely not be needed either. Realtors most likely would also be eliminated from these transactions, as the scope and complexity of the transaction becomes no more difficult than purchasing an automobile today and could be completed by filling out a form on a website and simply applying a credit card to make payment at the end of the process. Most likely we would also greatly reduce the number of jobs for contractors and building supply employees. Furthermore, digitally printed homes are not subject to damage from termites and other rodents, and so the number of jobs in the pest industry would be expected to decline as well. Needless to say, the creation of homes today is incredibly expensive and requires vast amounts of labor in order to support the industry. And what do all these people do with all the income that they create every month by working in this industry? They turn right around and pay a large portion of their income to rents and mortgages, so in essence we see another instance of people funding their own demise. In summation, what's really happening today is that we're all working towards a goal of creating, repairing and replacing inferior technology, which produces long-term debt as a side effect. When superior technology is introduced into the real-estate industry, it forever reduces the amount of monthly overhead expenses of the average citizen and the extensive need for jobs, long working hours and constant currency circulation is no longer required. In short, we can break the constant cycle of debt and overhead servicing, through labor for cash by choosing a path toward creating superior survival technology.

If we decide not to institute the proposed licensing system in this industry and continue on our present path—which is to randomly produce technology that eliminates income for Americans without directly address- ing their monthly overhead expenditures, then we are likely to run into a "period of waiting" where we have high, untouched overhead expenditures coupled with low minimum wage or government- supported incomes, and this will surely cause a collapse in our banking and credit systems as we see massive defaults and foreclosures take place in the real-estate industry. These real estate loan defaults, and will cause a chain reaction in the stock markets, further layoffs and reduced incomes, spiraling towards an eventual currency collapse. Either way, our extensive need for currency will be dras- tically reduced in the future, due to loss of incomes from technology and automation or a loss of jobs from creating superior technology in our four overhead industries. We can directly try to reduce our dependency on cur- rency now by reducing our overhead and thus permanently decreasing our need and dependency for currency. Working as a means to an end seems to be a better way of approaching our economic system, rather than attempting to randomly eliminate jobs with no concern for the overall welfare of our population, as we are presently doing today.

I firmly believe that ownership is an illusion. No one can really own anything, hence the reason I am so vehemently against patents and turning our thought processes that might seriously help humankind through patent law, over to our corporations, whose only intent is to hold technology at bay, rather than evolving and distributing the benefits to the general public. Ownership has always been an illusion based on a piece of paper, representing the ideals and beliefs of any given society at any point in time in its history. Over time the beliefs and idealisms of many cultures have changed and will continue to do so, this licensing system represents what I believe will be an eventual change in cultural beliefs, away from narrow-minded ownership principles towards a broad and evolving perspective of what ownership can become, which hopefully will be taking advantage of shared resources for the benefit of future Americans. In order to better understand the current system, let's take a look at the history of the United States and how its financial empire was essentially—built. The 1.9 billion acres of land in the lower 48 states, that we enjoy as citizens of the United States today was actually stolen from American Indian tribes, who had lived here before the United States colonies were settled. This type of acquisition was accomplished by openly squatting on the land and then shooting the native inhabitants if they decided to protest against this hostile takeover. In addition, the United States Cavalry was used to overpower those indigenous groups who would try to reclaim their land by force in large numbers. All the deeds to all the land in the lower 48 states are basically predicated on murder. Let's just think about this for a minute. If you owned land and someone came along and murdered you for it and then said that they owned it, would they be able to own it today? No, certainly not. They would be put in prison for murder. Nevertheless, all the deeds issued, by every county in the United States are based on an act of murder or at the very least the forced removal and eradication of the prior residents of that land. Perhaps the Indians killed other tribes to take the land that these tribes had once occupied as their territory in the past, and prior to that in the distant past Cro-Magnon man killed Neanderthal man for their access to new and undiscovered lands. Throughout history, for hundreds of thousands of years, we've developed this idealism that killing and conquering are the best means to enjoying the greatest amount of lasting prosperity.

So really you can look at the idea of the creation of wealth from two perspectives:

1. Mass exploitation and mass wealth are directly correlated with each other. Throughout history, the exploitation of land and the exploitation of masses of people in the United States were both required prerequisites in order to gain superior wealth for a small group of individuals. Wealth comes about by creating ownership, and all ownership laws are created or not created

based on the perspective or point of view of the group of people who agree to abide by these laws, regardless of that law's morality or consequences. So, if you can manipulate the population into believing the idea that something is good for them even if it hurts or destroys other people, you can make it a reality. If the mass population agrees with the idea, that a new law is a beneficial regardless of its morality, it becomes the law. In the case of the early settlement of the United States, there was no law protecting the ownership rights of the indigenous population; it was okay to murder people, in order to take their land and divvy it up to other people— in this case, the American settlers. This was a perfectly acceptable business practice based on the consciousness and level of technology of the people living in the United States colonies and territories in the 1700s and 1800s. Let's also be aware that these current lands were used to build empires that required lots of workers, repeating daily tasks over and over again, in perpetuity in order to create a vast amount of wealth for small groups of people over time. The development of the United States economy over the last several hundred years, has been a direct result of using human slaves in addition to taking land by force; these are the specific reasons I don't believe we should continue on with this type of manipulation by the wealthy. Today's manipulation has evolved to another scale, through the use of currency and patents and created another form of slavery—"debt slavery," where roughly 99% of the population has agreed to waive their technology rights, rights that are innately endowed to them by their Creator, and committed themselves to service in perpetuity as a result of their poor decision-making.

2. Wealth cannot be created without ownership, and all land ownership in the United States is enforced through a piece of paper, and that piece of paper represents an idealism, or shared belief system and nothing more. The true reality from a very-big-picture perspective is that a paper called a property deed is a meaningless pipe dream and has absolutely no physical relationship between the land and the human who owns it. Based on the interaction between this piece of paper and the general public, this paper is merely a

way to transfer a system of beliefs and ideals between humans. Therefore, the concept of land ownership is simply a thought process and nothing more. The piece of paper granting ownership is granted by another piece of paper, called currency. So, the reality of our current economy was really created through evolving perceptions and accepted business practices—that is, people universally agreeing that some acts are offensive or not offensive and how they react to them by creating laws to stop or regulate certain acts from being repeated. Once technology and information no longer remain constant and evolve beyond a certain point, new laws are required in order to reach another state of economic equilibrium. We've already reached beyond this breaking point, having already developed artificial intelligence that can simulate human thinking, free information through a worldwide internet and the creation of humanoid-type robots that can mimic human labor and communicate on a basic level with other humans. The current system ran successfully on constant economic variables: a low level of technology - that advanced at a snail's pace, slow communications, bad transportation and paper vs. digital currency, coupled with a vast supply of willing human laborers – who saw no other choice to end their plight. It is simply impossible to go on with the current system, as we know it, now that the variables of information and technology have exponentially evolved and are no longer considered unchanging economic variables.

A deed—a piece of paper—contains words referencing laws that bind other people in society to abide by them, and currency—another piece of paper—contains words that do exactly the same thing. Both pieces of paper are based on thought processes that were accepted by humans a long time ago. The thought process of creating the first deed of trust was considered the right process for a small group of humans, so that they might have exclusive control, over a specific area of the earth, not otherwise occupied by the ocean. Similarly, the thought process of currency is based upon a piece of paper with specific symbols on it, being a universally accepted medium of exchange for goods and services by the general population. It's very important to recognize innately that both these pieces of paper are based on thought processes and these thought processes, can be changed at any time by the collective consciousness and accepted beliefs of society. If society or American culture finds that another thought process serves the aggregate population in a more efficient and beneficial manner, it is likely that new laws will be passed to change the actions and accepted business practices of the entire country, so that some new level of equality can be attained. So, what does this all mean? Our economy is based on our emotional psychology! To solve the problems of the economy, you have to first solve the problems of the emotional psychology of the mass population, before you can solve anything else! The biggest problem America has today is being stuck in thought patterns that no longer serve the general public based on the advanced level of technology and information available to people today. Technology and information that were certainly never available to the Europeans who first came the United States and began killing Indians in order to fulfill some sort of dream quest that they had. People today accept the laws of capitalism and currency as immovable objects, innate truths that can never be changed, and this type of thinking will result in physically manifested failure—100% of the time. In summary, at some point in the history of the world somebody came up with the idea of currency as a medium of exchange, for goods and services between people; and as we progressed, somebody came up with the idea that a property deed was a good idea in order to perpetuate the concept of ownership between humans. Today nobody questions these concepts and they are hundreds or even thousands of years old! Do you think people back then were as intelligent and had access to as much information as we do now? Do you think it's a good idea to bow your head and go along with the status quo, or do you think it's a better idea to question the validity of ancient laws as they relate to our modern-day technologically advanced society?

Let's contrast the past ownership beliefs with our present-day ownership beliefs for a moment. Did the founding fathers of our country have access to timeshare condominiums? Homeowners can now rent out rooms in their homes through the internet for a second income. Businesses offer tools and appliances, from welding machines to refrigerators, that anyone can rent for a single day. Anyone can pull up information on hotels in any given area in the United States in a just a few seconds and compare room rates and amenities. Alternative currencies are now showing up in vast numbers, and blockchain technology is on the forefront of how we may be able to verify the results of our elections. We're coming to a new understanding of ownership, currency and how the two relate. This evolution of ownership and currency's relation to it, is going to continue exponentially faster as we get more intelligent, have access to more information and our world becomes more transparent, through a massively developing internet, cell phones with cameras and 24/7 media coverage. Robots and computers in just the next few decades may create new technologies without human intervention. Our idealisms and beliefs are changing about ownership as our technology advances, and correspondingly as out technology advances at an accelerated rate we should expect our idealisms and beliefs regarding ownership to change at a vastly faster rate than it has over the last several thousand years. I believe in the not so distant future; the citizens of United States will view a licensing system adapted to survival industries as an absolute necessity and welcome its enactment. I believe that there is currently a change of consciousness happening across the United States now. If you would've told a woman in the 1700s that she had the right to vote, the first thing she might've done was to look at her husband to validate such a statement, as innately she felt perhaps she didn't actually have the right to vote and perhaps felt unworthy to do so. Contrast that with the fact that in 1922 women were given the right to vote and some level of sovereign power over their lives. As we evolved further in our idealisms of equality, in 1974 under the Equal Credit Opportunity Act, we allowed women to live independently without their husbands, because the law no longer required their husband's signature as a co-signor, in order to obtain credit and live on their own. It seems that as our society increases its level of technology, access to information and level of intelligence as a whole, laws and human rights tend more towards equality between all humans. Creating survival technology through a system that is nonprofit, non-publicly traded and patent-free, allow us to take another logical step in the cultural and conscious evolution of humankind. I believe that we are understanding at this point in time, that is not a good idea to continue on with the practice of repeating tasks over and over again, tasks only create ever-increasing debt in our nation. This text deals with a pathway to eliminating debt slavery, but it will only be implemented and become a reality in our world if the majority of people feel that they are worthy of receiving a life that does not require their endless toil in order to survive. If people are willing to "receive" this new lifestyle, I believe that without question, they certainly will.

Let's ask ourselves how ownership actually helps people today? It allows us some degree of privacy and perhaps that is a good thing for the aggregate at this point, so maybe we should not be so hasty to just go ahead and make all land public. Does land ownership give people a certain feeling? A feeling of safety and security? A feeling of permanence? A feeling of having a secure future? Can these feelings be attained by different means? I keep asking you questions because I want you to understand that thought and perceptions, based on information and technology, have created the reality and the laws we know today, and the only means that can change our reality will be to interpret how to apply the best use of our technology and information in order to advance our society forward for the benefit of all our citizens. We must approach the understanding of our technology rights with a new consciousness and leave the past behind. Rioting in the streets won't help, holding picket signs is a waste of time, arguing on television will accomplish nothing. Occupy Wall Street led protests more or less asking rich people to give away their money; this is direct evidence that not having the right plan, results in achieving nothing. Had occupy Wall Street crowd funded attorneys to go to court with a specific plan, to change certain laws in our country, they would've been incredibly successful.

Do we need to modify our ideals and values toward what our rights should be, to match the advanced-level of technology and information we have access to today? Exactly what are our new priorities? Is it more important to have excessive currency or better access to the technology that the currency can buy? Certainly, the level of information and technology that we have access to now far exceeds anything we've ever had before and because of its progression, our ideals are now conflicting with past laws that are directly affecting its future progression and evolution. Let's look at some of the things we know now that we didn't know when the Constitution was originally written: we didn't have an understanding of DNA, we didn't have an understanding of computers or even knew what one was, we didn't have an understanding of light-speed financial transactions, we didn't have an understanding of how to retrieve almost any type of information in the world in just a few seconds, we didn't have airplanes, rocket ships, refrigerators, electric lights and so many other technologies. There have been mass changes to our society, its religious beliefs, its stances on civil rights, its understanding of currency and its mass education since the Constitution was originally written. Still, many of the laws of this country are antiquated and outdated and keep us from living the lives we truly deserve. It is only with a clear understanding of where we stand now, in this era, that we will allow ourselves to move forward and agree upon what laws need to be updated or changed in our country. We are in dire need of updating our Constitution again, and the individual laws governing the economies of our individual states, regarding technology and its relation to our present-day survival, in order for all of our citizens to finally share true equality.

CHAPTER 11

Living in Our New World: Old Persona Versus New Persona

Let's try to better understand what we can accomplish by licensing our energy, healthcare, transportation and housing industries by first reviewing briefly the power shift and dynamics that are created as a result of using currency for all types of goods and services in America— specifically survival technology. Through the current patent laws covering our survival technology industries that are heavily influenced by currency incentives, we can virtually guarantee that the development of technology will be sequestered in its evolution, severely slowed or even halted altogether in order to satisfy for-profit incentives. There are simply too many incentives for companies to keep superior technology off the market and keep their inferior product on the market, by directly purchasing any type of competing technology allowed through patent law. Based on the Invention Secrecy Act of 1951, the federal government also has the power to sequester or confiscate any patent it feels is in the best interest of national security. Forty states now have "at will" employment laws, there is no guarantee of a job for any length of time by your employer who can terminate your employment at any time for any reason under the law and has basically no responsibility to ensure the currency you need to trade for survival technology purchases will continue. This system openly and notoriously violates the technology rights of all humans on this planet, who have the right as a community and people to evolve technology in order to better their standard of living and pursue happiness. As we keep the current system in place, American citizens can expect more restricted access to technology at an increasing cost.

Let's follow the simple example to understand why. Since price × volume = revenue, and maximizing revenue is paramount to maximizing profit for any company, if companies that produce survival technology like pharmaceutical companies can't sell more product at some point, they're going to make up for the lost revenues by increasing the prices of their current products, without a doubt we should expect the price of survival products to continue to increase over time. Increasing prices is just another way that companies follow for-profit incentives. So long as our survival technology producing companies are working under for-profit laws, the price of your overhead is guaranteed to go up and your standard of living is virtually guaranteed to go down over time as work hours for full-time jobs, part-time jobs and wages decline due to automation. People will feel less empowered, they will feel they have less control over their lives, they will feel like they are a number, they will feel like they have no future and eventually if the regulations do not change, they will in fact become a "prisoner" of the for-profit currency-based system's antiquated laws and regulations. Is this the system you want to keep perpetuating through your daily work activities and thoughts?

Under a federal licensing system that can be propagated through state collusion, implemented into our energy, transportation, healthcare and housing industries, we can ensure cooperation, transparency and open sourcing of vital technology between companies to ensure we produce our survival technology at the lowest cost possible and provide the highest level of empowerment and standard of living to all American citizens.

Imagine a city, somewhere in the deep Southern United States or the coast of California, or even in the high desert of Arizona, where everyone owns their home free and clear, no one has a mortgage payment, healthcare payments cost $150 a month for an entire family of four, the average work week is about 15 hours and most of the mundane tasks are done by machines. Parents have extra time to teach their children all sorts of things and even homeschool their children. Everyone knows everyone in these small communities; elders are sought for their advice. The town lives in harmony and never worries about an economic recession because all their survival needs are met—by industries that are only incentivized to lower these costs over time, and at this point in time their monthly survival costs are so low that their thoughts rarely, if ever, turn to the possibility that they will run out of money to survive. No one ever worries about being evicted or having to relocate to another area of the country to get a better job during economic down times. This is just a glimpse of what the world can look like if we regulate these four core survival industries.

People should expect to feel empowered, in control of their own lives, confident and secure in their future. People will have direct control over their economy and their survival, and have peace of mind towards their children's futures as their survival needs will be completely taken care of by superior technology that requires almost no repair or replacement, over a 25-year or even a 50-year period. Humans will eventually become tourists on the planet Earth. They will need to find other ways to fulfill Maslow's hierarchy of needs: volunteering, educating, teaching, creating art, starring in a local play, inventing and building their own new superior technologies, perhaps helping and supporting the mentally ill, or just talking with a friend. The ways that people can help others with their new role or persona people will play in this new world are simply endless since people will no longer be tied to endless 40-hour work weeks. People will finally be able enjoy inner peace on this planet, without worrying about borders, limitations or scarcities, and be free to observe, create and enjoy the planet's beauty.

So where does licensing our energy, healthcare, transportation and housing industries specifically leave the American worker? Typically, we should expect major job losses over time, in all these industries and throughout our entire economy, but at the same time a decrease in the overhead expenses of every American citizen as well. These changes may leave Americans with more disposable income—income available for spending monthly, after rent, utilities and other expenses are paid. An increase in disposable income will most likely lead to an increase in the purchase of all other available goods and services offered in the United States. This would provide an initial boom to retailers and just about any business in the United States. Large amounts of long-term savings would no longer be required to be withheld from a person's monthly budget since the purchase of future survival technology, which is mainly what savings are used for, would be expected to become lower over decades of time, so the need for an extensive savings plan would be minimal. Almost all Americans would feel fairly confident in liquidating some of their long-term savings to purchase goods and services now available to them. This would result initially in a long-term boom to the economy. Since overhead is low, Americans will have tremendous opportunities to start small businesses, because these businesses wouldn't require massive incomes in order for the owner of that business to survive. New entrants to economic markets would only need to sell a small amount of product, rather than taking huge risks to sell products on a large scale, because large monthly overhead requirements are no longer a part of a technology-based economy. In addition, small business owners could hire employees without the fear of mass overhead expenses due to a healthcare system that was competitive in cost worldwide.

The best way to be competitive against other world markets would be to lower the cost of healthcare in the United States exponentially. As the United States is already a very technologically advanced country, it could potentially dominate world markets, with its cheaper exports of high-quality and technologically advanced products. There would be fewer incentives for acquisitions and vertical integration of markets by corporate America as small businesses would be able to stay competitive by lowering their prices in the event corporations attempt to aggressively flood the market with a high volume of product at a very low price to capture more market share. Large corporate conglomerates are typical for today's economy; they drive mass volumes of product in order to put their competitors out of business, and they may well become a thing of the past. An increased number of small businesses in our country allows our economies to become more localized and higher-quality products to be produced. It might be difficult for a large corporate conglomerate to produce such high-quality product at an even lower price than offered by the local small businessperson. There is more room for innovation, because businesses don't need to sell as much product and aren't drowning in high overhead costs anymore. A very positive chain reaction takes place, as labor costs will be exponentially dropped as the workers of small businesses also have low overhead and can survive on lower wages to maintain an increased standard of living. The incentives to accumulate large amounts of currency are also diminished as the biggest worry of all Americans, because their future survival needs have already been resolved. Americans might find themselves buying very-high-quality products at very reasonable prices from local companies, with robust competition and innovation throughout all markets.

In a for-profit currency-based economy typically we have over-hiring during times of economic booms and lack of employee hiring during times of economic recession. In a technology-based economy, consumer confidence and economic cycles have very little effect on the overall well-being of the human population of any given state, because again overhead expenses are incredibly low or nonexistent. For example, if a large majority of the population no longer needs to remain renters and is now able to purchase their home free and clear, this situation gives that person incredible confidence and peace of mind in times of economic recession. In a currency-based economy during times of economic recession, consumer confidence drops exponentially along with consumer spending, people are unemployed and are required to dip into their long-term savings or use credit in order to survive. Job loss from technology becomes less of a problem for most Americans in a technology-based economy, because overhead expenses are so low that the average American may be only working 15 hours a week in the first place, versus needing to work 40 hours a week or more while at the same time always on the verge of bankruptcy. The bottom line is that it's much easier to replace a 15-hour-a-week job for anyone than it is to replace a 40-hours-a-week job. Employers would prefer their employees to work fewer hours, to keep their overhead low, and are always more willing to take on part-time workers than full-time workers, especially if healthcare costs are no longer a concern to any company's bottom line. This also makes it easier to deal with full-time job loss from automation and outsourcing to other countries. Workers could find part-time jobs and still meet their monthly spending needs, because their overhead would be a fraction of what it is today.

Over the next several decades, keeping the current patent laws and currency-based incentives in place, Americans will find themselves retraining for new jobs more and more. This is going to place the cost of technology advancement on the American public, through the use of student loans in order to finance retraining themselves. Student loan debt cannot be declared in a bankruptcy, so the average American will be left with an insurmountable amount of debt headed towards joblessness and no income. In the long run all jobs will be eliminated anyway due to artificial intelligence and automation, and all debts eventually will be written off because there will be no income to pay them, once human labor is no longer a requirement in order to operate our economy. My point here is why go through all this, when a licensing system would eliminate all of this debt creation in the form of student loans from ever happening in the future?

Today, young people are more than willing to get into a pile of debt, to just get a chance at obtaining a good job and potentially receive a large amount of monthly income. Housing prices are higher than ever and young people, thinking of their future and not wanting to live with their parents their entire life, are looking for any way to get out of their parents' house and purchase their own piece of real estate. The accumulation of wealth for the 1% relies on continued mass manipulation of the population as the system runs on debt—which is a form of manipulation. Debt creation in this country now takes place on so many different levels. Today, the government has found another way to exploit young people and put them into huge amounts of debt which is very profitable for universities, technical schools and other forms of higher education. Student loan debt has become almost like another mortgage for young people who haven't even bought their first home yet. Student loan debt has risen to a staggering level of almost $1.5 trillion. Educational institutions are clearly taking advantage young people's willingness to complete higher educational courses in order to potentially receive a higher-paying job so that they can own real estate whose price only keeps rising. So essentially the battle cry for young people has become: Let's get into huge amount of debt through student loans, so we're able to earn an income and take out another huge debt—a mortgage—so we can be worse off than our parents! Educational institutions are clearly charging more for tuition and other educational needs then they were decades ago. There is absolutely and completely no possible way that the price of education in the United States has anything to do with general inflation numbers increasing over time. A 2014 article from *USA Today* by Amanda Reaume reported that educational expenses for higher learning that directly create student loan debt have essentially increased at a rate over four times the price of food, since 1978.[74]

---

74 https://www.usatoday.com/story/money/personalfinance/2014/11/08/credit-dotcom-tuition/18417721/

There are number problems with increased tuition that I looked into. Over time there has been less aid from the government in the form of dollars invested in education that have been sorely needed. Increased construction costs in order to build more buildings to accommodate a mass influx of new students with the rising population has also been a factor in the amount of tuition charged as well; in addition, incomes are not keeping up with the cost of living, resulting in less savings by parents for their children for college, and the overall result is more student loan debt. When you privatize your survival technology, the cost of every good and service, including education, in the United States is run with the central thought process and idealism of increasing the price for the product over time in order to gain more profit; but that's not the underlying problem here. The bigger reality is that teachers, faculty, staff, maintenance workers and construction workers of new buildings all require a massive amount of income in nominal dollars to cover their overhead; in other words, their survival costs for energy transportation housing and healthcare represent the biggest need to charge what educational institutions need to charge in order for their employees to survive. These costs are passed along to the students in the form of debt, since neither the students nor the parents on a mass scale can afford to cover these expenses from savings. Students are currently going into debt to finance the current incomes for all the employees and hired labor needed to run our colleges and universities. Are you starting to see how the system really works? One generation is simply a slave to the other, through the currency system. America runs on debt, because of its high overhead costs. The massive increase in student loan debt over the last 40 years in America is merely another byproduct of the currency system controlling survival technology, with the basic idealism that the cost of survival technology must increase over time. Many people who have student loan debt can simply defer these payments decades forward; no lender under traditional methods would allow this type of deferment, so essentially we are putting innocent people into debt that we know cannot be paid pay back in a reasonable amount of time, without any type of term limit set for the full reimbursement; this is usury and illegal.

In a 2016 article for CNBC, John Schoen told us that college tuition over the long term has been rising at a rate of 6% above the inflation rate. In 1971 it took the average parent 13 weeks' worth of income to pay the yearly tuition for their son or daughter to attend Harvard, and today that that same parent must work almost twice that to cover the same annual tuition.[75]

It isn't just an extremely expensive school like Harvard that is the problem here. If you do your research, you'll find across the board tuition prices are going up, far beyond what can be accounted for by inflation. Instead of the United States freely training people at a low cost or providing them a free education in order to keep young people fully up-to-date on various types of software and computer programming, biochemistry, agriculture and other knowledge; the state and federal governments of the United States have chosen to drop a heavy load of debt onto our young people. Simply put, if students carry a heavy load of debt, they will be more apt to look for an immediate income to pay off their debt rather than spending their time pursuing what they truly love to do after college or perhaps even inventing some new form of superior technology. Most students will just run to the first job they can and end up working over the course of many decades to pay their debt off. The United States government, through the guidance of corporate America, seems to want to create a workforce that has very limited knowledge and education, or if they are privileged enough to obtain a higher level of education, to make sure that the individual is highly debt ridden, so the average person in the workforce has no choice but to continue a lifelong pursuit of exchanging labor for currency, so they can continue to service debt for the majority of the rest of their life. The unmitigated evidence of this is almost $1.5 trillion of student loan debt that has already accumulated in the United States today. This debt cannot be discharged in bankruptcy. The reason this debt cannot be discharged in a bankruptcy is because a small group of people

---

75   https://www.cnbc.com/2015/06/16/why-college-costs-are-so-high-and-rising.html

made it the law. It had nothing to do whether it was right or wrong, immoral or moral; it was simply necessary for a successful corporate long-term plan to control Americans through long-term debt servicing. A large population of highly educated people who are debt free would overall be predisposed to leaving their jobs at some point in their life and possibly attempt to invent superior technology without regard to the amount of currency they might receive, by developing it and distributing it to the general public. Keeping the masses in debt allows employers to manipulate and exploit employees over their need for survival in the workplace, chained to a life of drudgery and endless 40-hour workweeks.

Technology continues to expand in its evolution, and in roughly the last 60 years we've invented and increased the floating operations per second of computer chips by literally over one trillion times. We can use machines and computers to help us design, build and distribute technologies covering every industry of our economy. Society at some point in its core beliefs will have to accept the fact that all human labor will be eliminated by highly advanced robotic technology and artificial intelligence, and this subject seems to come up more and more in the media and everyday conversations.

I would like to address some speculations made by the public on the future of the American economy as they relate to the licensing system I propose in this text. You're going to hear lots of speculation as we move forward, most likely for the rest of your life, about artificial intelligence and automation eliminating human labor. You're also going to hear propaganda from the government, that may or may not be true, and it's going to be up to you to discern what the truth actually is. Those who would say that artificial intelligence replacing human jobs is not a threat are most likely motivated to keep the currency-based, for-profit system in place for their own personal gain. Please listen to me carefully, because what I'm telling you here is: You have absolutely nothing to fear from losing a job to a machine. Why would you want to dedicate your life doing mundane tasks over and over again, Monday through Friday, 40 hours a week, if you no longer had to? No one in their right mind would want to do that or fear losing that endless drudgery from their life. The fear comes from needing cash for survival. If you have survival costs that are as low as possible and trending even lower according to the way licensed overhead industries are incentivized and run, then you would certainly welcome the elimination of all work from your life or at least the type of work that we know today, which is basically just a series of mundane tasks repeated over and over again, decade after decade.

A 2017 article in the *Chicago Tribune* by Samantha Masunaga noted a study by PwC that estimated up to 38% of all jobs in the United States could be eliminated by robots and artificial intelligence within the next 15 years.[76] Do you have the right to sue an employer that eliminates your job by automating it? Absolutely not; employment is basically "at will" in the United States and can be terminated for any reason with no fault obligated towards your employer. Good luck in getting a court to agree with a class-action lawsuit of this type. What happens if your job gets eliminated by technology? Where does this type of action actually leave you? The simple answer is, it leaves any person who's lost their job the responsibility of finding another one, draining their savings while doing so, financing the cost of any schooling or education that would be required to retrain themselves to work in a new industry and going through absolute hell emotionally, wondering how they're going to provide for themselves while they stave off homelessness. Let's not quickly forget that majority of this country lives basically paycheck to paycheck and has no real long-term savings to weather a financial crisis of this type. Most likely some of these people are going to end up on county, state or federal welfare, food stamps and other assistance programs, so the rest of the general public can look forward to paying for the loss of these jobs in the form of higher sales and income taxes. In short, the consumers and the remaining American working public will absorb the cost of technology's advancement through higher taxes; again, we see another example of people funding their own demise through the enforcement of antiquated laws.

---

76   https://www.chicagotribune.com/business/ct-robots-american-jobs-takeover-20170324-story.html

Why should any person suffer so much for so many years and incur such an enormous financial cost so that businesses can make more profit? Moreover, who is going to buy the same level of goods and service as they are today with reduced incomes? How do we get past these conundrums? In short, what's happening here is that we're trying to decrease our need for currency but we're doing it in a random, haphazard way with no specific plan to take ourselves through the process in the easiest, most efficient manner possible. This is why I have stressed throughout the text that it's important to bring down overhead first in order to eliminate the types of emotional and financial calamities that our people will certainly experience, unless we change the laws regulating our overhead industries.

A 2017 article in Quartz from Kevin J. Delaney stated that Bill Gates believes that robots should be taxed at the same level as humans if a human labor job is taken over by a robot, to slow down the process of automation.[77] I fail to see how this plan makes absolutely any sense. This idealism only keeps the same level of taxes going to the federal government, to help pay welfare and other assistance programs for people whose jobs are eliminated by automation. It also violates the technology rights of the majority of American citizens and allows corporations to keep superior technology off the market by purchasing and shelving it or the government openly and notoriously, confiscating it. Unless we change the laws governing the restrictions on our technology today, we can expect to be painted into a corner, with even fewer rights and freedoms than we have now. The cost of retraining people and incurring new student loans; the loss of long-term savings during periods with no income; the loss of homes and other property; and the mass emotional turmoil that could result in serious illnesses; is all unaccounted for in these types of plans. That's why I'm telling you that this plan or any of the other proposed plans to deal with automation and outsourcing will simply never work. Bill Gates is also telling you right here that we need to slow down the pace of automation, because the currency system simply won't handle

---

77   https://qz.com/911968/bill-gates-the-robot-that-takes-your-job-should-pay-taxes/

it. Technology destroys currency. Here's an example of a famed and noted person who is considered very intelligent and is well-respected by society, basically telling you that if we keep randomly destroying jobs, without a long-term plan, we're going to leave our country in a complete economic mess. A limited income limits the amount of technology you have access to, so again, to make this point: The level of abundance and prosperity you're enjoying in your life every day is based on the level of technology you have access to and not the amount of currency.

Let's examine a counterpoint to the fact that artificial Intelligence and robotics will not eliminate human labor and by some magical means, we will continue to create more jobs in this country that require more human labor, in our futuristic economy. A 2017 article in the *New York Times* by Ruchir Sharma cited a study by McKinsey & Company, that stated that about one-third of all the jobs created in the United Stated were jobs that did not exist or barely existed 25 years ago.[78] Lets' ask a few questions about this study. How is it relevant to the price of housing constantly going up in value? Why do we want to keep on perpetuating a labor-for-cash-for-survival system? Why do we want to keep creating new jobs requiring human labor at all? Creating new jobs does basically nothing for the standard of living of Americans, it just keeps them perpetually working. The only way to better, the standard of living for any American is to reduce their overhead and the number of hours they work per week. Furthermore, should we expect this trend of job creation to continue over the next 25 years? The answer is that it's quite unlikely, our level of technology, robotics and artificial intelligence is so much more advanced now then it was 25 years ago. Twenty-five years ago, Windows 95 was just made available for purchase to the American public and no one was really even thinking about what a home computer could for them. It took half an hour just to download a picture on the internet, robots were just a gleam in someone's eye as well as the idea that a computer might carry on a conversation with someone. Robots today can teach themselves to walk, beat

---

78   https://www.nytimes.com/2017/10/07/opinion/sunday/no-that-robot-will-not-steal-your-job.html

world champion Go players at their own game, do extensive mathematical computations and even engage in a conversation with another human being. It would be absolutely foolish to expect the same level of human job growth over the next 25 years as we've had over the previous 25 years. It's simply an inevitable and inescapable fact that humans will no longer work at some point in time in the future and technology will do all the mundane tasks that we are being paid to do today. Why do we want to keep on suffering? What's the point? The purpose of this text is to raise the awareness of what you should want and demand as a human being on this planet today, and that is superior technology to be implemented as soon as possible into your overhead industries. The benefits to you created by making this demand will be immensely greater than you could ever achieve by taking any other course of action.

Let's look at another example of how all jobs will eventually be eliminated, even the very highly skilled ones, and how there are few to no options for workers to transfer their skills from the field to the office in the future. A 2016 article in the *Japan Times* by Takamitsu Sawa tells us that a newly developed IBM Watson computer can identify the right types of medicine to treat certain cancers. This machine studied over 20 million medical theses and 17 million pieces of pharmaceutical information to aide it, prior to studying specific medical information from individual patients, and can make a drug diagnosis in as little as 10 minutes.[79] There is simply no way a human being could ever evaluate that type of data in that short a time span. There's simply no way around it; eventually all human jobs will be eliminated by artificial intelligence and machines. Thank God we have a way to welcome this type of technology into our society, rather than fear it, and can enjoy its benefits to the full extent to live longer lives, pursue the things we love, be happier and enjoy each other. Isn't that what life is supposed to be all about?

Let's look at another idea being postulated out there today in the media to combat job loss from automation: Universal Basic Incomes. This

---

79   https://www.japantimes.co.jp/opinion/2016/09/23/commentary/japan-commentary/ai-revolu-tion-begun/#.XlMn2GhKiUl

is a new type of welfare program in which all citizens of a country receive a regular sum of money from the government. The bottom line here is to put the entire population of America onto some sort of welfare system once they can no longer work. Limited income gives you limited access to technology. Limited income limits the amount that any person can purchase per month, the type of house they will live in, their access to an automobile and in general a limited basket of goods that they can purchase, with no alternative to better their situation. So again, the technology rights of Americans are being exploited and misused under this type of plan. If you think that this concept is something that is going to happen decades from now like some scenario out of a science-fiction movie, please realize that Universal Basic Incomes are already being tried out on a small scale in Stockton, California, today. You can expect similar welfare plans like this to start popping up all over the country, in cities, counties and states, unless another plan is implemented to combat vanishing incomes.

A limited income will leave people with limited access to pursuing their dreams or evolving and educating themselves, and most likely will put them in a high state of accumulated debt as their limited income is probably not going to cover their future lifetime survival expenses, relegating them to making minimum payments to creditors over the course of their lifetime, much the same way low-income and poverty-level-income households operate financially today through the use of payday and hard money loans. Universal Basic Incomes for people won't work. We've already established that Universal Basic Incomes do not give direct control to American citizens over their survival. The currency-based system under its current regulations severely limits and restricts the technology rights of all Americans and continues to allow corporate America and the government to shelve vital new survival technology, Our planet's population is expected to approach 10 billion within the next 30 years and is certainly going to need low-cost survival technology with no guarantees of future work, and our current system is headed on a course of inevitable elimination. We've seen specifically that the best way to increase the standard of living for all Americans is to cut overhead, but that unfortunately destroys real-estate collateral for loans, the banking and credit systems, the stock markets, and so on. The bottom line is superior technology will destroy the power structure being enjoyed by the super-wealthy today, so it is likely that you will continue to hear propaganda in order to prolong the inevitable; which is changing to a system that will eventually not use currency at all and rely solely on technology for the survival of all of its citizens as well as fulfilling all of its evolving extended desires and wants.

I briefly wanted to touch on just one more point about artificial intelligence. Today we're witnessing mass computer hacks of private information throughout the financial industry. Credit card companies, even credit reporting agencies and bank accounts are being broken into. I recently had fraudulent charges taken from my checking account on two different occasions within a 90-day period; in addition, my credit report was also hacked and compromised within the last year. I believe at some point that viruses and hacking software will be developed to the point where private information will no longer be able to be kept private. Artificial intelligence will be developed to the point where it will be able to think cognitively, troubleshoot and write code the same way a human hacker does, not only at blinding speed but at the pace of thousands or even millions of hackers simultaneously. Breaking any company's firewall and security protocols will become child's play. If artificial intelligence continues to be developed at the present pace, no electronic currency will be able to be kept safe in a bank account. It seems very easy to keep finding reasons to move away from a currency-based system, and as we look closer at the advancement of technology from almost every aspect, we can see that eventually the currency system will end. I personally believe that within the next hundred years it's inevitable, and within the next 10 to 30 years we'll see massive changes to technology and correspondingly a massive reduction in human labor for cash opportunities. I believe that by licensing our energy, healthcare, transportation and housing industries in a tiered system over the course of perhaps the next two decades, we could put ourselves in a to a position to receive extreme abundance as a country and that our individual citizens would enjoy a higher standard of living and enjoyment of life that they've never experienced before. I expect people to be more empowered, freely enjoying their lives and finally experiencing the happiness and dreams that has never been attained, by every generation before us.

CHAPTER 12

Solving Our Environmental and Domestic Problems

Let's try to define our beliefs today, by understanding that our beliefs change over time, based on the evolution of technology and information. At one point in time in our history, whale oil was all the rage and we used to burn it in lamps for light at night, prior to the invention of electricity and lightbulbs that could potentially burn thousands of hours. Imagine the whalers out in their boats, eating crappy food, far from their families, way out to sea. Their goal? To slaughter innocent whales swimming beside them. The whalers would spear the mammal, causing it to panic and dive deep into the ocean until it lost all its strength and then it floated to the surface, where the whalers would continue to spear it, over and over again, until it died a slow, bloody and horrible death. All of this so that some primitives could have a little bit of extra light to read by when darkness came.

We can't hunt whales anymore to resolve our energy issues; our population is too great. Throughout the evolution of our country, in the development of its technology we've adapted our business practices in order to obtain greater levels of success and prosperity. At one point in time people risked their lives to get whale oil. Today we would laugh at such a notion, because we've developed far more efficient energy technologies and all sorts of helpful devices powered by them. My point is that we moved on, we evolved and we adapted our business practices based on the problems that we were facing at the time.

The licensing system that I suggest we implement into our country is simply another step in our evolutionary practice. Even though there may be an abundance of oil now in the form of shale oil, extracted through fracking, that can potentially supply the world's energy needs for another 100 years, an oil-based energy system requires the constant repurchase of oil- and petroleum-based products like gasoline. Since we know that constant repurchases create waste problems and keep us in a state of debt slavery, it isn't a good idea to keep using this energy system moving forward as we evolve on our planet. Paying for this crude technology on a daily basis keeps the majority of our population in a paycheck to paycheck status.

The earth is merely a manifestation of the current consciousness of humankind. Our population is under the impression that we have reached a zenith of sorts and a golden age, when in reality technology has been invented in most cases as a response to extreme scarcity and a direct threat to the economies of civilizations that were in serious peril prior to their invention. Technology hasn't really changed over the course of our evolution in most cases until people's backs were against the wall. For example, there was a mass explosion of technology during World War II from the direct threat of the extinction of human life. In response to this threat, our country ended up producing one of our greatest technological breakthroughs in the history of the world: the atomic bomb. It was quite a feat to invent such technology and a special conglomeration of very intelligent people had to gather together for a period of roughly four years, in order to achieve such a breakthrough. No cost was spared, no egos got in the way, cooperation was used rather than competition to further its development and there was no motive for profit, only to save lives. If we only gave this type of effort into building a portable source of energy; a portable source of water, tires and brakes that would last for 300,000 miles; anti-gravity technology that would not require the production of tires or the building of roads; and houses that could be built virtually anywhere for less than $25,000—our world would be a completely different place.

Oil, as it stands today, is the main commodity of our world. Currently the United States is the world's reserve currency for oil purchases. Anytime oil is purchased around the world from OPEC (Organization of Petroleum Exporting Countries), other countries must first convert their currency into U.S. dollars in order to buy oil. This means the United States does not need to hold currency reserves like other countries do in order to buy oil. This also means that if the accepted business practice of purchasing oil in U.S. dollars no longer takes place, most likely our currency will collapse or at the very least we will develop serious, long-term fundamental economic issues, as a result of this changing business practice.

One of the main reasons we can afford to have military bases around the world is because we are the world's reserve currency. We can literally print money out of thin air to pay this worldwide military force with no consequences. If the United States loses its sovereign power and is no longer the world's reserve currency, there could be mass inflation effects felt and a short-term collapse of the economy. The relationship between the U.S. dollar and OPEC, commonly known as the "Petrodollar," runs great risk being tied to oil, due to two reasons:

1. Globally, green energy sources are becoming more competitive with oil.

2. The United States cannot stop producing an ever-increasing level of government, corporate and consumer debt.

Another currency may replace U.S. dollars eventually as the world's reserve currency for oil; oil may one day be purchased in any country's currency of origin or replaced by another form of electronic currency. If that happened, foreign countries would no longer be required to hold U.S. dollars to purchase oil, so these dollars would simply find their way back to the United States because there is no longer a use for them worldwide. Since our government will no longer be able to print money out of thin air and not incur a cost from it, most of the military bases worldwide would have to be closed and the ex-military personnel would become our future unemployed. Why do you think our past presidents, regardless of their political affiliation, have always supported a strong military? There are approximately 2 million people in the active military and reserves combined worldwide. Dismantling the military, or greatly reducing its numbers, would put these people basically on the unemployment line and competing for jobs with other Americans. In addition, the potential loss of government contracts to produce technology in order to destroy other human beings, through the creation of various types of weaponry would be lost and would have a huge negative effect on the gross domestic product of the United States economy. Any president who started decreasing the U.S. military budget would automatically incur a problematic economy, so they continue on perpetuating the illusion that a strong military is good for the country, when in reality what we're doing is simply propping up in an efficient system with debt - that eventually will become so great it will topple our economic system.

A 2015 article from Military.com by Richard Sisk tells us that prior to 2015, the U.S. Army had been pushing for years to halt the production and upgrades of Abrams Tanks, and despite their efforts in 2014 the U.S. government pushed through another spending bill for $120 million to upgrade Abrahams Tanks that the U.S Army directly stated it did not want upgraded, because the average age of the current tanks they already owned was two-and-a-half years. One government official cited the reason was to keep skilled labor jobs safe in the state of Ohio.[80] The United States government is basically

---

[80]   https://www.military.com/daily-news/2014/12/18/congress-again-buys-abrams-tanks-the-army-doesnt-want.html

perpetuating jobs that are no longer required by creating weaponry that the military itself states specifically it does not need to defend our country. If we put this money into the development of superior survival technology along with countless other examples of government waste in our ongoing federal budget, this newly freed up cash could provide our newly licensed industries with an ongoing budget to work and draw funds from, in order to fund their ongoing business operations. There are many sources of funds available to start a technology-based economy; this is just one example of many. This type of ridiculous habitual spending in order to propagate fake jobs through government contracts that you pay for, that have long past their useful life, is simply getting us nowhere. In the eyes of the government, the unemployment rate looks great and the politician gets reelected! The federal government would rather keep propagating a system of job welfare in the United States than changing our intellectual property laws and allowing open-sourced and transparent technology to be developed and implemented into the U.S. economy. In the future you can look forward to paying higher taxes in order to supplement someone else's income; so in essence under this system you are basically working for somebody else—in this case, people who create defense weaponry and military personnel we haven't needed for decades to support an artificial economy—who can't stand on its own two feet without constant taxation and intervention by the federal government.

United States currency is unsecured and not backed by any tangible assets that could be used as collateral in the event of a currency default. The United States government is at least $24 trillion in debt and has very few assets to sell off that could cover even a small portion of this debt. The government also spends 100% of its tax revenue per year, saves nothing and is unsure how to meet the demands of its long-term costs such as Social Security, Medicaid and Medicare. Potentially, it may be looking at a mass decrease in tax revenue as the baby boomer generation moves out of its prime earning years and stops providing income to the Social Security system; this large demographic of people will actually become Social Security recipients instead of contributors. The currency-based system leaves us walking in circles with no long-term goals and no long-term sustainable, survivable future.

Let's examine how incentives under the for-profit system not only create pollution throughout our ecosphere but pollute and destroy our human bodies as well. Do jewelry stores benefit by people getting married? Of course, they do. Does a jewelry store care if your marriage ends in divorce? Of course, it doesn't, and it might actually encourage your divorce because potentially you would be back at a later date to purchase another expensive piece of jewelry. Correspondingly, what we eat is massively affected by the incentives produced from running our food industry under a for-profit system whose only goal is to sell as much product as possible regardless of the long-term or short-term health effects to all Americans. The for-profit food industry is having a direct negative effect on the immediate health of Americans. There is also an emphasis on urging Americans to overeat by a for-profit food industry because selling a mass volume of product again, is part of the for-profit model. Over the long term, a mass increase in healthcare costs should be expected from an aging, overweight population whose organs will struggle over decades of time to process a daily imbalanced diet. Americans typically consume high-carbohydrate diets, and carbohydrates are broken down quickly by the body into sugar and what is not used immediately is stored as fat. This is one of the reasons you see diabetes running rampant in our country even in young children. In the long run, everyone in our society who supports the for-profit food industry, in order that it might make the maximum amount of profit by encouraging our population to consume mass quantities of unhealthy food, becomes very unhealthy. Usually things like grains, oats and rice, which are very cheap to produce, result in an unhealthy population getting unhealthier as time goes on. According to studies the average American consumes approximately 38 pounds of high-fructose corn syrup per year. Higher healthcare premiums result in the short run and continue to increase over time as the population becomes more and more unhealthy, while in the background corporate lobbyists push to continue to make this insanity happen on a larger scale every year. How does this make sense? All we do in this country is spend money on inferior food products and inferior technology, supported by inferior ways of thinking, in a never-ending cycle. What kind of affect does consuming 38 gallons of carbonated beverages per year have on the healthcare costs to Americans? What about the poor subsidizing their budget by continually purchasing unhealthy and cheap fast food? Everyone pays for it in the long run in the form of higher healthcare premiums. Can you see here again why for-profit is failing the country in every respect and that spending money on inferior technology only leads to spending more money and working continuously for nothing, never accomplishing any type of lasting sustainability?

Just like our for-profit real-estate builder, who slams as many condos as possible into a small lot in a crowded city, takes no responsibility for the increased traffic and other problems associated with more people confined to a small living area, the for-profit food industry, takes no responsibility for the consequences of selling its products to the general public, which directly affects the health of human beings in this country. I'm not asking you to consider banning for-profit food; what I'm merely pointing out is when you apply for-profit incentives to any industry, you end up with negative results. Price × volume = gross revenue, and the higher the gross revenue, the higher the profit. Any company in any for-profit industry will look to drive as much volume as they can, by selling as much of their product as they can, regardless of the consequences to the general public. Lower overhead and you reduce the incentives to sell as much volume, of any product, simply because you need to create less gross revenue, because overhead is lower. I cannot stress enough how much a licensing system will help people's lives and the entire ecosphere and bring ease to everything we do on this planet. The problem we have is with the system and the way it incentivizes certain behaviors. Only by bringing about a new system, by changing our current rules and regulations and breaking down our steadfast beliefs, will we change our manifested reality.

Another problem is that the for-profit food industry encourages the cultivation of a sort of monoculture of just a very few number of crops. Without a diversity of crops, we may have problems long-term with sustaining our current honeybee population and pollen propagation. We've torn down our diversified forests and ecosystems and replaced them with mile after mile of fields growing corn, soybeans, wheat and oats, across this country, just to go to the trouble of making people fat and increasing healthcare costs for everyone. This system incentivizes problem after problem after problem with no solution in sight. Let's remember that the only thing that determines your level of prosperity, abundance and the ability to pursue your dreams in your entire lifetime is your level of access to technology and not your amount of currency. If you remember the story of our pirates earlier in this text, you can certainly see that if I sent you back 500 years ago in a time machine with $300 billion, you would be far less happy than you are today because that $300 billion would buy you very little in the way of advanced technology to make your life easier.

Should we place a tax on fast-food items to help fund the healthcare problems that they cause us? I certainly think that we should, but by lowering our overhead, the general public would have more money to spend on organic and non-GMO foods, or more time to prepare healthy meals, because they would not be running around in chaos trying to keep up with a never-ending 40-hour work week. "All roads lead to Rome," as the old saying goes; and when it comes to solving our economic problems, all roads lead to overhead reduction. Instituting a licensing system into our overhead industries will still not deter the problems of crime, people eating things that they shouldn't, people living in crowded cities because that's their preference, unplanned pregnancies and a host of other problems; but by reducing the 40-hour work week we can certainly give more of our time and attention to solving these problems. In general, the more disposable income people have to spend on food, and the more time they have to prepare food, the more likely they are to eat healthy food rather than sustaining our current economic situation, where people have very little money to spend on food as part of their monthly budget and are more likely to choose cheaper low-quality fast foods, in order to sustain themselves. If people had more money to spend on food, it's more likely that in the long run restaurants and even fast-food chains would offer higher-quality, nutritious food alternatives on their menus. If the public has the money to spend on it and time to sit down to eat it, companies are going to provide access to high-quality food for them and our food industry will adapt itself quickly to this increased demand.

A plastic bottle is simply a convenience provided by the for-profit food industry in order to sell its product and maximize profit. The reason that single-unit consumption (e.g., smaller plastic bottles) are so prevalent in our society today is that the sales price per ounce of liquid is higher in a smaller-size container versus a larger- size container holding a larger amount of liquid. The reason we have oceans filled with plastic is because of the food industry's need to drive volume and sell as many units as possible, while at the same time creating the greatest price per ounce sold for its soft drinks. In order to maximize profit, the for-profit food industry's main goal is to provide the maximum amount of convenience to you, the consumer, to purchase their product to the point where regardless of your need for any given quantity of the product, you can find it in a vending machine or on a local grocery shelf. Do you want 8 ounces of soda? We have a container for you. You want 12 ounces? We have a container for you too; and so, on and so forth. Could we make a law that required you to only purchase soft drinks in 68-ounce containers or greater? Certainly, we could, and this policy would directly limit the amount of plastic thrown away annually in our country. Let me state to you unequivocally that the only way to solve the problem of plastic in the oceans is to require the general public to use reusable containers to consume various soft drinks and other drinks sold in stores and vending machines. Perhaps through the advent of technology your refrigerator could dispense soft drinks directly to you at home or in the office, and you would just use your reusable container each time you had a need to consume various types of soft drinks. Unless we have a law stating that all citizens must use a reusable container every time, they need to purchase a soft drink, regardless of location, you'll never reduce the amount of plastic in the oceans. It just won't change, folks, unless you change the laws governing the industry. If we pass such a law here, we can clone the system around the world and we can stop many poorer countries around the world from throwing away plastic bottles into rivers, about 1,000 rivers around the world create about 80% of the plastic pollution in our oceans. If we can provide an alternative form of technology to these poorer countries, we can eventually stop all plastic pollution of our oceans. Boyan Slat is a person I really admire who is taking a proactive approach to clearing plastic from our oceans and rivers; please check out: The Ocean Cleanup.com online when you have some free time and donate to a worthy cause that actually provides results. Boyan's ideas are a perfect example of new technology making a permanent change to our world. New hardware is what we need to make these large physical changes and not another phone app. Silicon Valley has sold its soul to for-profit and is only interested in obtaining more currency by cashing in stock options, driven by software sales, which in no way at this point is going to do much at all to our bottom line.

California recently passed a law in regards to purchasing paper bags at the point-of-sale, in the form of Proposition 67. This forced consumer like me to buy a set of reusable bags or be forced to purchase a paper bag for ten cents at the point-of-sale every time a purchase was made at any grocery or retail store. Initially this was kind of a pain for me, but I bought reusable bags and have gotten in the habit of bringing them to the grocery store every time I go. It isn't really that hard to use them over and over again. I don't think it would be that big of a stretch for me to use some sort of reusable cup or container to consume soft drinks with, rather than using a container one time and then throwing it away, so I finally switched over and I now use reusable drink containers daily. For-profit looks to constantly sell products over and over again, and thus the containers provided by the manufacturers in order to physically consume the product must be implemented on a mass scale in various sizes and forms, so that the consumer has the greatest ease of use of them. If the ease-of-use decreases, a competitor may very well steal their existing market share, or consumers may stop buying their product altogether. For-profit basically has no goal other than to create profit. Despite environmental laws, antitrust laws and laws protecting consumers, really for the most part, for-profit companies are completely exempt from taking responsibility for the problems that result from the constant repurchase of their inferior goods and services and their long-term effects on our health-care costs and ecosphere. For-profit creates massive waste on our planet and pollutes our ecosphere. The for-profit currency-based system will always require massive repurchases of inferior technology over and over again; your rent, your healthcare, your automobile every 5 to 10 years, common household items and almost everything you purchase requires constant repurchase, and as a result, all the containers used to house these constant repurchases, ends up causing environmental problems to our planet with no direct responsibility for the costs borne by the perpetrators. A 2016 article in the World Economic Forum by Erik Van Sebille reported on a study that showed that about 8 million metric tons of plastic was dumped into rivers or on land worldwide in 2015, that eventually entered our oceans.[81]

What's the real cause behind most of our pollution problems, like plastic in the oceans? It's not having access to portable energy so we can live anywhere, lower our overhead and change the basic operations and incentives of retail food industries, so that potentially if workers lose jobs as a result of lost revenue from reduced container production, their overhead remains low and the workers as well as soft-drink companies need less income to survive. Energy isn't just your $100 utility bill per month; it drives our rents and mortgages perpetually higher by making our lot costs scarce and the need to drive a higher-volume sales of all products, in all industries, in order

---

81   https://www.weforum.org/agenda/2016/01/how-much-plastic-is-there-in-the-ocean/

to cover ever-increasing overhead costs, resulting in the mass pollution of our ecosphere.

If you want to solve our pollution problems, the first thing we must do is drive down overhead, to increase disposable income. Once you have a higher standard of living and a relatively higher disposable income through lower overhead, it's easier to tackle things like: requiring consumers to purchase soft drinks in a reusable container and gearing soft drink machines to dispense liquid only rather than in a pre-packaged product. I look for other states to adopt California's policy requiring the purchase of bags, whether paper or plastic, at the point-of-sale by all vendors. Cardboard waste is also another problem caused by excessive repurchases that are directly incentivized by the for-profit currency-based economy. We can also look at things like a mass launch of satellites, to decrease our cell tower costs and essentially make phone service free or provided at a very low cost to everyone in the world, but first we need to tackle our overhead problems and make sure our long-term survival technology is developed properly. Trying to change everything at once would be a mass misdirection of energy and most likely cause mass failure. A carefully vetted and strategic plan would be the best option to follow.

I would like to briefly touch on the mass media hysteria of global warming, which is overtaking our media and the internet. The bottom line is, you can debate global warming but you can't debate debt slavery. Are you going to work on Monday morning? If the answer to this question is "Yes," then you're probably a debt slave, like 99% of the rest of the country. Technology is your only way out; technology is your only way to a better and more prosperous life and a reduction of your never-ending 40-hour work week. I can tell you with 100% certainty that the majority of the people in the United States, will continue to work their entire lives for meager benefits, based on the laws binding the currency-based, for-profit system. Shouldn't we look to solving our own demise of constant drudgery, prior to saving the planet, as a greater priority? Implementing a licensing system into the energy industry will certainly allow a faster development of superior technology than we could ever hope for by eliminating a private equity-based, patent-shelving industry, using improper energy sources in order to proliferate maximum profit. Implementing a licensing system helps us move away from debt slavery and saves our planet at the same time!

Another great debate about how we can affect the consumption of energy on our planet is the implementation of a carbon tax. This is the most ridiculous response to a technology-development problem ever invented. In essence, what the government wants to do is make people pay more for the same inferior technology, by raising the cost of petroleum-based energy to a point where it will make it feasible for new forms of inferior and centralized energy production to be comparable in cost. This is an absolutely blatant lie, because the government at the same time, as I already outlined in this text, is sequestering patents that would compete with centralized energy systems and quickly replace them. There is simply no substitute technology right now that can compare with our petroleum or centralized electrical utility services, which most of the general public could afford to purchase on a monthly basis. This is not like substituting cable for satellite and raising a mass tax on cable services, so that people would be incentivized to switch to satellite technology. There is no established form of energy technology on the planet that is remotely comparable to the energy technologies we have now, in terms of costs per unit. So basically, people will just be paying more money for the same crappy technologies we have now with the hopes of emerging technologies in the future replacing them. Those emerging technologies will be confiscated, through patent purchases by corporate America and hidden government sequestration. We will continue to walk in circles and deepen the paths that we are on, with no results. I believe it is a much simpler to manipulate countries like China and keep free energy technology or a technology that creates more energy than it uses, off the market than it is in the United States, which is a far more liberal, open and willing country, to provide some forms of advanced yet limited technology to its population. Yet even within the borders of the United States, we know superior technologies that could change our country and world forever, are deliberately being kept from our possession.

Over the last hundred years we have stripped the diversity of our ecosphere, and it is having a massive effect on our wildlife, lands and oceans and the health of our human population. If we can bring down our overhead, people will have more money to accomplish the following:

1. Americans will have more disposable income and thus more money to spend on higher- quality organic, non-GMO vegetables, and more time to prepare foods at home, eat meals in more expensive and differentiated restaurants, and avoid unhealthy fast foods, although I would expect fast-food restaurants to vastly increase the quality and nutritional value of their products, to capture this extra income, if it became available.

2. There will be fewer stress-related diseases and organ failures, due an overall reduction in the number of hours worked per week and potentially more available savings to draw from in uncertain economic times.

3. Potentially fewer traffic accidents may result by mitigating the crowded commute hours normally associated with an eight-hour workday as companies can stagger their start times due to shorter work hours per day. Countless construction accidents could be avoided through automated labor, further reducing our healthcare costs.

4. People would have more money in general to spend on other household goods and services as their overhead costs reduce, creating a boom to the other industries within the nation. This resulting increase in disposable income, coupled with low healthcare costs, may result in local businesses finally being able to sustain themselves in the United States and remain globally competitive over the long run.

5. Consumer confidence will be elevated to a much higher, sustainable base level than it is now because the public will have confidence that their basic amenities needed for human survival are taken care of and expected to decrease in cost over time. Employers will hold less power over employees, and employees will perhaps be free to choose from multiple part-time jobs and have more choice as to where they would like to work, and more specifically what type of work they would like to accomplish. Perhaps the average employee will start speaking their mind again in the workplace and not fear the loss of their job as they do today, and perhaps this new line of communication will help to foster more efficiency and precision within American businesses. Overall, the population will reduce its level of emotional stress due to the fact that there will be less worry about job layoffs and future potential reduction of incomes due to outsourcing and automation.

6. There will be less worry about paying back the national debt, corporate debts or personal debts as we move into a technology-based system where technology is not predicated on the constant movement of currency through repurchases of inferior technology and the constant creation of debt by the general public. Being able to scrap the entire national debt and write it off as a loss could easily become an option after several decades of time, as our dependency on currency continues to diminish to the point where currency transactions will become less and less commonplace and have little effect on our technology-based economy.

7. Overall I would expect a constant decline in visits to hospitals and clinics as a domino effect created by this licensing system in boosting the overall health of our population due to fewer hours worked per week, more time spent being able to prepare and eat healthier foods, less stress from no longer having to fight survival issues due to lack of currency, and more general inspiration and happiness throughout the public as a result of being able to spend more time with their children,

to do the things we love or just simply having more time to relax and enjoy life.

I hope you've seen what a wonderful effect this licensing system can have on the rest of the industries in the United States, our overall health and well-being as a population and the long-term evolution of our species on this planet. I believe these changes are completely necessary and will confer a golden age of technology, prosperity and happiness upon not only the United States but the rest of the world as well. It is my hope that you can see we're on the verge of greatness and that we possess all the fundamentals as a people to move forward into a great period of abundance. I hope that so far, I've raised your awareness about the currency system and your hopes and inspirations for beginning the creation of a technology-based economy. We have a lot to do yet, but I hope you'll come along with me on this wonderful ride. The entire world is waking up and changing its consciousness from serving themselves to helping others, and we'll create an incredible world as a result!

CHAPTER 13

Cloning the System Throughout the World

Once we have developed and implemented a licensing system into our four key overhead industries, and have reached a successful conclusion to developing a technology-based economy here in the United States, it will then be time to clone the system around the world. A technology-based economy will promote a more harmonious world filled with peace and happiness, and will drastically alleviate and eradicate wars, global poverty, global suffering, starvation and unsanitary living conditions in Third World countries whose infrastructures are meagerly developed or simply not developed at all. Every part of the world will receive a boost from enhanced and superior survival technology, increasing world harmony and drastically reducing our long-term environmental and ongoing ecosphere concerns.

United States government is attempting to clone the currency-based for-profit system around the world. This is an incredibly bad idea for several reasons. Let's take a look at just a few.

Our government's goal is to spread democracy around the world, and this requires installing an extensive for-profit, currency-based system in other countries supported by strong financial markets and credit systems. Any country that mirrors the United States economy can expect higher levels of debt, a high consumption of petroleum-based products, an increase in pollution of its ecosystem, massively sequestered or shelved technology and a population that works endlessly with no other direction to get to its next paycheck.

The difference between the standard of living for a citizen of the United States and a citizen of Mexico is simply based on the fact that the United States offers better financial markets and access to credit and its citizens better access to technology then a country like Mexico. Technology, not currency, drives our standard of living.

The United States' current problem concerning the number of jobs being filled by Mexican immigrants who are undocumented seems to be an unsolvable one. A technology-based economy looks to eliminate as much human labor as possible over the long term as the driving force of the economy, and is not concerned with the creation of jobs; rather it is concerned with the elimination of human labor through the development of superior technology. It would be better for the people of the United States to rely on superior technology to meet their survival needs rather than on the ups and downs of human-labor-driven cyclical economies. The United States would be wiser to invest its money into the development of superior technology, which would benefit both the citizens of Mexico and the United States, rather than investing money into building a physical wall between Mexico and United States. Most of our military defense budget should be directed towards the creation of superior technology rather than creating weapons, under long-term government contracts that are either simply outdated or not required at all, as our inventory of weaponry is already over-stockpiled.

I find it interesting that Americans are so preoccupied with the possible filling of American jobs by undocumented U.S. immigrants, most of which include fieldwork for the harvesting of crops, that most Americans would never even think of applying for; when at the same time American companies are not restricted in any way in outsourcing American jobs to any country across the world that they choose. U.S. law does not specifically regulate job outsourcing, based on what I have researched on the subject. Not all jobs can be outsourced, if the outsourcing specifically would interfere with laws affecting currency or the privacy of financial accounts or other national security issues of American citizens; but that basically leaves pretty much 99% of the rest of jobs in the United States unprotected. We can definitely count on more outsourcing through the next several decades, for all the different industries in the United States and all types of jobs, both blue-collar and white-collar, skilled and unskilled. Everyone will be affected by outsourcing over the next few decades, regardless of their level of education, job skills or current level of income; and at some point, even those with connections to power will no longer have power to protect their own jobs.

It certainly would be a wiser course of action for the United States to develop a technology-based economy and attempt to clone this economy throughout the country of Mexico, providing Mexican citizens with a much higher standard of living than they subsist on today. Instituting a technology-based economy in both countries would vastly reduce incentives for Mexican citizens to cross our border illegally with the advent of superior technology being available in both countries. The U.S. government is simply chasing rainbows trying to spend money today, keeping people out of our country to compete for jobs that should be automated anyway or most likely will be lost in the long run to Asia, in the next decade or two. We can apply automation to replace human labor, if we apply superior technology to our overhead industries to offset the reduction in loss of job income, rather than continuing to turn away people from Mexico who are simply seeking to meet their basic survival needs through the current system.

World poverty and slavery still are part of the global economy, and the only way we will ever see this eradicated in Third-World developing countries is to implement low-cost survival technology into their infrastructures, to replace slave labor.

The central theme of a technology-based economy is about honoring the technology rights of all humans on the planet and getting technology to our world population at the lowest possible cost to help reduce their struggles in times of economic downturns. People have a much easier life in the United States because of the commitment our society has to getting at least some basic survival technology to the majority of our population, at a low-cost. Can you imagine what the United States would look like today if it had no functioning electrical power grid? What kind of businesses do you think we would have? How do you think we would compete with the rest of the world in exporting goods? The simple answer to all these questions is that we couldn't. Each citizen is basically allowed access to a power grid, some sort of potable water through a tap, a sewer system, basic heating and cooling technology, public transportation and access to credit to purchase homes and transportation. Access to these basic life-supporting systems allows all citizens a very high standard of living compared to most countries around the world. Just having readily available technology to dig water wells makes life in this country so much easier. We've built reservoirs and water treatment systems and provided 24/7 access to water to our citizens through pipes that run right into our homes. Still, the process to obtain water, for the average American home is very expensive and time-consuming, and contributes massively to ever-increasing real-estate lot costs, due to the massive costs associated with attaching new home sites to centralized water utilities. The United States, by prioritizing basic access to utilities and other basic survival needs, has allowed our economy and our people to thrive. Many Third-World countries are still at least 100 years behind us in terms of their survival technology; people still walk many miles a day for water, burn wood and have no sewer systems whatsoever. Many Third-World countries in Africa and

Asia still require their residents to walk miles a day just to get water because they have no centralized water utility systems whatsoever. A 2016 Ecoloodi article by Soofia Mahmood stated that a survey by UNICEF revealed 66% of the households in 45 developing nations had no drinking water on their premises and were forced to walk up to three miles a day to collect drinking water for their homes.[82]

A portable source of water would solve so many problems not only in our country but around the world. Instituting extremely efficient Atmospheric Water Generators—machines that create water directly from the air—in these countries on a mass scale would vastly change the standard of living for residents of all of these countries. Atmospheric Water Generators have already been developed for commercial use that produce at least 4,500 liters of water per day. I'm sure it wouldn't be a stretch to install these units in Third-World countries so the residents could enjoy pure, clean water for drinking, bathing or any other industrial or economic needs they might have. How about using ground-penetrating radar, from satellites, to find caches of water in order to decide where to dig wells? It seems we never use our advanced military technology for the benefit of our own citizens. Ground-penetrating radar would certainly be able to identify water in remote areas in the United States. We could build cities around water caches rather than continuing to bemoan the state of our reservoirs that never seem to be filled by rain.

Why do we want to continue to build reservoirs and pipe water for hundreds of miles, relying on weather systems to create water for us? If we simply created a law that mandated the use of portable water (water produced on site) in every home in the United States, and developed superior technology in order to make it a reality, we could then clone the system around the world and the residents of Third-World countries would no longer be required to walk for water, daily.

---

82   http://ecoloodi.org/en/people-walk-water/

The problem with implementing our currently inferior technology here in the United States into Third-World countries is that it is so expensive and labor-intensive that charitable organizations and government donations could not cover the costs to bring the type of survival technology that these struggling people need. The simple reason we cannot implement our technology in Third-World countries is because it's bad technology! It simply costs too much, it's not portable and it's too labor-intensive to build. Our current system of distributing water, for example, is based on building reservoirs that rely on rain to fill them; and coincidently, when it doesn't rain, they don't fill up. Then there's an elaborate aboveground or underground system of piping and aqueducts that have to transport the water to homes, all of which have piping in them, faucets, toilets and so on, that are all geared to receive water from a centralized system. Most homes in Third-World countries do not have any type of way to receive water; they have no piping, no sinks and no toilets. So, building a reservoir would only serve the purpose, for most people in those countries, of providing a place to dip their buckets and walk back to their homes to satisfy their daily water needs. Their system of technology simply does not match up with our elaborate system of technology, and there is no way that we can replicate it in their country on a mass scale; the bottom line is that it's just too expensive and time-consuming.

Third-World countries also need access to electricity. As I noted earlier in the text, running power lines in the United States—which is obviously a well-developed economy and extremely adept and efficient at producing low-cost power poles, transformers and electrical lines—still costs up to $90,000 per mile. There is absolutely no way we can clone this type system on a mass scale in Third-World areas that don't have access to electricity. The process is so expensive it's simply unattainable, unless we build a highly developed economy around these power lines in order to justify their expense, and we know this will never happen due to outsourcing and automation. We're in dire need of portable utilities in the United States to lower our overhead just as much as other countries around the world are in need of these portable utilities in order to meet their basic survival needs. We need to keep the emphasis on localized portable systems and stay away from centralized systems. Centralized systems generally have massive costs associated with them, are very labor-intensive to build and once implemented, discourage the development of competing technology. Centralized energy and water systems increase lot costs and make the price of real estate high. Centralized systems are very hard to evolve out of, once they have been implemented in any economy. Nothing competes with the centralized water system currently in place in America, because once you've spent all this money to build reservoirs and bury expensive piping to connect homes to them, there are virtually no incentives to create any competing technology.

As an American citizen you're actually participating in an economy that directly reaps great benefits from cheap overseas labor, and quite frankly I don't hear a lot of people complaining about it or wanting it to change anytime soon. My point here is that we're all guilty of practicing some sort of hypocrisy by participating in a currency-driven economy, and we all need to accept our responsibilities and the consequences of our actions when it comes to being stewards of our world rather than owners. Most of the goods you buy online or at your local department store are made in Asia by people who work long hours and have a fraction of the standard of living of workers in the United States. Let's take a look at some of the overseas labor practices, which are in many cases inhumane or actually still use human slaves to create these products that directly support the United States economy.

A 2016 article by Annie Kelly for *The Guardian* reported that the Democratic Republic of the Congo produces up to half of the world's cobalt supply. Cobalt is a precious metal used to build computers, smart phones and other electronic devices. Humans as young as 7 years old work 12-hour days hand-carrying rock and dirt on their backs, and are beaten and fined if they do not keep up with their company's mandated work pace.[83] Children that

---

[83] https://www.theguardian.com/global-development/2016/jan/19/children-as-young-as-seven-mining-cobalt-for-use-in-smartphones-says-amnesty

are forced into slave labor are directly helping to keep the cost of your smart-phone, computer and automobile electronics, as low as possible. Wouldn't it be better to fully automate the plants than to have children continue to live this way? Wouldn't it be better to create superior technology, so we didn't have to keep repurchasing these items and thus create a smaller constant demand for this raw material? Wouldn't it be better to implement superior technology into these countries, so that their people could enjoy the basic utilities and amenities of survival that we enjoy today? Fining electronics companies or boycotting their product here in the United States isn't going to change these labor practices any more than it's going to change the labor practices here in the United States. People in the United States just have a higher standard of slavery, better known as debt slavery. In either case, the system relies on humans performing mundane tasks over and over again and walking in the endless circles of income and spend.

The United States economy would have serious problems operating today, without the support of cheap overseas labor performed by humans whose standard of living is massively lower, than what we enjoy in America today. A capitalistic, currency-based economy does not attempt to solve any of the problems the citizens of Third-World countries currently experience, including their low standard of living, basic sanitation and healthcare. Technology to grow food at an incredibly low cost, for example, is the only solution that can help eradicate global starvation. The for-profit, currency-based system directly contributes to and accelerates the forces that create global starvation, poverty and slavery because the countries abiding by this system directly limit their citizens' access to technology.

In the 1960s, roughly 95% of all the clothes people bought in the United States were made in the United States. Today, roughly 98% of all the clothes bought in the United States are made overseas. There is simply no way we can expect manufacturing jobs to pop up in the United States to produce clothes with a privatized, publicly traded healthcare system that represents ever-increasing labor costs in the United States. The United States garment-manufacturing force, or any other labor force, under these circumstances, will never seriously be competitive with overseas labor.

A 2017 article by Michelle Chen for *The Nation* reported that workers in call centers who answer customer service calls get paid around two dollars per hour for the same job that might pay a living wage here in the United States.[84] American businesses are going to continue to outsource labor, and nothing can be done to stop it. The American economy as we know it is dying right in front of our eyes; this is exactly why we need a licensing system here in the United States to reduce our overhead—there is simply no other way around our economic problems. We can't solve these problems by increasing our income—that's simply not an option anymore. Automation and outsourcing basically guarantees that the: labor for-cash for-survival system is phasing itself out of existence as we speak. To be quite honest, based on the facts that there are container ships running across the ocean 24/7 and that most of the major express carriers can get a package across the world in two business days now and the entire planet is connected through a global internet system, I simply see no reason to open a business in the United States at all. There are overseas consulting firms that can handle the hiring and management of employees, so my physical presence in the overseas country is no longer even required for daily business operations, and I can drop my labor costs by 75 to 90%, reaping all the profits for myself. There are no incentives under a for-profit currency-based system to create any product or service here in the United States unless the certain economics of a particular industry would force businesses to do so. Our jobs are going to continue to go overseas, and eventually this alone is going to destroy our economy, coupled with the facts that we have an enormous amount of debt that is never going to stop accumulating, ever-increasing healthcare costs and ever increasing real-estate costs, which make it simply impossible for the United States labor force to compete with the rest of the world. Our world population is expected to increase to 11 billion by the year 2100; the population of the United States is

---

84   https://www.thenation.com/article/the-workers-who-answer-your-customer-service-calls/

only 325 million now; so, you can expect that the vast majority of the world population's increase to come from overseas countries, providing more cheap labor to compete with American jobs. The U.S. economy and its financial and credit markets are headed on a direct course for failure, explosion and eventual elimination. At this point we should plan on all jobs on this planet becoming automated, but first let's make sure our overhead costs us as little as possible and continues to decline over time, through a well-placed and planned licensing system.

Americans are also under a great illusion that slavery ended throughout the entire world in 1863 with the passing of the Emancipation Proclamation. The currency-based economy has always relied on slave labor, whether from actual imprisoned slaves or debt slaves, in order to run at a high level of efficiency. Examples of slavery are not hard to find in the world today. Even child slavery is still very prevalent in Africa in many forms, such as cotton farming and gold-mining. There may be up to 1 million children held in slavery worldwide to produce raw materials for the world's economy. If you want to look at a product that is close to home, look no further than your own chocolate bar. Childhood slaves are used to harvest cocoa beans and are often paid no money; they may be kidnapped or abducted from their families or tricked into slavery. Americans have traditionally taken strong stances against these labor exploitations. Isn't it time we stop turning a blind eye to labor exploitations around the world? In essence, the population of the United States has replaced the slave masters of the early eighteenth century because we consume all the products from the raw materials that these overseas slave labor forces provide. Concentrating on a solution for everyone is a much better path to follow than just condemning the system and heading down to the local bar for a drink.

Perhaps at one time slavery was acceptable to the world, due to the limited amount of technology and information available to people during that era. Today we have no more excuses to perpetually exploit people to complete repetitive tasks over and over again for the rest of their lives, for our benefit. It would be an incredibly great idea to just eliminate the concept of human labor altogether. Slavery throughout history has never been specific to any race but rather specific to exploiting humans, who have always needed to perform some sort of physical task in order to survive. The tradition of slavery is not isolated to just one country or continent; look no further than the country of India. In a 2017 Article in the *Equal Times*, Aarthi Gunnupuri reported that over 25 million people in India are forced to work as debt slaves making bricks. Families are never allowed to leave the site as a unit, and one family member is held hostage whenever family travel is required. These companies provide less income or pay advances than these people need to survive, and even when these advances are paid in full, they may not be able to leave. If any protest arises, they may be beaten or starved by the withholding of money, they desperately need. [85] Americans are just another version of advanced debt-slaves; the obvious difference in America is that we are granted access to higher levels of technology, and the technology that is not directly offered to us we are able to finance using an advanced credit system. The similarity between all countries and their mass populations around the world is that they are all exploited to work perpetually in order to survive. It's time for privatized survival industries to end! The solution is up to us and no one else.

Roughly 2.1 billion people on this planet live on less than $3.10 a day. Let's contrast this extreme poverty to the extreme wealth of a small percentage of people in the world: 42 individuals now have a combined net worth greater than half the population of our planet of over 3.7 billion people! Any person can easily discern from looking at these incredibly unbalanced statistics that that the mass population of the planet has access to a small amount of technology and a small percentage of the planet has access to an incredibly vast amount of technology and attains that vast access by exploiting the mass population through the existing laws covering currency and patents. Anyone in a position to make wholesale changes to this separate right

---

85 https://www.equaltimes.org/the-horror-of-modern-day-slavery?lang=en#.Wu9jLYgvyUl

through currency system is heavily incentivized, and works in lockstep with government interests to keep the system intact, perpetually.

We can end global poverty, slavery, starvation and the horrible sanitary conditions that breed all sorts of diseases and propagate global suffering on a mass scale by forming an economic committee in each state that works in our best interests—a committee that is no longer incentivized to defraud or manipulate the American public. And by implementing a licensing system governing our energy, transportation, housing and healthcare industries right here in the United States, we can literally transform ourselves from perpetual debt slaves to tourists on our planet within the next 50 years, each enjoying the same individual freedoms as one another. And then we can clone this system throughout the world to create one of the happiest planets in the universe!

It has been an absolute pleasure presenting this text to you. I hope it's raised your awareness and given you a new understanding of the way the currency system works and the fact that our economic system will never change unless we change the laws currently regulating it. Together through mutual cooperation, with the best interests of all in mind, we can make a technology-based economy a new reality, change our world forever and enjoy a world of abundance and prosperity like we've never known before.

Please discuss this book with your friends, to help to raise their awareness about the currency system, its serious drawbacks and the unlimited benefits that a technology-based economy would provide to the United States and the world. In time we will be ready to take action and make this new thought process our reality. It's inevitable that what you think about becomes your reality. Look around you: Every man-made item that you see was once a thought in someone's head. Today you're armed with a new set of thoughts, and I suspect that by continually pondering these new thoughts, you'll eventually create a new reality for yourself and eventually together we'll create a new technology-based economy that provides us unlimited time to create and enjoy life. Thank you!

Additional Books and Videos Recommended for You

Smarter, Faster, Better and The Power of Habit
Charles Duhigg

No Contest: The Case Against Competition
Alfie Kohn

The Source Field Investigations
David Wilcock

Resilience from the Heart
Gregg Braden

Morphic Resonance: The Nature of Formative Causation
Rupert Sheldrake

You Are the Placebo: Making Your Mind Matter
Dr. Joe Dispenza

Outwitting the Devil: The Secret to Freedom and Success
Napoleon Hill

The Complete System of Self-Healing: Internal Exercises
Dr. Stephen T. Chang

Videos at Gaia.com
Nassim Haramein

You may also find additional videos for many
of these authors at Gaia.com.